A WOMEN'S DIARIES
Miscellany

Edited by Jane DuPree Begos

MagiCircle
10 Hyde Ridge
Weston, Conn.
06880
PRESS

Library of Congress Catalog No. 88-092539
Copyright © 1989 by Jane DuPree Begos
Cover by Adele Aldridge

All rights reserved. For information
regarding reproduction contact Jane Begos

Most of the articles in this book appeared
in *WOMEN'S DIARIES, A Quarterly Newsletter,*
Vols. 1-4, 1983-1986. Several have been
slightly revised, and six appear here for the first time.
ISBN 0-913660-23-X hc
ISBN 0-913660-24-8 pb

Preface

I n 1977, I self-published an *Annotated Bibliography of Published Women's Diaries*, the first of its kind. It filled a need, but the content and scope quickly became dated. In 1983, I began the publication of WOMEN'S DIARIES, *A Quarterly Newsletter*, as an effort to update the bibliography and to stay current with the wealth of newly published women's diaries. In 1986, a family relocation to Europe forced me to cease publication of the *Newsletter* because it was impossible to coordinate the production and mailing from that distance. However, I still had much good material for future issues, and I hated to see it go unpublished. Also, I felt it was a good idea to put previously published material in a more permanent format. I herewith offer *A WOMEN'S DIARIES Miscellany* as a solution to both problems.

Most of the articles presented in this collection originally appeared in the *Newsletter*. Some that I would like to have included were not made available for this book. Some that I was unable to include in the *Newsletter* have been added and are published here for the first time.

I want to thank all the authors for their participation in this work. They have been most generous. I also want to express my appreciation to Valerie Harms of Magic Circle Press for handling its publication. She steered me through many pitfalls and was always ready with her encouragement.

Contents

PART II
In Particular

PART III
Applications

Introduction

*W*hat is a diary, and what is a journal? Are they the same, or different? According to Webster's *Third Dictionary,* a diary is "a register or record of events, transactions, or observations kept daily or at frequent intervals." A journal is "a daily record of personal activities, reflections or feelings. The distinction seems to rest in the addition of the adjective "personal." Remember, however, that the keepers of these documents usually decide that one term or the other applies to their own exercise in recording whatever they choose to record, whether it be "diary," "journal," "notebook," "daybook," or even "log."

The history of diary keeping is a long and honorable one. It is important to remember that personal records have, of necessity, been produced by educated people with enough leisure time to write down their thoughts and observations. There are very few diaries of working-class people, and none from illiterate and primitive peoples. The earliest English diaries are bare-bones records of daily life. They began as household records on large estates, business records, if you will, through which the personalty of the keeper gradually began to push its way. The diaries of American farm women are also usually these bare-bones records. Many people consider this type of diary dull because there is so little of the diarist in them. But these "dull" diaries can be chock full of information for social and public historians. They deserve a careful reading, because they can tell us very much indeed about how people lived in earlier times. They give us a sense of the seasons and how time was used. They tell us about place, either a specific house or a locale, both important in historic recreations.

There have been historic trends in diary/journal keeping, as in human life styles. At an early stage, they were religious in nature, serving as tools for recording one's progress in fulfilling one's Christian duty. The Quakers have long advocated the keeping of diaries as an exercise in religious education. This approach is comparable to today's use of the journal as a therapeutic tool. Joanna Field, pen name of English psychoanalyst Marion Milner, wrote the first book about the process of journal keeping, *A Life Of One's Own*. Christina Baldwin explores the theme of journal writing as therapy with great sensitivity in her book, *One to One*. Ira Progoff, a psychologist, has developed a psychological tool, *The Intensive Journal*, and Tristine Rainer devotes a chapter of *The New Diary* to the journal as therapy.

The most interesting question we can ask about diaries and journals is why are they kept? "Why did I start writing a diary? What makes one do such a thing?" asked Frances Partridge, a member of the Bloomsbury Group. She goes on to answer her own question: "The desire to pin down or preserve happiness, one might say, except that it is often in times of misery or stress that one rushes to confide in it. It is a form of talking to oneself of course. . ."

Exactly. It is a conversation with the self, a personal laboratory for making observations and examining feelings. As Beatrice Webb, co-founder of the London School of Economics, wrote, "What a blessing I can write in this little book. . . That has been the attraction of a 'diary-book' to me—one can talk one's little thinkings out to a highly appreciative audience, dumb but not deaf." Webb, in fact, had a great deal to say about the why of diary-keeping, and her reasons changed through the years.

For many, the diary/journal is the non-judgmental confidante, the friend to whom one can "tell all" without fear of criticism. Anne Frank began her diary, which she addressed to an imaginary friend, Kitty, with the wish that "I hope that I shall be able to confide in you completely, as I have never been able to do in anyone before, and I hope that you will be a great support and comfort to me."

Journal keeping is also a means for getting a grip on reality, especially when the world is in chaos or an important relationship is ending. Many become journal keepers in time of war for instance.

Although Sarah Dawson began her diary in a confident and frivolous mood, as the Civil War progressed and the horrors crept closer, she wrote, "There is no use in trying to break off journalizing, particularly in 'these trying times.' It has become a necessity to me." Journal keeping is also a support system for times of emotional stress, such as the break up of a marriage or a love affair. Loran Hurnscot was subconsciously aware that her masochistic love affair was a "prison" and through journal writing came to see it objectively as not good for her. Jan Fuller's journal gave her the "space" to accept her divorce.

Journal keeping can allow one to come to terms with old age, a terminal illness, or the death of a loved one. Gerda Lerner was able to deal with the impotence of watching her beloved husband dying of cancer by using her journal to record its progress. Alice James recorded the progress of her own cancer in her journal, and even edited the final entries with her last breath. As Helen Keller wrote after the death of her dear friend and long-time teacher, Anne Sullivan Macy, "This journal is a godsend. It is helping me to discipline my mind back to regular work."

Although many men have kept and do keep diaries and journals, the form is considered as being particularly suited to women. Certainty it is true that it is one of the non-literary forms that women have made great use of. And its form—fragmentary, interrupted, non-linear, emotional— is analogous to a woman's life. One stage of life at which the diary is a peculiarly feminine expression is during adolescence. Confused, and frequently embarrassed by the changes that her body is undergoing, the adolescent girl turns with relief to the non-critical confidante, and by conducing a dialogue with the self is able to guide herself through the shoals and reefs of young womanhood. Even for the pseudonymous "Alice," the journal was a place to record where things went wrong, where roads were taken that led through drugs and indiscriminate sex to death.

Obviously, the diary or journal is a literary tool. It is a proving ground for finished works of art, a place to try out ideas for more creative works. Journal keeping is, for a writer, similar to an artist trying out visual ideas in a sketchbook. As Anaïs Nin so aptly put it:

"The very process of the diary resembles that of a painter making a series of sketches each day in preparation for a final portrait." She was speaking of the self-portrait of the diarist, and she created one of the great self-portraits in the history of women's literature. But Nin also used her diaries as the mother lode from which to mine the jewels of her fiction. Passage after passage from her diary can be compared with those in her works of fiction, and one can see, dramatically, how the one nourished the other.

Anne Morrow Lindbergh is another writer who used the raw material of her diaries to fashion her non-fiction adventure books. She states: "Writing in a diary is my tool for the development of awareness. It is the crucible through which the rough material of life must pass before I can use it in art."

Some diaries are works of art in themselves. Hortense Calisher, who has published sections of her diaries and written works of fiction in the diary form cautions that we should "never trust the private journal of a writer; give her confidence, your sympathy, and before you know it you may be standing in the middle of what is merely another work of art. The journals of May Sarton, for example, however full of insight and truth they be, are works of art. She writes them, knowing that they will be published.

Another type of diary, also frequently meant for publication, is the travel diary. Because travelers want to share their impressions of new places and different peoples, they want to show the stay-at-homes that the place visited was interesting, the people unusual, and the adventures exciting. Some of the best known travel diary keepers are Isabella Bird Bishop, Freya Stark, and Christina Dodwell. Even Mrs. McAuliffe, on the ill-fated Challenger space shuttle, had planned to keep a diary of her experiences on the journey, in the manner of early explorers who compiled guides for those who followed.

Prison diaries, kept for the period of internment, have served as a means for the prisoner to hold onto sanity in an insane situation; sometimes, they serve as a document of social protest, such as Barbara Deming's *Prison Notes*.

Naturalists keep nature diaries. Dreamers keep dream diaries. Artists keep sketchbooks. Visual diaries reveal a wide range of individual approaches. They too, are a way to preserve history, whether it be in the scrapbooks of Louisa, Lady Antrim, lady-in-waiting to two Queens, or whether it be through the eyes of a photographer such as Dorothea Lange, who wrote of her camera that "it became for me a little notebook, a sketch book. . . I always photographed what the moment told me."

There are contemporary spiritual diaries which are quite different from those of early Quakers and Methodists who kept theirs to emulate the founders of their religious sects. Dorothy Day used her journals to record the internal development of the soul. As Marie Noël expressed it: "If only I had had someone to help me with my inner self, I would not have needed a notebook as a refuge."

The diaries and journals of writers are used by scholars for insight into the writer's life; they even serve as a basis for literary criticism. They have been used by writers as a basis for works of fiction, such as Ben Ames Williams' House Divided, based on the diary of Mary Chestnut. Certainly much fiction has been written in the diary form, as it hints at being allowed a peek into forbidden, hidden secrets. Diary keepers themselves use their diaries as a basis for autobiography, including Enid Bagnold, Margo Asquith and Helen Lawrenson, all of whom quote their diaries in their respective autobiographies. Biographers use every source available when trying to capture the essence of another person's life, and they ignore diaries at their peril, even though they may be led a merry chase. Lady Cynthia Asquith writes, "I wonder if all diaries are as unrepresentative of their writers as this is of me."

In this volume, I have tried to introduce a wide sampling of the rich diary/journal literature. "General" articles have been chosen to give some historic background of the genre, its importance to scholars and journal keepers today, and its literary and historical applications.

"Particular" articles deal with individual diarists and journal keepers. My aim has been to expand the reader's knowledge of the diversity of women who keep diaries and their reasons for keeping them.

The "Applications" articles show current trends and methods of diary/journal keeping, as well as some of the concerns of contemporary journal keepers and some ways that these non-traditional private writings can be used as source books for traditional, public writings.

The book reviews have been culled from those published in *WOMEN'S DIARIES, A Quarterly Newsletter*, and were chosen because they seemed to best support the articles included herein.

By choosing the term "miscellany" to describe this volume, I have tried to indicate its character. It is a miscellaneous selection and does not pretend to be complete in any sense, nor does it try to deal with all or even the most important women diarists or with all the issues to be considered in either the keeping of a journal or the study of others' journals. My hope is that it will be informative and stimulating, and that it will provide guideposts for further reading and research in women's diaries.

Jane DuPree Begos

The Guest House
Steen Valetje
Red Hook, New York
January 1989

PART I

In General

Since 1980, Jo Gillikin has been teaching a junior-senior course entitled Women's Written Expression. Her syllabus grew out of ideas generated at an Institute on Women's Nontraditional Literature, jointly sponsored by the National Endowment for the Humanities and the Women's Commission of the Modern Language Association.

For essays on diaries and oral histories and their use in the classroom, Gillikin considers *Women's Personal Narratives: Essays in Criticism and Pedagogy,* edited by Leonore Hoffman and Margo Culley, to be invaluable.

In this essay, Gillikin concentrates on the four collections which she considers to be necessary reading for an introduction to women's diaries. It is an adaption of an article which appeared in *The CUNY Women's Coalition Journal,* Spring 1986.

FIERCE WITH REALITY

by Dure Jo Gillikin

> *You need only to claim the events of your life to make yourself yours. When you truly possess all you have been and done, which may take some time, you are fierce with reality.*

Florida Scott-Maxwell

A diary is by its very nature a series of fragments that come together at the end to make a whole. With little time left over from housekeeping and mothering, with little sense of the significance of their words or their lives, women jotted down in their diaries phrases or a sentence or two—words enough, however, to summon up the days from that infinite book, their past lives. A diary is autobiography in miniature, sometimes as perfected as those scenes carved in a walnut shell, sometimes as rough as hands forced to scrub clothes all day.

With no publishers or readers to please, most diarists have no constraints. They write what they want to, when they want to, and how they want to. Such freedom allows new forms to develop, new narrative structures, and the steady, bit-by-bit creation of one character—the diarist herself. A combination of individual essences, diaries present us with a variety of original expressions. They also offer a democracy of perspective. For diaries, at their best, are the texts of lives, the distillations of day's deeds, thoughts, and feelings recorded only for the diarists' personal reasons. An accumulation of such selective entries over weeks, months, and years shows us individu-

3

als in a process of creating what may be called spontaneous autobiographies, narratives of the self as the self unfolds. Multitudes of such diaries, supplemented by volumes of conventional printed material, will help to provide us with a composite text of multifaceted humanity, showing the human creature varnished and unvarnished.

As Virginia Woolf wrote in her introduction to *Life as We Have Known It*, a collection of memoirs by Cooperative Working Women, these writings by everyday people make it "possible to meet not as masters or mistresses or customers with a counter between us but over the wash-tub or in the parlor casually congenially as fellow beings with the same wishes and ends in view, [and from this], a great liberation would follow and perhaps friendship and sympathy would supervene." Today, thanks in large part to the democratization of research that has come as a result of the feminist movement, many lives of everyday women are available to us in print and on tape. More lives are being recorded in the handwritten diaries we ask our students to keep.

By reading, appreciating, and analyzing diaries by the famous and the unknown, we become engaged with narratives in which the self is in conversation with itself. These girls and women who just write in their diaries what they want to put in them—and that selection of wants, presented in hundreds and thousands of diaries—provides us with a text and a context of humanity undreamed of until now. For centuries, we have had primarily the published, polished, and manipulated narratives we have told about ourselves. Now, it is possible to place beside them these unguarded, previously undervalued, handwritten scattered writings to the self about itself. As Florida Scott-Maxwell wrote, "You need only claim the events of your life to make yourself yours."

Diaries are invaluable resources for the bedrock narratives of our day-to-day existence. These private words also show us that to be human is to be a character in a universal and unending narrative that sometimes seems to have no author, and therefore to have no direction, no theme. Yet, diaries are imitations of this open-ended narrative of existence, providing us with the stories of individuals who,

4

because they most often are not consciously telling a story, reveal the innate patterns, quests, and questions in what it means to be human. Diaries are written to serve any purpose under the sun. The format requires a date; after that, it is up to the individual as to what words fill the entry. There is no required number of words, no required subject to be discussed, no person to be mentioned, no style to follow. The diary is a place of complete freedom within the boundaries of the space allowed for a day's words. More often than not, those words are used as a means to grow, to see where the diarist has been in her life and what she can do to change for the better. Often, the diary is a means of survival, of getting through inner and outer nightmares. At other times, the diary is a way of proving that the diarist exists; that there is a listener, even if it is only the words she has put on the page. Diaries are written, for the most part, in private, without any audience but the responding, recording self.

Written as records of unusual events while they are happening, diaries tell us what it was like to climb the Himalayan Mount Annapurna, to cross an ocean or a country, to begin a new world or a new life. Written as records of one or more periods in ordinary or extraordinary person's lives, they tell us what it was like to be those persons and how much like them we are. Diaries reinforce our commonality, help us search deeply and extensively until we find the distinguishing essence of an individual which may also help us discover our own.

Immediacy, authenticity, accessibility, accretion, density, fragmentation, and repetition—these are the chief characteristics of diaries. Written in the moment about the moment or moments recollected from a day, diaries draw their readers into their moments of being, sometimes so much so that the readers become constant companions of the diarists. Readers are with Carolina Maria de Jesus as she wakes in Sao Paulo, Brazil, dreading another day in the *favela*, which she calls the garbage dump, fully understanding that she and the other women and men and children who live there are considered garbage, that they are the people their society has thrown away. Awakening holds terror for Carolina, for she knows her desperate

5

search for food for herself and her three children must begin. Each day, as she writes about her necessity to find food and her fear of not finding it, as she writes about her scouring the streets, picking up paper and scrap iron, hoping to collect enough waste material to earn money for the family's food that day, the readers are there beside her, feeling the heaviness of the sack she carries on her back, rejoicing with her when she has collected enough pennies to buy bread, even if it is hard bread, gaining strength with her on the days she is able to buy rice and beans and bread, exulting with her when she raises a pig in a pen within the larger pig sty in which she lives and savoring with hope every piece of the slaughtered animal.

Carolina, with only two years of education, has learned to read and write, enough so that she writes poetry and plays and novels about the romantic, rich life she doesn't have. But it is her diary that gets her out of the *favela*. When a reporter overhears her threat to include in her diary the names of the older men who are trying to deprive the children of the teeter totter, he asks to see it. The diary's abiding value is contained in the brutal details of daily life of the *favela*, of what it is to be so poor, so miserable, to have to wait in line every day for water from a spigot, to have to wash clothes in water that the authorities have told them carries snail disease. Our horror, sheltered as we are, is nothing compared to that of the mother who, with her own hands, must pick the worms from her children's bodies. Only a miracle of fiction could rival the authenticity of the poverty Carolina experienced. Not *The Color Purple*, not *The Grapes of Wrath*, not even *The Lower Depths*. In her early diaries, Anaïs Nin details the poverty of artists, but that poverty is distinct from Carolina's because it is the artist's choice to sacrifice necessities for the time to work on her writing. But Nin's mastery of words, melded with reality, softens poverty, almost romanticizes it. There are, of course, shades of authenticity, of reality. For Anaïs Nin and for Henry and June Miller, their poverty is authentic and they suffer; but to know the very worst about poverty, read Carolina Maria de Jesus.

The accessibility of most diaries is part of their power, for they are written without any audience in mind other than the writers themselves. Thus, for the most part, the language is lucid and direct, making the reading of dairies as easy as slipping one's feet into a pair of old slippers. Almost immediately, the reader becomes at ease with the diarists, for the words they set down are workaday words, although they, too, on occasion, capture the artistry that is innate in existence. It doesn't take long to be at one with most diarists, whether they be the hardy pioneer women in Lillian Schlissel's *Women's Diaries of the Westward Journey* and in the *The Diary of Mollie Dorsey Sanford* or that of the longtime invalid Alice James: whether they be the seven-year-old Scot Marjory Fleming or the eighty-two year old Florida Scott-Maxwell. Even so distant a diarist as the tenth-century Japanese Sei Shonagon, who was in the service of a Japanese Empress, becomes a familiar presence.

Diaries by women have such a range that it is possible to enter the minds of women climbing Annapurna; of female writers—Virginia Woolf, George Eliot, George Sand; of the wives of male writers—Sophie Tolstoy and Anna Dostoevsky; of artists—Kathe Kollwitz and Emily Carr; of Sylvia Ashton-Warner, teacher and writer; of Ruth Benedict, anthropologist. Diaries draw readers into the *dailiness* of extraordinary women as they clarify what is extraordinary about everyday women. Not so surprisingly, there is a plentitude of common experience; for, after all, the patterns and possibilities in living day by day are humanity's common ground. The range of perceptions differ, but those perceptions are often centered around the experiences of everywoman: working, eating, sleeping, clothing and caring for children, observing the natural world, despairing over war, deriving consolation from religion.

Diaries, by their very nature, are fragmentary—selective siftings that are not always concerned with the most important events, thoughts, or feelings of a particular day. Within one entry can appear comments on the weather, on sickness, on an action, on encounters with another person, on what books are being read, on what has happened in the outer world. All of these topics are placed side by side, sometimes ordered chronologically, sometimes logically, but most of the time arranged with a disarming discontinuity that imitates the randomness of memory and of life itself.

A diary develops by accretion, as each entry adds one more detail, one more thought, one more accomplishment, one more love to the diarist's life. One entry or several entries often give no hint of the direction the diarist's life is taking. Although each entry is fragmentary, dense with details about the diarist's day, the life the diarist is living and recording is the unifying thread. The plot is itself the process of living—the slow day-to-day experience of growing older, the adding of events and observations, bit by bit, until a year is ended. Then the diarist can look back over the entries and see the patterns of a narrative building or concluding, a friendship developing or dissolving, an aspiration budding or fading. Viewing her own accumulated evidence from a year's perspective, the diarist can accept or can resolve on a pattern-breaking, even a cataclysmic change.

The diary of Hannah Senesh, who is often called the Jewish Joan of Arc, is a prime example of a diarist living through a year and then, at its end, analyzing it. For example, on Rosh Hashana and on Yom Kipper Hannah considers her past, connects it with her present, and then projects it into the future. The goal propelling her is to find and then fulfill her special mission, first by pioneering in the Holy Land and finally by parachuting behind enemy lines during World War II in a hectic attempt to liberate her mother and other Hungarian Jews.

A diary's method of construction consists of one relatively short entry followed by another on a daily, weekly, or monthly basis, building many small narratives until there is the one long narrative that unfurls a goodly portion of the diarist's life and times. As the diarist writes, and as the diary reader reads, there is no sense of manipulation as there is in deliberative writing, yet there is suspense—not heightened purposely, but there, nevertheless. For as surely as the sun rises and sets, a diary will tell not only one long story but several. There is a beginning, middle, and end for every entry, as there is a beginning, middle, and end for every diary (even an unanticipated or accidental end— a simple stopping or failure to continue past some point). There is reassurance and comfort in seeing this pattern reflected in the predominantly spontaneous writing that has come from our sometimes self-designed, oftentimes improvised living. In a diary, the meaning can't be found until the last word has been reached, until all the entries have been assimilated into order and significance. So it is with a life fully lived up to the moments of recollecting and evaluating. From those few but telling words that a diarist jots down on paper comes a life—one that must be largely filled in by the tangible, visible words the diarist set down on particular days and that thereafter serve to jog the memory and recreate a time, place, set of circumstances, and a series of emotions. Lacking the diarist's memories, the diary reader must create the story as an archaeologist recreates a civilization based on its surviving artifacts.

The voice of the diarist, along with the major and minor narrative threads, holds the seemingly disparate entries together. The voices of diarists have common ground, for we are more alike than we wish to admit. Probably, we are much more alike than we are different. Read several diaries by members of the same age group, teenagers, for example, and you can see the experiences they share, although 400 years might intervene. The mind and perceptions of the seventeen-year-old Mathilde von Buddenbroch of the sixteenth century are not much different from those of the twentieth century Hannah Senesh, who is a teenager during most of her diary. True, one wrote about the problems of the Reformation and the other about World War II, but both voices, although unique are accessible to all readers, no matter what their century or culture. The seven ages that Shakespeare delineated for humans in *As you Like It* have not changed. Even the voice of the tenth century Japanese woman Sei Shonagon is closer to ours than we might expect. The voice of Kaethe Kollwitz as she writes about the loss of her son and then her grandson to two World Wars is the voice of every mother who has lost her children to violence.

From the book reviews of years past, records of published writings once favored, then forgotten, and now remembered, today's women are seeking to piece together their composite past, determined not to let it sink into oblivion ever again. Restricted as they were to such spheres as sewing and gardening, our female predecessors mastered those forms, so much so that now, belatedly, their quilts are exhibited in museums, while at craft fairs today, new quilts command high prices and are more likely to adorn a wall than a bed. Our grandmothers' gardens remain in our memories; our mother's gardens, in our photographs of them. Through oral histories, captured on tape, transmitted to print, we corral our unrecorded past through the always known, but never fully acknowledged storytelling abilities of the older women in our lives. Anecdotes—familial, tragic or humorous, historical and personal—demonstrate that narrative has always been women's province.

In *Revelations*, the Foreword by Moffat and the Afterword by Painter, contain cogent distillations on diary writing by women. The thirty-two international diarists excerpted in this book range in time from tenth century Japan to the mid-twentieth century and range in age from seven to eighty-two. The diarists they chose to include were "those that demonstrated character as the ability to make moral distinctions and choices according to a personal code rather than the social or religious codes of the age in which they wrote." Side by side are known and unknown diarists; for example, Marjory Flemming, a seven-year-old Scottish diarist, whom Mark Twain saw as a female version of Tom Sawyer or Huck Finn, is followed by Louisa May Alcott; Ruth Benedict, the famous anthropologist, precedes the diary excerpt of an unknown Japanese woman. Anna Dostoevsky and Sophie Tolstoy present the other side of the story as they write of their "work" as wives of famous male authors. Although Anne Frank and Hannah Senesh were victims of the Holocaust, Moffat and Painter have also included excerpts about their traditional roles as women: Anne's sexual awakening as she is forced to share her life in the annex with Peter; and Hannah's pinpointing the dilemma common to most women: "The problem I now face is whether to marry a man 'just like that,' to disrupt my plans, give up my independence. Naturally, it's difficult not to be impressed and flattered by love of a man of character, a man you respect and esteem. But this is still not love, and thus there is really no reason to continue." The Anaïs Nin excerpt on her sexual attraction to June Miller, Henry's wife, has all the art of a short story. *The Pillow Book of Sei Shonagon,* penned from 990 to 1000—is not only the oldest diary in

10

this collection, but the most unusual. A contemporary of Lady Murasaki, sometimes identified as the first novelist, Shonagon compiled a work, as Moffat and Painter describe it, which is "partly diary, partly reflection and reminiscence, partly poetry," revealing "courtly custom and manners of love." Certainly, the excerpted passage in which Shonagon describes the proper behavior of a lover after he has left her chambers charms and delights as it exhibits the woman's freedom to respond to male behavior.

Each diarist has been subsumed under one of these three categories: Love, Work, and Power. However, the editors have defined these words nontraditionally: "What united these disparate lives for us was what we heard as an unconscious call by the women for a redefinition of these concepts into a less divisive, more organic pattern for existence, one where their capacities for both love and work blend, allowing them to be fully human and balanced, true to the power of their individual natures."

Joanna Field, a pseudonym for the English-born Marion Milner who later became a psychoanalyst, was one of the first women to use her diary for self-analysis. Published as *A Life of One's Own,* in it she sets forth several techniques for self-improvement, one of which was to write about those things which made her happy. Another approach grew out of her realization that she "could not *decide* to grow but could only discover conditions that made her own individual growth possible, and try to encourage them."

Revelations has excerpts from two diaries by sisters of famous brothers—one by Dorothy Wordsworth, which shows that she germinated some of the seeds of her brother William's poetry, and the other by Alice James. Overshadowed as she was by her brothers Henry and William, through her diary Alice attained a reputation for wit and for courage as she struggled through a long siege with cancer. On September 27, 1890, she wrote of her illness: ". . .these doctors tell you that you will die or *recover!* But you *don't* recover. I have been at these alterations since I was nineteen and I am neither dead nor recovered—as I am now forty-two there has surely been time for either process." So determined a diarist was she that she died shortly after revising, through dictation, some diary passages.

For the immediate experience of what it was like in the South prior to the Civil War, there is Frances A. Kemble's *Journal of a Residence on a Georgian Plantation in 1838-39.* A noted actress, Kemble unknowingly married a man who owned slaves, and when an illness forced him to go to Georgia, she joined him on his plantation. Her efforts to better the conditions of the slaves are vividly portrayed as is her recognition that the changes she makes are neither permanent nor wide-ranging. Many passages in the diary substantiate historical and novelistic accounts of the evils of slavery. Inevitably, she divorces her husband and returns to her acting career rather than live on money earned through slave labor. On the other side is the Civil War *Diary from Dixie* by Mary Boykin Chestnut who delineates the gradual decline and eventual collapse of the Confederacy. Her March 14, 1861, passage reveals how thoroughly she understood the corruption in which she and her kind were embedded: "God forgive us, but ours is a monstrous system, a wrong and an iniquity! Like patriarchs of old, our men live all in one house with their wives and their concubines; and the mulattoes one sees in every family partly resemble the white children. Any lady is ready to tell you who is the father of all the mulatto children in everybody's household but her own. Those, she seems to think drop from the clouds." Here is an eyewitness account of a situation fictionalized in *The Color Purple.*

O Rugged Land of Gold by Martha Martin is an account of a pregnant woman who was isolated by an avalanche and left on an island in Alaska for some months. How she gave birth by herself, how she foraged for food, and how she made clothing from an otter's skin are examples of her resourcefulness. This diary is an excellent counterpart to Robinson Crusoe, and indeed, it may be partly fictional. Martha Martin is, perhaps the adult version of Ayla, the heroic survivor in *The Clan of the Cave Bear.*

Hundreds and Thousands is the diary of the Canadian artist Emily Carr, who eventually achieved such fame that Vancouver, Canada, has a separate gallery of her work. On November 23, 1930, when she was fifty-eight, she began a new diary by giving two reasons for keeping it. Her first reason is one that many diarists have—keeping a diary gives them a time and a place to truly be themselves: "Yesterday! I went to town and bought this book to enter scraps in, not a diary of statistics and dates and decency of spelling and happenings but just to jot one down in, unvarnished me, old me at fifty-eight . . ." The second reason has to do with her thoughts, her art: "It seems to me it helps to write things and thoughts down. It makes the unworthy ones look more shamefaced and helps to place the better ones for sure in our minds. It sorts out jumbled up thoughts and helps to clarify them, and I want my thoughts clear and straight for my work." Her diary places us within the mind of a painter: "The artist herself may not think she is religious but if she is sincere her sincerity in itself is religion. If something other than the material did not speak to her, and if she did not have faith in that something and also in herself, she would not try to express it." [Male pronouns have been changed to female ones.] There are many more diarists' excerpts in Moffat's and Painter's *Revelations,* all of them well worth reading.

The second notable anthology of women diarists is Laurel Holliday's *Heart Songs: The Intimate Diaries of Young Girls.* This collection contains excerpts from the diaries of nine girls, from age eleven to eighteen, from the 1500s to the 1940. It provides new teaching material, as suitable for elementary and high school classes as it is for college. Selma Lagerlöf and Anaïs Nin are the two most famous writers, the former being the first woman to win the Nobel Prize for literature and the other being a woman of her own times who achieved fame through her numerous diaries. Two forerunners of Nin's are the diarists Marie Bashkirtseff and Nelly Ptaschkina. Sadly, Russian, multi-talented Bashkirtseff died in 1884 before her diary's publication. Her preface reveals her honesty and her healthy ego: "Not only do I always write what I think, but I have not even dreamed, for a single instant, of disguising anything that was to my disadvantage, or that might make me appear ridiculous. Besides, I think myself too admirable for censure. . . ." Aware of the limitations placed upon her ambitions because she was a woman, she wrote: "If I had been born a man, I would have conquered Europe. As I was born a woman, I exhausted my energy in tirades against fate, and in eccentricities." Even when Marie's painting is awarded a medal, she is accused of having been given assistance. Of this suspicion she writes, "But to suspect that my picture is not all my own work is too serious a matter. . . ." Bashkirtseff's diary received the plaudits she had so desired, yet never heard. Alice James, recognizing a competitor, refused to read it.

Ptaschkina, forced, with her family, to flee Russia, writes of things political and personal. Of particular note are her passages on women's rights. In her entry of October 1, 1918, she says: "Yes, woman must have all the rights, and in time she can earn them fully. At present we have still many women who are satisfied with their empty lives, but if we raise the standard, and improve the social conditions of life, which are connected with her, woman will also rise. Even now there are many among them who would be capable of leading a conscious existence successfully. Give them that possibility."

Maggie Owen Wadelton is the Irish counterpart to Scottish Marjory Fleming whose diary excerpt opens *Revelations*, for her diary provides the reader entry into the mind of a young girl who is unintentionally funny as she narrates her encounters. Feisty, eleven-year-old Maggie had a way with words: "Twas Vincent gave me the eye. He sneaked up behind me with a cold pigs tail and dropped it down me back and away with him, and I after him. I caught him up and licked the porrige out of him. I got the eye and me drawers were torn off me almost on a hedge. I larruped him well. He got a bloodied nose and I am glad of it. Nothing can stop me from being glad of it am I kept here forever."

And Maggie is not the only one of these girl diarists who can hold her own with her contemporary or an elder. At seventeen, Mathilde von Buddenbroch, has her verbal skirmishes with her older cousin John Calvin, producing these thoughts about predestination: "If we cannot become other than we are, then what can we hope to accomplish in life? If a man develops from a child, and corn grows from the stalk, then don't we all possess hidden, natural genius? And if God has already chosen his favored creatures, and endowed them with genius, then why do they have to struggle so to develop and perfect their creations?"

Who the real Kathie Gray of Ohio was we do not know. What we do know from the diary is that her life seemed to be the epitome of the life of a small-town American girl of the mid-nineteenth century. That life was neither dull nor dreary. The intensity of Kathie's friendship with Jessie is matched by the harrowing near-drowning episode in which she is rescued by the outcast Harry whom she had earlier befriended. Jibing with Carrol Smith-Rosenberg's work, in which she analyzes letters of friendship between women and girls of the nineteenth century, is this excerpt about Kathie's affection for Jessie upon receiving a valentine: "I almost jumped out of my skin when I got it. She called me her Dear Precious Friend and Pet and Dear Darling Kate and Precious and at the end she said Of coarse I like my new playmate Mamie but don't ever think I can ever find in the biggest citty anyone that can ever fill your place in my heart." For a different reading experience, novels and diaries are dynamic duos: Kathie's diary and *Anne of Green Gables* validate each other. The same is true of real letters and imagined real letters. Teach *The Maimie Papers*, written by a former prostitute from Philadelphia to the Boston Brahmin Fanny Howe, and follow that book of letters with Alice Walker's novel *The Color Purple*. Dorothy Bryant's fictional *Ella Price's Journal* vividly captures the dilemmas of adult women students returning to college.

Also in this collection is a diary excerpt by Gretchen Lainer (a pseudonym), which Sigmund Freud encouraged the publishers to print. Written in the early 1900s, it relates the conversations and events by which Gretchen and her friend Hella, both adolescent, received confirmation that all they had heard about men and women having sex together was true. "I know all about it now!!!" writes Gretchen. "That's how babies come. And *that* is what Robert really meant. Not for me, thank you. I simply won't marry. For if one marries one has to do it; it hurts frightfully and yet one has to. What a good thing I know it in time." But only Gretchen's witnessing of the sexual coupling of naked newlyweds convinces her of the truth. The diaries of two French sisters—Benoîte and Flora Groult, counterpoint typical teenage concerns with Hitler's encroaching terror.

Lyn Lifshin's *Ariadne's Thread: A Collection of Contemporary*

Women's Journals is important because it presents excerpts from the diaries of women writers of the immediate past—Sylvia Plath and Anne Sexton—and the present—Maxine Kumin, Alix Kates Shulman, Marge Piercy, Gail Godwin, Denise Levertov, Linda Pastan, and Rita Mae Brown. Equally valuable, however, are the not-so-well-known diarists she introduces. Lifshin subsumes the forty-nine diarists under seven categories—Work, Self, Love and Friendship, Family, Being Somewhere Else, Society, and Nature.

Since Lifshin, for the most part, solicited diary excerpts for her collection, there is the assumption that the diaries had been edited somewhat before they were submitted to her. This anthology, then, shows that diary-writing has become "infected" with the desire for a public, not a private audience. Therefore, diaries are now more manipulative. Instead of the automatic self, these excerpts present a more deliberate self. A major consequence of the diary form going public is that we are confronted with the partially-constructed self of the diarist that is an intermediary between the private diary and the formal deliberate self in autobiographies.

It is interesting to contrast these diaries with those written by women who did not expect eventual publication. What saves Lifshin's diarists from self-absorption is the rendering of daily events without too much elaboration as in the passage from Rita Mae Brown's diary: "This morning thick gray mist wrapped around the house. Damn, I hate February. It's useless as tits on a boar hog. The wind is sharp as a needle. Still, I couldn't stay in the house one more minute." True, the first simile is an exception, but it is part of Brown's Southern background and the inherent humor that goes with the territory. The diary excerpt of potterwoman Moraff is less self-conscious in detailing the aspects of her craft. "Alesia is melting the wax for today's glazes. I told her to watch it carefully, as it's highly flammable. . . .Glaze dries so fast you have to practically have painted your design before the brush even touches the glazed pot."

Writing about travel, or as Lifshin puts it—being somewhere else is seldom a subject of the diarist in the other three anthologies. Going to different places gives women an excuse to leave where they are, providing them with the chance to be someone else. Brooklyn-born Michelle Herman, in her opening sentence embraces and savors nature as she experiences it in the Blue Ridge Mountains: "Everything here is green and brown and red, slow and smooth and old and thick and lush." Rachel De Vries, although she is writing in Kenya, is more concerned with customs and women's lives than with nature. Sarah Arvio takes us along with her on her travels in Milan, Bari, Ivangrad, Paris, and Hamburg and, as she observes the people, places, and customs, we become Sarah for a while.

Lifshin's collection adds many missing pieces of women's lives to the other three volumes. The four together give the reader of diaries a comprehensive picture of women and girls in their times and places.

Margo Culley's *A Day at a Time: The Diary Literature of American Women from 1764 to the Present* is the most recent diary anthology. This work also has the most complete bibliography of women's diaries. The book groups diaries under three headings: In the Fatherland, The Journey Out, and Personal and Political. For the most part, these are the diaries of everyday women, some of which are record-keeping diaries and a few of which are diaries of self-analysis, such as those discussed in Tristine Rainer's *A New Diary.*

The anthology opens with Mary Vial Holyoke's record-keeping diary. It contains the bare bones of narrative, talismans that recall the day's essence: "Jan. 8, 1764. First wore my new Cloth riding hood. [Jan.] 9. My daughter Polly first confined with the quinsy. Took a vomit. [Jan.] 10. Nabby Cloutman watch'd with her. [Jan.] 11. Very ill. Molly Molton watched. [Jan.] 12. Zilla Symonds watched. [Jan.] 13. My Dear Polly Died. Sister Prissy came. [Jan.] 14. Buried." A compressed narrative of sorrow's impact compacted. Such are the diaries of those who record self or family history as well as social, political, meteorological, or artistic events. Today's *self* is not so concise, so factbound, and outer-centered.

Culley's modern diarists are the successors to those anthologized by Moffat and Painter and Holliday. There is Joan Frances Bennett, a native of South Carolina, attending Barnard College and writing her diary as part of a course requirement. As fate would have it, Martin Luther King, Jr. is assassinated that semester. Her response to his death and her experience as a Black woman in New York are the substance of this diary. The one page excerpt from Bonita Wa Wa Calachaw Nuñez is a vision of the future when American Indian women will be freely exercising their intellect, their creativity, and their political expertise.

Friendship between women is beautifully articulated in the excerpt from Mary MacLane whose diary, *The Story of Mary MacLane,* created an excitement that must have matched the publication of Marie Bashkirtseff's. Joyce Mary Horner's diary is self-explanatory: *That Time of Year: A Chronicle of Life in a Nursing Home.* A retired English professor from Mt. Holyoke College and a writer, Horner's account is all the more moving because she is so articulate. Her March 11, 1975, entry concisely captures the atmosphere of a nursing home: "Everyone wants to go home. Perhaps that says too much. Everyone 'wants out.' Or there may be some who are beyond wanting as much as that. But the woman who calls 'Martha' over and over, the woman who calls 'Eileen,' want what they used to have and sometimes think they can get it if they call loud enough." Added insights come through her poems about death's ubiquitous presence. An excerpt from Barbara Smith's journal concludes Culley's collection. Its content informs as it ruminates about the 1979 murders of twelve Black women in Boston whose deaths never captured the press's attention as did the murders of primarily Black male children in Atlanta two years later.

These four anthologies of diary excerpts bring a host of female voices and experiences that resonate inside us, modifying and often blending with our own voices, much as Celie's does in *The Color Purple,* perhaps in a way that Elizabeth Bennet's or Jane Eyre's do not. Celie's letters, written to God but posted to us, enter our being as diary entries do because they are often so intense, so private. In the same way, the letters of Maimie Pinzer to Fanny Howe enter our consciousness by a more direct, more invasive route. Diaries have easier access to our inner selves, drawing into us voices that are, and yet are not, our own. These many and varied texts reflect, no, are, as Culley writes, "life itself—the ultimate text."

According to Harriet Blodgett, women were among the first in England to keep true diaries, and the extant sixteenth century Englishwomen's diaries are among the earliest known. In this essay, Blodgett delves into the history of these important roots and gives us both a genealogy of the genre and some interesting conclusions. It was first published in *WOMEN'S DIARIES, A Quarterly Newsletter*, vol. 4, no 1 (Spring 1986). This material will also be part of her forthcoming book, *Centuries of Female Days: Englishwomen's Private Diaries*, Rutgers University Press, 1988, and is used here with permission.

ENGLISHWOMEN'S DIARIES: HISTORICAL BACKGROUNDS

by Harriet Blodgett

*E*nglish women have written diaries since as early as the sixteenth century, when the English diary began emerging as record-keepers gradually moved away from public events to private ones and from impersonal commentary to a more personal mirroring of themselves. The tradition of female record-keeping is significant, for women were among the first in England to keep true diaries.

Robert Fothergill has traced the history of the diary form in England in his *Private Chronicles* (Oxford University Press, 1974). He states that in the larger tradition of English diary-keeping, the diary as a book reflecting the daily life and impressions of an individual personality was a common form by the eighteenth century. Behind it lay sixteenth century standardized and fragmentary record-keeping habits to which the recorders increasingly brought more of themselves and which were to persist as foci within the more developed diary form. The travel diary existed by the sixteenth century; so, too, did the public diary—a regular-entry record kept largely as a duty, such as a military campaign annual or a record of an embassy, a profession, or the like. A handful of such diaries, all written by men, are extant. By the seventeenth century, the regular-entry record had evolved into the public diary, a form which focused on public events and persons of interest to the writer. Of these early public diaries, still only male versions are known. The formulaic diary of conscience was introduced in the late sixteenth and seventeenth centu-

21

ries and practiced in time by by male and female Puritans and Covenanters, as it would be later by Quakers and Methodists. Such standardized recording of religious soul-searching in forms prescribed by devotional manuals and embodied in celebrated models would serve as the ancestor for the personal diary preoccupied with the inner life. Last, and most important here, is the diary consisting of brief entries of memorable personal records and impressions, and of family records. This was the germ of the diary as we think of it today. Sparsely existent by the sixteenth century in both male and female versions (two women's diaries are extant, though only one in its original form), the personal record had lengthened and become comparatively well-established by the seventeenth century, when both genders kept such books. During the eighteenth century, its potential contents expanded enormously to include anecdotes and accounts of the famous in the manner of the public diary, and self-realizations of the sort found originally only in religious diaries. As the century advanced, romantic self-dramatizing expressions of feeling might also be added. In earlier practice, even emotion was spoken of dispassionately, but after the 1740s, novels of sensibility inspired some readers to undertake their own passionate explorations of consciousness. However, many diaries still remained bare factual records, conspicuously lacking in subjective introspection. Englishwomen over the centuries have kept diaries with all four sorts of focus—travel, public events and persons, conscience, and personal events and impressions. They began early to blend the latter two types and increasingly practiced a form whose contents were imported in the early twentieth century—the French *journal intime*, a serious exploration of the psyche, with characteristic manner of mercurial responsiveness to stimuli.

By the eighteenth century, the eclectic diary was flourishing. Also, the practice of keeping letter-diaries had begun. Writing an ongoing, daily, dated letter addressed to a specific recipient functioned simultaneously as a diary and as correspondence, for the writer retained a copy as a personal record. Moreover, it was established procedure for women (and for men) to keep bound pocket diaries that allotted a set space per day wherein to note appointments and other personal notes. Like letter-diaries, bound memo books continued to be used into the nineteenth century and, with much diminished popularity, still exist. While encouraging women to keep such books, the anonymous American conduct manual, *My Daughter's Manual: Comprising a Summary View of Female Studies, Accomplishments, and Principles of Conduct* (D. Appleton, 1837), describes the practice with a bit of circular reasoning: "Many persons, of both sexes, accustom themselves to keep a journal of their daily engagements. It is for this purpose that so considerable a number of pocket-books are yearly sold; a fact that substantiates the numerous persons preserving such a diary."

The bound memo books of the eighteenth and early nineteenth centuries, which were designed for women, are fascinating curios, at once reference books and diaries. For example, *The Suffolk Ladies Memorandum Book: or Polite Pocket Museum for the Year 1793* contains, besides its ruled diary pages and frontispiece, no less than "A Poetical Address to the British Ladies;" a poem by Burns, with a note about him. "Signs of the Planets and Zodiac, together with Eclipses, Moveable Feasts, Ember Days, Common Notices, Holidays, and Remarkable Days;" "A Table of the Moon;" "The Most Favorite New Songs and Airs Sung at Public Gardens, &c;" "The Flower Basket of Poetical Blossoms (original poems by diverse ladies" answers to puzzles, charades, and enigmas posed during 1792, with a new set for the diarist to work at during 1793; and, finally, "Country Dances for 1793." The two small pocket-books bound in red leather kept by diarist Harriet Grove (1791-1867) in 1809 and 1810, demonstrate another, less frivolous version of the type. After an engraved frontispiece with appropriate verses and "New Songs Sung at Vauxhall and other Public Places," plus the rules for Thomsons' Dances for 1809, *The New Ladies' Memorandum Book for 1809* settles down to a dated entry diary. This is printed in red, one week to a page, each page faced by a ruled page for cash accounts. The second book is even more business-like. Its title page declares it to be *Silvester's Housekeeper's Pocket Book; and Ladies's Daily Journal for 1810*, and its preliminary pages are a "Table of Expenses," a "New Marketing Table," and a description of Hawkstone, Shropshire. The

23

diary section, now printed in black, has on its ruled page a line for each of various household expenses, such as "Meat and Poultry," "Bread and Flour," "Cheese and Butter," "Rent," "Servants' Wages," and "Washing." According to the editor of the manuscript, the diarist in this case simply turned the accounts ledger into extra space for words. One suspects she was not the only diarist to do so. Grove also suggests how important such pocket diaries may have become to women. Her mother had given her the first two books as New Year's gifts, but Grove herself was quick to prepare for the future, and on December 25, 1810, she wrote: "Went to Church being Christmas Day . . . Bought pocket Book for next year" (*The Journal of Harriet Grove for the Years 1809-1810*, London, 1932).

One could keep both a pocket book and an expanded diary. Thus, for example, Samuel Johnson's friend, Hester Thrale (1741-1821), kept not only her massive *Thraliana* diary, but small pocket diaries as well. Not everyone was ambitious enough to keep two diaries, however, or even to expand on all the entries when doing so. Some women merely used their memo books as the basis for an annual summary, after writing which they destroyed the originals. Whenever a diary appears with summaries, one may well suspect memo-books antecedents.

The supposed diary of Lady Grace Mildmay, covering the period 1570 to 1617, is not in fact a daily diary but rather reminiscences written many years later for her daughter. It was probably based on daily memoranda (though not, of course, kept in a bound memo book; her records well predate that custom), which she afterwards destroyed, unfortunately for her right to fame as the first English woman diarist.

To go back to the beginnings of the history of Englishwomen's diary-keeping means, therefore, bypassing Mildmay for Lady Margaret Hoby, whose diary for 1599 to 1605 is extant. Hoby is doubly interesting in being one of the earliest true diarists, male or female. William Matthews' respected bibliography of British diaries lists only two fifteenth century embassy and diplomatic diaries earlier than Hoby's plus a scattering of sixteenth century travel, religious, and public ones, which become more personalized after mid-century. Bibliographer Baron Arthur Ponsonby, in *More English Diaries* (Methuen, 1927), marvels at how Hoby and, later, Lady Anne Clifford, manage "to jump into the correct daily diary method, although it seems unlikely that they were copying any model." The most significant "model" may have been the female engagement with daily trivia and the female concern with private life in the absence of the active public life. However, as a pious Puritan, Hoby apparently found the initial impulse for her diary-keeping in the instruction to keep a record of moral and spiritual self-examination and correction. Yet faith alone is inadequate to explain her diary, for it escapes doctrinal justification and account-keeping as it progresses through the years, and becomes more simply a record of what interests her in her days.

When Lady Hoby's extant diary begins, she has been married for three years to her third husband, Thomas Posthumous Hoby, second son of Sir Thomas Hoby, who was not only the translator of Castiglione's *Courtier*, but also author of an autobiographical memoir, *A Booke of the Travaile and Lief of me Thomas Hoby*, covering the period 1547 to 1564. For the last eight years of his record, Thomas Hoby included brief annual entries concerning his domestic life. Since Lady Margaret kept no diaries during her first two marriages—or at least no evidence shows her to have done so—her father-in-law's manuscript may have served as some inspiration for the personal, rather than devotional, diary she gradually began to keep during her third marriage. If Lady Margaret knew Thomas's *Booke*, which was accessible in the family archives, she had proof that one may properly write of one's domestic affairs without relating them to the divine will, as, increasingly, she does in her diary, making herself an early true diarist, circumstantially, one of the earliest in England.

But whether or not Thomas influenced Margaret, the difference between their books is instructive. Margaret's diary is uniquely hers. His brief, personal, annual entries are strikingly different from her daily ones. To illustrate, Thomas's complete 1559 entry looks like this (*The Travels and Life of Sir Thomas Hoby, Kt. of Bisham Abbey, Written by Himself: 1547-1564*, London 1902):

This yeer cam to the Court Monsr. Monmerency, the Constable's eldest sonn, to confirm the peac betwene England and France.

The Queen was visited with sundrie messagers from great princs, as th'Emperor, the King of Suevia, and divers other.

The viii day of July I came to Bissham with my wief, there to remaine.

The ix day of August I entred into a siknes that continued upon me the space of iij weeks.

The xij of November my wief went from Bissham to London, and there continued iij weeks in phisicke for her great belly, which was supposed to have bine a timpanie or dropsie.

Sample whole entries in Margaret's diary move much closer into her life (*Diary of Lady Margaret Hoby*, London, 1930):

After order taken for the house, and priuat praers, I writt notes into my testement and then brak my fast: after, I wrought, and kept Mr Hoby compenie tell allmost diner time: then I praied and, after dimer [sic], I walked awhill and went to church Wth. Mr Hoby, and when I Cam home wrought tell 6:, then I examened my selfe and praied, walked tell supper time: then I hard the Lector, and after wrought a whill, and so went to bed: Lord, for Christs sack, pardone my drousenes which, with a neclegent mind, caused me to ommitt that medetation of that I had hard, which I ought to haue had.

(Sept. 14, 1599, p.71)

this day, in the afternone, I had had a child brought to se that was borne at Silpho, one Talliour sonne, who had no fundement, and had no passage for

excrementes but att the mouth: I was ernestly in-
treated to Cutt the place to se if any passhage Could
be made, but, although I Cutt deepe and searched,
there was none to be found.

(Aug. 26, 1601, p. 184)

Mr. Hoby, my Mother, and my selfe, went to the
dalls this day: we had in our Gardens a second
sommer, for Hartechokes bare twisse, whitt Rosses,
Read Rosses: and we, hauing sett a musk Rose the
winter before, it bare flowers now. I thinke the Like
hath seldom binn seene: it is a great frute yeare all
ouer.

(Oct. 5, 1603, p. 206)

The difference between 1599 and 1603 in sample entries is con-
spicuous. Margaret's recorded religious fervor abates considerably
as her diary continues; increasingly, the entries become simply
domestic. The diary, which breaks off abruptly in 1605, may have
been abandoned, in fact, because Hoby recognized how far she had
strayed from her pious intentions. Although through the years she
continues laconically to report private prayers among her activities
on many (not all) days, her last few entries concern the visitors and
guests who came to dine on Sundays. Even before that time, however, entries are devoted to recording gossip garnered from friends.
On May 5, 1601, she writes an entire entry on a precise description
of a two-headed calf. Clearly, she was fascinated by the oddities in
creation—and not just as God's handiwork. But contents aside, Margaret, unlike her businesslike father-in-law, who merely kept records which included a few about his personal life, transmits, from
the beginning, some sense of her feelings—penitence, puzzlement,
delight. As the first extant English female diarist, she anticipates
much of what is to come in women's diaries. The sample entries
give one a good sense of her daily activities: praying, attending
church, performing chores—and hers were endless, involved as she
was with both house and estate—doctoring, entertaining visitors,

and taking conjugal walks. Meanwhile, without being confessional or introspective, they convey the sense of her thoughts, self-concept, and reactions. One can see why Cynthia Pomerleau, in her essay "The Emergence of Women's Autobiography in England" (in *Women's Autobiography: Essays in Criticism*, Indiana University Press, 1980), all but implies that diary-writing proper is the creation of women, when she claims that "the idea that oneself, one's feelings, one's spouse and domestic relations were properly and innately worth writing about was essentially a female idea, however tentatively conceived at the time. There is little or no precedent for such a notion, at least in England, in male thinking or practice." Men's diaries do offer some scraps of precedent, but women's offer more than scraps. Before Hoby, Grace Mildmay's missing diary was also apparently a record of herself and her domestic relations. After Hoby, the early seventeenth century diary of Anne Clifford, Countess of Dorset, later also of Pembroke and Montgomery (1590-1676), though still not introspective, is even more personally informative both about states of mind and activities (Anne even includes taking a bath in June 1617.)

The diaries Englishwomen have kept belong to the historical tradition of English diary-keeping, but they also inevitably represent a contribution of the women's own. They are an expression of female lives, perceptions, and behaviors.

Metta Winter, a practicing Quaker and a long-time journal keeper, has done a great deal of research on Quaker diaries, both at Woodbrooke College in Birmingham, England, and at Pendle Hill, Pennsylvania. Her research gives us further insight into the roots of women's diary keeping, and shows that published Quaker journals provided a forum where women were able to hold their own. Also, the Quakers' use of journal keeping as an educational tool for recording spiritual growth offers interesting parallels with today's journal keeping. This essay, first published in *WOMEN'S DIARIES, A Quarterly Newsletter*, vol. 1, no. 2 (Summer 1983) is an adaptation of an article published in the *Friends Journal*, vol. 26, no. 16 (November 1, 1980).

A LOOK AT QUAKER DIARIES
AND THEIR USES

by Metta L. Winter

H istorians disagree as to the number of journals, or "spiritual autobiographies" as they were often called, that were published by Quakers in the early years of the society. Howard Brinton, in his thematic survey entitled *Quaker Journals: Varieties of Religious Experience Among Friends,* believes there are at least 1,000 published journals extant. Luella Wright, in her *Literary Life of the Early Friends,* refers to over 3,000 spiritual journals and confessions published before 1725, which well exceeded all non-Quaker autobiography printed in England during the first seventy-five years of Quakerism. Regardless of which figure is correct, we know that, from the beginning of the Society, Friends kept daily private diaries on which the later published accounts of their "gospel wanderings" were based. Also, from the very beginning, women traveled in the ministry and were seen as spiritual leaders in the meetings equally with men. Since the journals were published as examples of spiritual leadership, Quaker women were much more likely to appear in print than women of any other denomination. The numbers, showing the ratio of women to men are as follows: in Brinton's book, of the total 129 cited, twenty-nine were by women; in Wright's book, of the total 176 cited, twenty-three were by women. Additionally, of the 219 spiritual autobiographies footnoted in Owen Watkins' *The Puritan Experience,* twenty-three were written by women, only two of whom were not Quakers. Since the two major studies cover only the very early period before 1725, it is probable that not very many women's books on any subject were in print before that date.

Over the centuries, women continued to hold their place in Quaker publications. The numbers, from "Women Writers Among Friends" in the 1918 *Journals of Friends' Historical Society*, break down as follows:

total Quaker women writers	Century
84 in print	17th
63 in print	18th
250 in print	19th

This covers diaries, tracts and autobiographies. It was not until the 19th century that censorship was lifted and more individualistic books were published, such as *The Journals of Caroline Fox, 1835-71.*

Why did early Friends keep these private diurnal jottings? Why did official bodies of the Society posthumously publish edited versions of these writings? And why did the Society as an institution so heartily exhort its members, especially the young, to read them?

In the seventeenth century, the keeping of a daily private record was a socially accepted and educationally sanctioned activity, for literate adults as well as children, both in "the world" and in the novice Society. Owen Watkins in his book speculates that the overall popularity of keeping a diary was largely due to the abolishment of the English priesthood during the Reformation. As oral confession became illegal, the practice of daily confession took the form of a written diary. It was here in privacy that one could write of progress or set-backs in life and of the ongoing struggle with sin. It was here that one could remain grateful in spirit to God, as God's daily mercies were enumerated.

If, as Friends believed, life was a search for the Light Within—for "Christ residing in the Heart"—and that all external action, both verbal and physical, should emanate from this Source, then it was incumbent upon believers to become attuned to it. Processes were thus needed to assist the seeker in developing this habit of waitfulness and self-examination. The keeping of a diary filled this need most naturally. Writing in the diary provided a reviewable record of the seeker's spiritual changes wherein progress in cultivating the attitude of "heart watching" could be charted. Indeed the contents of the early published journals give evidence of a passionate concern for purity of heart.

In addition to this documentary function, diary keeping provided a vehicle for obtaining clearness on an idea or action. The early writings illustrate this process of differentiating between a genuine leading of the spirit and self-will, of working through opposing desires, and of challenging sources of fear which could cripple effective action. The joyful declaration of the validity of one's call and the recording of states of spiritual peace obtained from obedience to it shows how this writing process could additionally act as a means of solidifying the seekers' convictions and of reinforcing their commitment to them. Thus, the journal was used not only as the record of a life of practical mysticism, but as a tool which could be actively used to achieve and sustain this life orientation as well.

The officially published version of George Fox's *Journal* became the prototype upon which the editing of all subsequently published journals was based. Typically, they included a demonstration of the miracle the Inner Light created in the writer's life, including the successive steps by which she or he obtained spiritual harmony; a recounting of religious crises and how these were resolved; and the carrying out of the commands of the spirit in outward action with an account of the resulting inner peace.

Careful selection of content from the private diary entries was most important, for the ultimately published "official journal" was intended to serve a proselytizing function. All passages in the original which portrayed ideas or actions contrary to those of the sect were edited out. Only those passages which gave an unequivocal testimony to the new way of life were included; passages which would arouse the "slumbering seed of God" in the reader and excite him or her to action. It was the spiritual basis of human nature, not the intellect, to which these writings were intended to appeal. Journals published before 1825 rarely contained references to "the world's learning" in terms of history, philosophy or current events, but rather those passages were chosen which portrayed spiritual truths through biblical imagery, dreams, openings and visions. Yet, in spite of the editorial uniformity of these early journals, the richness of the individual writer's own experiences showed through and spoke to the condition of the reader. The experimental truths of Christianity embodied in these accounts and specific examples of the consistent way in which God deals with people brought many converts to the Society.

As time went on, the publication of the journals took on a more pastoral function. Editorial decisions on the content of the journals emphasized those descriptions of facts, emotions and experiences depicted by individuals who had the welfare of the group at heart. Studying this common body of literature was a way of strengthening relations between geographically dispersed groups of Friends, fostering group solidarity and reducing internal schisms by portraying a "unanimity and concurrence" in all affairs concerning the individual and the corporate whole. Quaker women's diaries did not differ in content from the men's because in the very early period of Quakerism, all diaries were censored and made uniform in content before publication. No doubt their own early jottings were different, but research remains to be done in this area, and all the original material is in London.

Having served the Quakers well for over 300 years, the tool of journal keeping is still relevant today. Its power in the naming process cannot be over-estimated. While the traditional as well as historical uses of the journal apply as much now as ever, we, today, have great advantages over our ancestors in keeping journals. While they had superb intuitive sense of the use of the tool, we benefit from the insights of the social sciences which help to illuminate how this process of journal writing actually works. In addition, we can exercise freedoms to use our journals experimentally, which our forebears did not possess.

We know from psychology, for example, that until an emotion, idea, event or object is named, its nature cannot be understood—in fact, for the individual it does not exist in any truly useful way. Viewed most simply, then, when we write descriptively in the journal, we are engaged in applying names to experience. Through our choice of name, the characteristics of the experience are brought to the fore so that they can be examined and the nature of the experience can be more fully determined. The journal writing process is, however, not as simple as that; unlike with other forms of writing, we need not struggle to find the most illuminating words the first time around. This type of writing is by definition a repetitive, evolutionary process, mirroring the ongoing changes in our own development. It is a structured way of keeping an ongoing conversation with ourselves.

Also, our privacy as writers can be assured, and we are consequently freed to write both copiously and without censorship, making the most effective use of the journal's experimental dimensions. We can write about an experience not just once but many times, for journal keeping at its most fruitful is cyclical and often contradictory. As we take advantage of the distancing perspective which comes from rereading previous entries, we find that in writing from various points in time and points of view, different qualities and characteristics of the experience emerge. We can use this process of review and reflection to pose the right questions to ourselves, thus evoking still more diverse meanings. Calling upon the resources provided by our daily experiences, our dreams, waking fantasies, or sketches (for journals can be visual as well) provides additional depth and richness. Unhampered by sanctions against the world's knowledge, we are free to incorporate into our writings the wisdom of other seekers, conveyed through literature, the arts, the spoken word. Thus over time, the journal becomes an accumulated store of names—of truths gleaned from both our inner and outer worlds.

This uncensored style of journal keeping may seem to be creating a jumble of contradictions aiding confusion instead of clarifying it, but this is not so. After writing in the journal over a period of time a number of things begin to happen. When we pay careful attention to dreams and waking fantasies, the more potent these sources of knowledge become. So it is with journal writing itself. As we attend seriously to all our sources of wisdom, as we treat them respectfully in the act of writing them down, the quality as well as breadth increases. Our ability to wait, to watch, to attend with confidence begins to increase; as our skills of observation develop, a heightened perception of what is important, a kind of unconscious selectivity begins to occur. Along with this goes the curious facet of journal keeping that upon rereading material written over a period time, it seems to sort itself out, refine itself, and coalesce into discernable patterns. The significance of happenings which could not be so clearly known at the time can be seen to fit into a whole The path on which we travel becomes more visible to us. With the emergence of these patterns comes a synthesis of all the truths, which we may not have been aware of having guided us.

The contents of the journal provide a grounding for self reliance, a source of self validation, for the assumption of an appropriate sense of responsibility for our words as well as our actions. But beyond all this, the most fundamental use of the journal has always been as a source of comfort—companionship on the solitary journey of life.

To many, the diaries of farm women seem very dull. The days pass without variation, and the diary entries, too, seem to reflect a life of unrelenting boredom and small scope. And always there is some mention of the weather. Why, we may wonder? But Thoreau himself wrote that it was important, in keeping a journal, to describe the weather, or character of the day, as it affects our feelings. "That which was so important at the time cannot be unimportant to remember." So, too, with the entries that describe the daily chores, the births, illnesses, deaths, visits and church going. All these make up the patchwork of lives as they were lived, harsh, perhaps, but true. We can learn much from them, if we give them the attention they deserve, but, as Gould points out, they must be read without our twentieth century mind set which obscures the meaning. This article was first published in *WOMEN'S DIARIES, A Quarterly Newsletter,* vol. 1, no. 4 (Winter 1983).

ON READING THE DIARIES OF AMERICAN FARM WOMEN

by Emilie W. Gould

*D*iaries may reveal the drudgery, intellectual poverty, and social subordination of rural women in the nineteenth century America . . . or, they can show the symmetry, values, and beauty of a vanished way of life. Country women have left few records that speak so directly to the heart as do their diaries. When we read their stories of endless chores, sick children, farm accidents, deaths, and the cirumcscribed lives, we weep for the writers. But perhaps our tears are wasted. Contemporary values may color our judgment. In particular, our feminist perspective—our assurance of the sisterhood of women—can lead us to assign to nineteenth century women emotions that *we* would feel in certain situations.

Obviously, we do share basic human instincts and many cultural assumptions with women of the past. But Freud and Erica Jong were not part of their collective consciousness. A century ago, women operated in a different psychological and political context. We may overlook what the diarists felt was important in their own lives in our search for double meanings, deliberate evasions, personal guilt, psychosis, and social pathology. We may also ignore the message in other creative expressions—the quilts and coverlets and well-seamed clothing—artistic creations which demonstrate that women's lives were not entirely bitter and that hard work was not without its intrinsic joys.

Another factor makes the lifestyle of traditional country women problematic: until recently, printed records were conspicuously ab-

39

sent. In the vacuum, society created a number of mythic stereotypes—the pioneer woman was drudge, helpmate, or feminist radical; the country woman, lacking the pioneer spirit, toiled in inarticulate silence. These stereotypes may have a measure of statistical validity, but they fail to capture the pragmatic spirit of these nineteenth century women. Recently, researchers have discovered, catalogued, and published a variety of reference works and diaries. Some editors have directly confronted these biases and stereotypes; others reflect them.

In *Farm Women on the Prairie Frontier: A Sourcebook for Canada and the United States* (Metuchen, NJ: Scarecrow Press, 1982), Carol Fairbanks and Sara Brooks Sundberg combined an excellent bibliography of nineteenth and early twentieth century diaries, memoirs, and fiction with interpretive essays on the cultural geography of agricultural settlement in the interior grasslands, the helpmate image of women on the Canadian prairie frontier, women's perspectives in fiction, and the "creation of a usable past." The last is a vision of the past—an idealization of how society could be recreated in the wilderness—that nourished and sustained frontier women. The essays concentrate on the mythic dimension of the frontier in the nineteenth century, looking to contemporary diaries and literary sources for validation. On the other hand, the very project—a book that concentrates on frontier women alone—reflects the mandate of feminist historians in our own times and carries mythic overtones of its own.

While such a sourcebook is an excellent guide, original sources are obviously superior references. Annotated diaries of rural women have often appeared as a byproduct of genealogical research.

For example, Blanche Brown Bryant and Gertrude Elaine Baker have edited *The Diaries of Sally and Pamela Brown, 1832-1838. . . . Plymouth Notch, Vermont* (Springfied, VT: The William L. Bryant Foundation, 1970). First one sister, then the other, kept a diary in the same book. Both describe the settled way of life in rural Vermont that each, in turn, gave up for marriage and migration to Schoolcraft, Michigan.

Particularly in the light of the prairie sourcebook, it is interesting to scan the Brown sisters' diaries for any factors that might have "pushed" them into marriage, or "pulled" them west. But both sisters write in an objective and abbreviated style that gives little indication of unrealistic ambitions or excessive regrets. The tone of the diaries is almost stoic. The narrative style displays a philosophical orientation that owes more to the kind of fatalism aligned with "primitive Christianity," than to self-actualization and modern psychology.

Another excellent diary displays a similar voice. *And a White Vest for Sam'l: An Account of Rural Life in Western N.Y.* was edited and published by Helene C. Phelan in 1976 (Almond, NY). Day by day it covers a period of five years in the life of Maria Whitford of Alfred Station, NY—from January 1, 1857 to July 17, 1861. (Two weeks after the last entry, Maria died at the age of 30.) The yearly round of rural work, the weekly calendar of religious gatherings, and a full account of daily social contacts comprise a mass of detail that gradually lets the reader understand Maria's nineteenth century world-view, without undue extrapolation from the reader's twentieth century experience.

Maria's religious perspective is crucial to reading her diary. She was a Seventh Day Baptist, or "Sabbatarian," and celebrated the Sabbath on Saturday (the Seventh Day of the Creation). Her denomination originated in a religious schism among the Puritan settlers of the early seventeenth century Massachusetts, and the group migrated to the Alfred area after first establishing settlements in Rhode Island and the Hooskick Valley of eastern New York. Although a distinctive group, the Sabbatarians were not unusual in the Burned-Over District of western New York State; religious revivals and evangelical religions dominated New England, New York and the Mid-West at this time.

Maria's attitude toward work is the first feature of her life and religious attitudes to claim the reader's attention. A second is the separate but linked worlds of husband and wife—the separate domains of men and women. A final feature, Maria's treatment of illness and death, is particularly tragic; one hopes her vision of the hereafter reconciled her to her own fate.

As Phelan reminds us, we must analyze Maria's workload with

critical detachment. The catalog of chores tends to obscure the character of the diarist. Her days were exhausting, and it is difficult to visualize the work required for tasks that are now performed with the flip of a switch. "For Maria, work was an obsession; but she did not think of it that way. She had grown up in a society where survival was dependent on work. . . In addition, she also was the product of a Protestant-Christian heritage that equated work with virtue, and virtue as necessary to one's ultimate destiny."

Also, one was proud of one's work. Throughout the diary, Maria describes the occasions she found to sew, quilt, and weave bed coverings and cloth. She made bonnets, children's clothing, lamp mats for gifts, and endless shirts for her husband Samuel. Some things were intended for sale; some of her handiwork went to support the local minister; but much of her sewing was done for her husband, cousins, and friends. Almost every day, Maria visited in the community and, at least once, she and Samuel left their farm for a long trip to visit relatives.

Maria's statements vary from the view of farm women bowed down by farm work. She rarely mentions any other chores than washing, cooking, cleaning the house, and tending poultry. Her home kept her very busy, but her husband handled the rest of the work—and, when she was sick, he washed the clothes, cooked the meals, and once even sewed a carpet together. This close cooperation was rarely commented on by Maria because she found no reason to question the validity of dividing work into different spheres for men and women. Underlying her own sense of merit was the Biblical assurance that men and women complemented each other and were equal as souls in the eyes of God.

The Bible also supported Maria in illness and grief. After her cousin's death, Maria writes: "Death has taken another of my choicest friends but I will not complain for tis from 'him who doeth all things well.' She was pure in heart and I loved her dearly, but she is only added to the LOVED ONES that have gone before. May my life be spent in such a way that I may meet them in a BETTER LAND where parting shall never come and we shall see the brighter glories of the New Jerusalem and sing songs with our dear Redeemer round the throne of God."

Such deep religious belief is hard to credit today; we live in a skeptical, secular age and even evangelical denominations have adopted more humanistic theologies. Nonetheless, we should try and accept Maria's belief and sincere faith in the certainty of her redemption. Religious certainty is manifested throughout the diary in her relationships with husband, family, and church, and in her calm acceptance of illness, death, and fate.

As readers, our contemporary struggles for equal opportunity, equal recognition, and equal pay for equal work can blind us to the symmetry of the traditional life. Or we may disparage those lives. Many commentaries written about rural women in the nineteenth century focus on the struggle and not the caring spirit of frontier settlement, the sacrifice and not the feast. In reading diaries we should recognize the incremental pride the authors felt in meeting the challenge of farm work day after day, the reciprocal benefits of traditional marriages, and the real consolation of religions when death won another battle.

We have much in common with nineteenth century rural women, but some attitudes we do not share. We need to recognize our biases in interpreting their diaries, and we need to accept the biases that animated their lives.

It is a matter of history that the doors to higher education gradually began to open to women in the mid-nineteenth century. Prior to that time, women were certainly educated, but either at home or at a variety of religious or ladies schools. Since they were not admitted to the practice of the three professions for which colleges and universities educated the man—i.e., the law, medicine, and the ministry—there seemed no need to make such education available to them. But with the advent of higher education in the liberal arts and in science, it was no longer possible to keep degrees as an exclusively male prerogative. In short, women also insisted on being allowed into the male-dominated professions. This inevitably created problems, forcing women to choose between their traditional roles and new roles which were to be forged with difficulty and pain. By looking at the diaries of educated women of the nineteenth century, Erickson gives us some insight into the process of change which is still giving rise to educational innovations today.

This article is an edited version of part of Erickson's Senior Project for Bard College, "When the hand that penned it shall be dust:" Women and Their Diaries in Nineteenth-Century America. Permission to quote excerpts from the diaries of Ellen Skeel Adee, Ida Frank Guttman, Abby Rankin Holden, and Elma G. Martin is courtesy, Vassar College Library.

WOMEN'S EDUCATION IN THE NINETEENTH CENTURY, AS REFLECTED IN THEIR DIARIES

by Jill E. Erickson

> O this learning
> what a thing it is
> Taming of the Shrew, I, ii

*T*he educated woman in nineteenth-century America faced a difficult problem, for, as Barbara Welter states in *Dimity Convictions* (Ohio University Press, 1976), "she could not be truly womanly if she was truly intellectual." The challenge of reconciling the heart with the intellect was faced by every intellectual woman, though some confronted it better than others. Margaret Fuller, for example, wrote in her diary, "I shall always reign through the intellect, but the life, the life! Oh my God! shall that never be sweet!" Maria Mitchell, Lucy Larcom and Alice James chose not to marry as their solution to the problem. However, remaining unmarried did not diminish the difficulties of being an intellectual woman, as their diaries indicate: Lucy Larcom resorted to religion; Alice James, to invalidism; and Maria Mitchell, to polemics on female education.

But younger women, just being subjected to the opening up of educational opportunities, were not yet aware of the complex problems that these older women had encountered. For the younger women, education was a chance to be away from home and to establish close female friendships with other students and teachers. Often, it was a religious experience as well. The diaries of these young women vividly point up their reactions to these new opportunities.

The diaries under consideration here vary widely in style from the matter-of-fact listings of Ida Guttman to the verbose religious musings of Lucy Larcom. The Vassar students considered here structured their diaries around the daily routines of attending classes, going to chapel, and, in the case of Ellen Adee, recovering from illness. The structure of the diaries of older women reflects the random pattern of their lives. Naturally, the younger women exhibited a greater interest in romantic stirrings. All the diarists adhered to the traditional dated entry form, kept more or less frequently. Sections of the diaries of Lucy Larcom and Maria Mitchell are travel diaries, documenting their trips. What is crucial, however, is the essential struggle between the heart and the intellect.

Early nineteenth-century educators believed in education for women only insofar as it might reinforce the dominance of sensibility and feeling over intellect. Until the middle of the nineteenth century, women's education consisted of instruction in the womanly skills: embroidery, painting, French, singing, and playing the harpsichord. Gradually, the curriculum began to change. Between 1830 and 1860, women's seminaries and colleges introduced courses that required thinking, though they always sought a balance between the intellect and feminine nature. Because the majority of the students were ill-prepared, most women's colleges had to lower their academic standards. Smith was the first to insist on the same entrance requirements as the best men's colleges.

Typically, the limited curriculum for women was rationalized on medical grounds; medical opinions on the dangers of higher education to women's health were rampant in the nineteenth century. In his book *Sex in Education,* published in 1872, former Harvard Medical School professor Edward H. Clarke concluded from a study of six patients, that "women who went to college . . . were likely to suffer mental and physical breakdowns and possibly sterility." In 1895, the faculty of the University of Virginia announced that "women were often physically unsexed by the strains of study."

Diaries reflect the changes which education underwent during the nineteenth century. In 1811, Nancy Maria Hyde went to school, when her family was in financial difficulty, in order to learn the arts of embroidery and painting so that she might be a better teacher. Elma Martin, who attended Vassar College in 1892, enrolled in German, mathematics, Latin, hygiene, and rhetoric. However, although the educational emphasis changed, the position of the educated woman remained problematic, for one of the major drawbacks of women's education was that the students had no way to use their education after graduation. The reactions against higher education for women at the turn of the century was partially in response to the difficulties faced by college women in attempting to put their education to practical use. In spite of the availability of higher education, women were still expected to play the same roles: wife and mother. The diarists considered here pour onto their pages a great deal of self-hate, hesitancy, and insecurity—much of it rooted in the dilemma of the educated woman.

Educated women began diaries for the same reasons anyone begins a diary. In *The Writings of Nancy Maria Hyde* (Russell Hubbard, 1816), Hyde wrote that her diary was "a daily account of [her] life" which she began in order to "render the work of daily self-examination more perfect." "I never kept a journal before," began Abby Holden, whose manuscript "Diary" is in the Vassar College Special Collections, "but in this one I am going to write down facts or feelings in my daily life, just as I wish." Later, in a discussion with some friends as to the good of keeping a journal, Holden came out in favor of it, as it was the only place where she could express her feelings. Ellen Skeel Adee described her journal, also at Vassar, as a "brief record of the thought and deeds for one year," and later suggested that journals were really quite useful because "when you really write down your feelings in black and white, you often see how foolish they are and so drive them away altogether." Even in their brief statements on the purpose of keeping journals, these young women expressed a sense of freedom denied them in day-to-day life.

Nevertheless, there are some diaries that give no clue as to the reason for their existence. Ida Guttman's, in the Vassar College

Special Collections, is a case in point. It consists of almost identical entries throughout the entire diary. Typical is the following:

> Arouse about 7; breakfasted at 7:45; made bed; studied and recited all day as usual; lunched at 12:15; spent about an hour on the lake in the P.M.; was excused by Miss Goddsell for Thursday; had dinner at 5:15; made a call on Miss Leech; Chapel at 6:30; read a little in ? had a very pleasant call on Miss B ? She is so kind and lovely. Met Miss Acker in her room. Came back to my room and returned about 10.

Some indication of her aim in keeping a diary occurs in the following entry, which appears almost in the middle of the diary:

> Am not satisfied with my diary; as it is composed of only the facts without comments; but I have so little time, and so many come into our room. Of course, I am always glad to have them; but when they are here I can not write.

Unfortunately, Guttman's realization that her diary was somehow lacking did not inspire her to new heights; it remains the same throughout.

Lucy Larcom is the most outspoken about why she kept a diary. In fact, her extensive commentary on the use of her journal is more interesting than anything else she wrote, most of which is sentimental nineteenth-century religious commentary. In *Lucy Larcom, Life, Letters, and Diary* (Houghton, Mifflin & Co., 1895), she described her journal as "a ventilator from the interior," and said that she wrote in order "to keep track of myself, and give account of myself to myself."

Larcom did not want to to write a journal of the "'subjective'" which she always thought foolish. She faced a dilemma in her diary, the book of the self, because the nature of the diary is private communication rather than shared language. She wrote, "I don't want to feel interested in anything which is only to benefit myself, and I don't want to write these trifles for other people's eyes." She resolved the dilemma by imagining that she was writing her journal for someone else—her friend Esther.

The oddity of such an attitude cannot be sufficiently underscored, since privacy is one of the most accepted rules of journal keeping, although probably there are few diaries that have not been shown to some other person at least once. To a twentieth-century reader, Larcom reveals the most traditionally feminine sense of self when she writes that "self is a mere speck on the great horizon of life," and "it is never good to make self the centre of thought."

At one point, noting that she had not written in her book for months, Larcom wrote that "while there is so much to be lived outside, who cares for the little self-life of a journal?" However, this negative self-image was balanced by another entry:

It may be good for me to read the record of myself
as I have been, —cheerful or morbid,— and of what
I have read, thought and done, wisely or unwisely.

Of the educated diarists discussed here, Charlotte Forten is the most self-critical. The editor of *The Journal of Charlotte Forten: A Free Negro in the Slave Era* (Collier Books, 1961) attributed that entirely to her "constant awareness that she was a Negro." There is no question that race was a major factor in Forten's low self-esteem, but the fact that she was female must also have exacerbated her feelings of insecurity. When asked to write a poem for a school event, she declined the honor because she felt "unworthy." Eventually forced to write it, she still feared the task was "quite beyond [her] powers." Finally realizing that she would have to depend on herself, she asked, "What can that self produce? Nothing, nothing but *doggerel!*"

Often entries on birthdays and at the beginning of the new year tend to be most self-critical for any diarist. Forten is no exception. On her twenty-first birthday, she wrote:

My birthday. Twenty-one today! It grieves me to think it; — to think that I have wasted so many years. I dare not dwell upon the thought!

On another birthday, she wrote:

My birthday. — How much I feel today my own utter insignificance! It is true the years of my life are but few. But have I improved them as I should have done? No! I feel grieved and ashamed to think how very little I know to what I should know of what is really good and useful.

Another diarist, Nancy Maria Hyde, was also frequently self-critical. On her birthday she reflected:

I behold continual imperfection in duty, and constant inability to reach the standard of excellence which imagination has formed. In all my past actions, I discover error and frailty, and self-knowledge leaves me justly fearful that my future life will be equally frail, equally imperfect.

With this penchant for self-deprecation, which she shared with many of the educated women, Hyde always expected the worst and was frequently surprised if anything went right. Of her teaching position, she wrote:

Considerable encouragement is received, in an undertaking, begun on my part with fear and trembling; continued in doubt and perplexity; but which at last, has been crowned with unexpected success.

Ellen Adee, a Vassar student, was required to read one of her papers in chapel, before all her classmates. Convinced it was awful, she tried to reassure herself with little success. She measured her intellect in terms of the heart—in terms of whether or not her friends would like her—and she was convinced she would fail. Afterwards, she wrote:

> Well gloria in the highest glory—glory be to God in high! It is over! What I have dreaded and dreaded is over. . . . The girls say I did nicely, but I have not the remotest idea how I read it . . How sweet congratulations are! Gloria.

Teachers played a crucial role in the lives of these young educated women. Combining love for a teacher with the intellectual process avoided the judgment of heartlessness because of being educated. Close relationships often developed between female students and their female teachers. One of the first entries in Elma Martin's diary, also at Vassar, was a list of her teachers with a description of each. Fraulein Neef "talks as if she had too many teeth," while Miss Richardson was "of medium height, rather slender [with] iron grey hair and steely eyes [and] a nose which is an acute angle." There is no doubt that these teachers had considerable influence over their students. When Fraulein Neef told Martin that she had written "a very good paper" in German, Martin noted in her diary that she "could have embraced her."

Charlotte Forten also developed a great intimacy with her teacher, Mary Shepard, and uses romantic language to describe a walk they took:

> My beloved teacher and I walked home in the quiet starlight— . . . And more delightful it seemed to me with that dear friend, the remembrance of whose kind words and loving sympathy will remain even after I have parted from her, one of the happiest of my life . . .

Abby Holden was even more enamored of her teacher, to whom she referred as "Dear Dear Miss Clarke." The bulk of Holden's journal is filled with expressions of love and devotion toward the older woman. Holden's one sadness at going home for Christmas vacation was that she had to leave Miss Clarke:

> . . . there is one, whom I am sorry to leave, Dear Dear Miss Clarke, I love her so much, I never loved a Lady outside of my relatives, as much as I do her, I would be so happy if she would only love me a little . . .

Just before summer vacation, Holden learned that Miss Clarke would not be returning in the Fall. The last entry in her diary is filled with expressions of despair:

> All my longings and prayers have been in vain she does not love, not but that she is always lovely and kind, so very kind to me, and yet why should she love me when there are so many beautiful and smart girls who are so much more worthy to be loved than I, and yet I don't believe one of them loves her more than I do. She has been a dear kind friend to me, any way, and I think she may love me a little.

Holden obviously wanted more from her teacher than kindness, and her unrequited desire for love resulted in an extremely negative view of herself.

Religion was an intrinsic part of the education of nineteenth-century women. Mt. Holyoke's catalogue promised to make female education "a handmaid to the Gospel and an efficient auxiliary in the great task of renovating the world." According to a student, Mary Lyon's "first aim was to make us christians; her second to cultivate us intellectually." In 1872, the *Smith College Official Circular* described the role of the woman's school as follows:

> . . . to furnish young women with that general yet

appropriate discipline of all their powers and faculties which will qualify them, in a fully developed womanhood, with a sound mind and a pure heart in a healthy body, to do work of life for which God has made them, in any place to which in His providence they may be called.

Vassar students were required to attend chapel regularly, and detailed accounts of the sermons they heard can be found in many of their diaries. Religious belief was considered appropriate to the female nature that was dominated by the heart. The union of religion and education allowed the educated woman to combine the heart and the intellect without finding it necessary to succumb to marriage.

Religiosity was so embedded in the education that it pervaded the lives and diaries of these young women. Elma Martin, at Vassar in the late 1800s, kept a diary that, though quite tedious, intricately combined religious beliefs with day-to-day college life. Chapel was regularly recorded in the diary, but it did not take precedence over fudge making or taffy pulls. An entry on the righteousness, sublimity, and powerfulness of God was followed by the information that Miss Witcome was to be "Queen of Hearts" because she had received fifty-six valentines, rather than Miss Cobb who had received only forty-seven. The knowledge that Christ appealed to man's good side was dutifully noted, but so was the fact that the maids wore green ribbons on St. Patrick's Day. She wrote very little about her actual studies.

Although Abby Holden's diary was filled with her love for Miss Clarke, an occasional expression of religious thought did occur. If she tried to live nearer to God, she expected all her problems would be solved. Her perception of death was infused with pious sentimentality. When angels came to take her baby sister "never to know sin or sorrow," Rankin wished that she, too, had died when a baby. But on reflection avowed that "Perhaps God has something for me to do in the world. I am sure he has, and I will try to do his will . . ."

The diary of Ellen Adee similarly reveals an intelligent, loving young woman, who is in addition very religious. Most of her diary was written when she was at home recovering from typhoid fever, which resulted in her losing most of her hair and prevented her from graduating with her class. When asked which she regretted most, she decided it was the latter because "hair will grow, but I never can graduate with '69 now."

Religion for Adee was not blind faith. She was not afraid to ponder on, or even question, religious conventions:

> . . . last year my opinions as regards fasting, were
> received as almost heretical by the Church girls. . .
> I have always thought it right to give up gaieties
> such as opera, theater, parties and dancing, but as
> regards fasting I am undecided.

She viewed consecrated bread and wine as "*holier* than ordinary bread and wine," for if it were only bread and wine, why should it be revered, and why should we "be so exhorted to try and examine ourselves before we par[take] of the holy sacrament"

On the one hand, the church served as an intellectual stimulus when she was away from Vassar. "What an interminable day this has been," she wrote: "I don't know what I would do if I never went to church!" On the other, it demanded an emotional response which was easily aroused by fire and brimstone sermons. She described one of the Sunday sermons:

> A sermon from Dr. Loomis on the uncertainty,
> frailty and disappointments of life . . . A hymn on
> hell and its dangers, and a dirge in conclusion set
> some of the girls in tears and made them all feel sad
> and desolate.

Adee concluded her diary with a few thoughts on her commencement once she was away from Vassar. She found the mere possession of an academic degree did not provide the "beautiful joy" that she had expected, for she realized that a diploma was "not quite the philosopher's stone." Adee was coming to the disappointing conclusion that she had no way to use her education now that she was graduated. She regretted no longer being part of Vassar College, which "home excepted, had become the dearest place upon earth."

Lucy Larcom is best known as a representative of the Lowell factory girls. She wrote a great deal of poetry for *The Lowell Offering*, a literary magazine produced by the working girls. She had a strong sense of herself as a woman, as this entry from her diary indicates:

> I am so glad to be needed, as I seem to be now, by several of my friends: my thoughts, my care, my suggestions seem of some value. It is a woman's want, and I feel a woman's gratification in being allowed to think a little for others.

Although she suggested the role of "giver" for women, she was by no means oblivious to the limitations put upon educated women. In a rare moment of revelation, she wrote, "Girls will be ill-educated, until their teachers are allowed the time and thoughts which teachers of men are expected to take. " Intelligent women probably realized they were faced with the handicap of an inferior education, and were also aware that it was a consequence of sex.

Larcom was an older woman, but she too, was devoted to religion. Its influence in her diary is overwhelming, and suggests a need to fill her life with something which was socially acceptable. Even as a teacher and writer, she was faced with the emptiness of her life. Religion provided a direction and a meaning which she viewed as a necessity for any woman: "Oh! what is any woman's life worth without the friendship of the One ever near, the only divine?" Larcom was no doubt correct in her conclusion that a single, childless, educated woman needed religion in order to make her life meaningful in a society which gave women no credit for intelligence, but praised them most for their roles as wife and mother.

Astronomer Maria Mitchell, an intellectual woman in a scientific field entirely dominated by men, was acutely aware of the injustices which a female had to face when getting an education. She became involved with astronomy because her father was devoted to it, and involved all his children with his passion. Mitchell was aware, however, that this set of circumstances which encouraged her to pursue her intellectual interests was not commonly available to women. For twenty years, she was librarian of the Nantucket Atheneum, where she bought "not such books as the people want, but books just above their wants, and they will reach up to take what is put out for them." She spent the next twenty years as a professor at Vassar College. The plight of the educated woman in nineteenth-century America is the subject of many of the most striking passages of her diary, published as *Maria Mitchell: Life, Letters and Journals* (Freeport, NY: Books for Libraries Press, 1971). She felt that educated women had to make the decision that their lives would encompass more than simply "women's work." She used the needle as the symbol of the chain that "fettered her more than the laws of the country." Later, however, she suggested that stitching was in fact good training for the study of astronomy, for it trained the girl's eye from early childhood to be keen.

Mitchell was also well aware of the difficulties in combining intellect with romance, and was herself intellectually driven to the love of women over that of men. She wrote that "the love of one's sex is precious, for it is neither provoked by vanity nor retained by flattery; it is genuine and sincere. I am grateful that I have had much of this in my life." For her, marriage was not a viable alternative because in nineteenth-century America marriage extolled the superiority of the husband over a submissive, dependent wife. She felt that the single life was the only possible life for the educated woman if she wanted to retain her self-respect. She also believed that every woman was born "with more than the average heart," and saw love as a necessity, but felt that a woman need not sacrifice her desires in order to follow her intellectual pursuits.

In conclusion, the diaries of these educated and intellectual women testify to the struggle that women had to undergo to obtain even a meager education in comparison to that received by most men. The diary served as a place where they could vent some of their misgivings and dilemmas about being educated women. The diaries often captured the emptiness of these women's lives, an emptiness which came, at least in part, from the absence of that social security that could only be achieved as wife and mother. Nancy Hyde wrote of the monotony of her days which "are so much alike, it is difficult to distinguish them, or to avoid mistaking the lying sister for the same." Charlotte Forten wondered why it was that she had "this strange feeling of not *living out myself.*" Her existence seemed "not *full* not expansive enough."

"My whole life has lost the feeling of reality: I cannot tell why," wrote Lucy Larcom. She imagined she felt as "the world might have felt, when going through some of its slow transitions from chaos into habitable earth,—waiting for sunshine, and bursting buds, and running rivers." She adds, "I suppose I am not ready for life yet." And Ellen Adee lamented, "so often it seems to me that I am leading a worthless life."

Young women were often waiting for a husband so that their role might be established, but older single women had resigned themselves, in one way or another, to being educated and single. The diaries document the loneliness of women who had defied the traditional role models in an attempt to establish new ones. They also illustrate the importance placed on religion in the education of women, for the religious sphere was considered the natural and proper place for a woman's heart. By infusing education with conventional notions of womanhood, society could continue to control the most educated of women. A tension was created in the lives of these women between their status as educated women and society's definition of what a woman was qualified to learn and to be.

On September 25, 1854, at the age of thirty-six Maria Mitchell wrote of her life, "The best that can be said of my life so far is that it has been industrious, and the best that can be said of me is that I have not pretended to what I was not." Although Mitchell was fortunate enough to find a career to match her talents and capabilities, most educated women found professional doors closed to them.

All that remains of their promise and potential, their distress and ambivalence, are their diaries.

In 1974, the publication of *Revelations: Diaries of Women* did not cause a ripple on the literary scene. In fact, according to Moffat, the first edition was not even remaindered, but sent almost immediately to the shredder. Since then, however, the editors' faith has been vindicated, for this seminal work, revolutionary in the field of women's studies and research into women's nontraditional writings, has enjoyed wide-spread use as a text and has remained in continuous publication in a paperback edition. In this article, Moffat takes a look at a few of the diaries that have been published since *Revelations,* and gives an insightful analysis of the value of these records of the shortened lives of highly gifted young women. This article was first published in *WOMEN'S DIARIES, A Quarterly Newsletter,* vol. 2, no. 1 (Spring 1984).

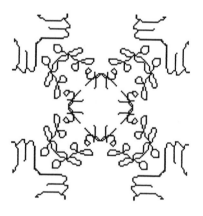

ON READING THE DIARIES OF GIFTED
WOMEN WHO DIED YOUNG

by Mary Jane Moffat

*I*n 1974 when *Revelations: Diaries of Women* was published, one reviewer noted that "an alarming number" of the girl diarists whom Charlotte Painter and I included in the anthology died young. Keeping a diary during one's formative years, is not, of course, a passport to an early grave. Rather, it is that instead of being lost, ignored or destroyed—as they might have been had the authors lived—the diaries were preserved by survivors as memorials. The most notable example of this reliquary tradition is *The Diary of Anne Frank.* Out of the human need to try and wrest some beauty from tragedy has come the opportunity for the reading public to explore the very private emotional realities of young women and the historical periods in which they hoped to find worthy exercise of their gifts.

There is inherent pathos in the story of any young person whose life is cut off before its season of full ripening. In the case of sensitive, intelligent and articulate young women, there is a double sense of mourning, of sad irony. Did the world lose a potential George Eliot, Käthe Kollwitz, Margaret Sanger or Eleanor Roosevelt? Or might the complications of their gender, which the adolescent diaries I examined all address, have consigned them to obscurity even if they had survived?

In reading for *Revelations*, I was struck by the common themes that preoccupied the girls and young women. Despite their different periods and cultures, the diarists sound like avatars of one voice as they advance from girlhood to the threshold of maturity and the opportunity to act on their dreams and aspirations. "I cannot be good without God's assistance, I will never again trust in myself," says the fortunately irrepressible eight-year old Marjory Fleming in early nineteenth-century Scotland. "I can assure you I'm not at all keen on a cramped existence like Mummy and Margot," Anne Frank confides. "Marry? Paint? What should I strive to become?" asks the late nineteenth-century French artist Marie Bashkirtseff. In flight with her family during the Russian Revolution, fourteen-year old Nelly Ptaschkina resolves, "I shall arrange it, so as not to depend on love. . .but I *shall* live all the same." And on the eve of a dangerous wartime mission, Hannah Senesh, often called "The Joan of Arc of Israel," writes, "I long for satisfying work."

Vocation, love, sex, marriage, motherhood, spiritual development, the life of action versus the life of contemplation: questions moved about and rearranged like pattern pieces. As if they intuited that the pattern might prove too complicated to complete, Nelly Ptaschkina and Marie Bashkirtseff admit presentiments of early deaths. All anticipate that their notebooks may have some higher purpose, may one day be read by others.

The recent publication of two memorial diaries kept by exceptional women, both of whose lives ended violently at the age of twenty-nine, provides us with an opportunity to compare the aspirations and innocence of gifted girls with the realities of a woman's early maturity. Both books suggest the continuing importance of the diary process in enabling the writer to locate a true self with which to keep faith in a darkening world. And I believe that the books suggest why we readers, who know the inevitable outcome, participate out of our own needs in transforming these private diaries into sanctified images that come to possess a numinous power to reassure.

Jenny Read, In Pursuit of Art and Life: The Journals and Letters of a Young Sculptor, San Francisco, 1970-1976 (Celo Press, 1982) is a handsomely produced memorial put together by the grief-stricken friends and family of an engaging and complex artist shortly after her murder. *An Interrupted Life: The Diaries of Etty Hillesum, 1941-1943,*

The Intimate Journal of a Young Jewish Woman in Holland During the Holocaust Years (Pantheon, 1983) has kept its own faith in waiting almost forty years to be published. It is a document so unusual in its psychohistorical and philosophic implications, that it seems destined to become a classic text.

In terms of the writers' psychic progress, it seems appropriate to look at the more recent diary first. Before twenty-nine year old Jenny Read was raped and stabbed in her San Francisco warehouse studio in May, 1976, by an unknown killer, she listed Things to Do in This Life: "Make one good sculpture. . .Be a grandmother. . .Write a novel. . .Die at home near soft soil where the climate is gentle and birds sing even before dawn."

Antioch-educated Jenny Read lived in San Francisco from the age of twenty-three until her death, supporting herself with odd jobs and modest help from her parents. The inner questions of her diary are also reflected in her art, which initially reached out into many styles and had, she felt, "not enough of a message—a tune but not a song." The book includes lithographs of her progress from small, charming pieces to increasingly powerful, androgynous figures of wood and bronze that loom, Christ-like, over their freckled-faced creator.

She commits herself to her art and to the ideals of living decently in relation to others, to "the inner life lived deeply" as the only weapon against human indifference and evil. The inner life is made manifest through her eventual decision to produce art for the church: ". . .religion is as ancient a part of our society as art, and has the advantage of being one of the clinging remnants of brotherhood. . ."

Secure in her choice of vocation, and living in a period of greater freedom for women than did many of her younger sister-diarists, Jenny, at age twenty-eight, reiterates the age-old feminist dilemma. With characteristic moral severity, she begins a new journal with the resolution, ". . .No writing down what has already been revealed." The theme she keeps returning to is the conflict between Jenny the artist and Jenny the woman. How does one become a grandmother and still make a sculpture "that will last at least 100 years?" Although she recognizes the need for an abiding relationship in a fully realized life, her love affairs are unsatisfactory. "I guess I'm asking for a saint," she writes, describing the characteristics of a man who would be supportive of her work and spiritual quest, be the kind of father to their children that her father has been to her. "Am I doomed to hunt forever what I least desire to find?"

Related to this conflict is Jenny Read's search for affordable space where she could live and work, under one roof, alone, but within reach of a community. The recurring theme of this search adds another requisite to Virginia Woolf's metaphor for the needs of a woman artist: a little money and a *safe* room of one's own. Jenny loved San Francisco, its gentle climate, tolerant way of life, but she was not oblivious to the increasing violence of the 1970s: "I long for . . . unlocked doors and easy sleep but where is the peace of Christ if I cannot carry it in my heart?"

At first, a warehouse in a neighborhood where she felt comfortable seemed to provide a solution. Yet, even though there was room for her enormous sculptures, she spent increasing time in the upstairs cold-water living quarters, reading, writing, exploring existential questions of life and death, defining religion as "what man does with his solitude. . ."

In May of 1976, she awakened from a scary dream and wrote, "I am living in a perishable place." Possessed of the same generosity of spirit toward the nature of humanity as Anne Frank, but sadly wiser, Jenny Read recorded her last entry the day before her murder, a dream of being hunted and diving into a hole: "There are two other men there and I'm not sure whether they are friends or enemies. We are not all brothers."

She also wrote, "I do not believe that we end." That belief is the transforming power of a preserved diary on the reader. Even in its most brutal forms, mindless evil has not triumphed; it is as nothing compared to the brilliant light of even one small figure seeking to live a full life in accordance with the highest human principles.

Etty Hillesum kept her diary in an even more perishable place, in Amsterdam in 1941, in a friendly room with books and a vase of ox-eye daisies, not far from the Secret Annex where the following year Anne Frank would begin hers. Etty had resolved many of the questions that the girl diarists pondered. She'd taken her degree in law and was embarked on an intellectual career. She had achieved autonomy from her parents whom she regarded from an affectionate distance as "people with a destiny of their own." Secure in her sexuality, she'd had several lovers and lived in a Bohemian atmosphere of free thinkers. There was no ambivalence about bearing children: "The mother instinct is something of which I am completely devoid." Yet something essential was lacking, which at twenty-seven, she hoped the diary would help her find.

> ...so much fear of letting go, of allowing things to pour out of me, and yet that is what I must do if I am ever to give my life a reasonable and satisfactory purpose. It is like the final, liberating scream that always sticks bashfully in your throat when you make love.

The diary more than accomplished its purpose. From the state of "spiritual constipation" with which she began, Etty became the transcendent being, at one with the suffering of all humanity, whose last note before being taken to Auschwitz from a transport camp was, "We have left the camp singing."

Early on, Etty perceives that "woman's handicap" is that she looks for one man on whom she can bestow all her wisdom, warmth, love and creative powers, when she should long instead for mankind. "We still have to be born as human beings." The catalyst for her own birth is a remarkable relationship with Julius Spier, a fifty-four-year old Jew who had fled Berlin. Spier had trained under Jung and had an uncanny ability to read character through palm prints. A month before starting the diary, Etty consulted Spier for help in sorting out her life. In him she recognized the ability to love the human being in all persons—even the enemy—to which she aspired. Strongly attracted to each other, intellectually and spiritually as well as physically, they gradually work upward from the "not very high level" of their first "impure impulses" to a nobly unpossessive communion of body and soul that, at least as observed through Etty's eyes, seems rare and wonderful.

Etty wanted to write a novel called "The Girl Who Could Not Kneel." When she feels herself born as a human being she learns to love life and mankind, and thereby God. The diary frequently becomes a fervent address to that deep well within herself, "which for convenience' sake, I call God." Even the increasingly menacing restrictions against Jews do not prevent her form finding life beautiful. ". . .above the one narrow path still left to us stretches the sky, intact. They can't do anything to us, they really can't."

Etty's refusal to kneel to no force but God and that which is real brings her, by July, 1942, to an inescapable conclusion: "Very well then, this new certainty that what they are after is our total destruction, I accept it. . . I must try to live a good and faithful life to my last breath: so that those who come after me do not have to start all over again. . ."

She considers marrying Spier so she can follow him to the camps and share his fate. But shortly before he was to be deported, he fell ill and died. Etty's sorrow speaks of none of that loss of self so prevalent in the literature of mourning; instead she believes that her "great friend, the one who had attended at the birth of my soul," lives on with her, "nameless."

Through her work for the Jewish Council at the transit camp at Westerbork, where trains departed for Auschwitz and camps in the East, Etty was exempted from deportation for almost another year. Her diary maintains that this was an onerous reprieve, that she wanted to be at every one of the camps scattered over Europe: ". . .a camp needs a poet, one who experiences life there, even there, as a bard and is able to sing about it." Her final letters from Westerbork, where she helped those boarding the daily death trains, are such songs: fierce with reality, a voice that cannot be murdered.

Etty's train left for Auschwitz on September 9, 1943. Her death at the age of twenty-nine, on November 30 of that year, transcends the pathos we feel for lives cut short too early. If we can believe the record she left in the diary she entrusted to a friend before she left for the transit camp, this was a completed life, one she meant for us to read, so that those of us who come after her "do not have to start all over again." By the age of twenty-nine, Etty Hillesum, had achieved a generativity and oneness with the universe that few lives attain even in old age. Her preserved diary is more than a memorial to the lives wasted by barbarism throughout history. These eight closely written exercise books bear witness that it is possible to create an inner world not governed by threat of extinction. There is vast consolation for survivors in the message that if we will develop our capacity to see the truth clearly, we will thereby endure it without violence to the hard-won, essential self that resides within.

The process of editing an intimate diary for publication inevitably does violence to the authenticity of the original documents. In the matter of memorial diaries, in particular, the human tendency to sanctify the dead, or their cause, might seem to influence editorial decisions. Can we trust these published versions?

The friend to whom Etty Hillesum entrusted her notebooks passed them on to a Dutch writer who attempted to interest several publishers with no success. In 1980, J. G. Gaarlandt became fascinated with the hard-to-decipher handwriting of the notebooks and selected entries for publication. In the introduction he says, "To publish a 400-page diary by an unknown woman was too much of a risk. I have tried to convey the contents. . .as carefully as possible, taking out repetitions and many quotations. [Etty had read widely in Freud and Jung; Tolstoy and Rilke were particularly beloved authors whose books she packed in her small suitcase when she left for the camps.] No word has been added."

It's difficult not to credit Gaarlandt's sincerity, for aspects of the Etty of the published diary may shock some readers: she maintained a tender love affair with a much older man in the midst of her passionate relationship with Spier; she writes of efforts at a self-induced abortion when she believes herself to be pregnant. Gaarlandt also has the objective advantage of distance in time and no personal relationship with the dead diarist.

In the case of Jenny Read, the publication of the diary and letters was conceived by a family friend and writer, Kathleen Doyle, who began to edit the material in grief's first aftermath. I asked Doyle if she had a preconception as to the theme of Jenny's life: she says the pattern of a young woman in conflict with her role as artist and female only gradually emerged as she read the documents that amassed after the murder. No one to whom Jenny had written from 1970 to 1976 had failed to save her letters, which were unusually candid and read like an adjunct to her journal. The family exerted no censorship that would keep readers from a true Jenny. If anything, Doyle says, the family "wanted to put in every dream, every visit to a doctor for a menstrual problem—things that didn't belong. It really takes an outsider." In the first draft of the book, Jenny's stepmother, Dallas Johnson, wrote explanatory notes in her own persona. In the published version she subsumes her own role and her connective commentary is always helpful, never intrusive, allowing Jenny's voice to speak for itself.

Portions of Anne Frank's diary, withheld from publication by her father, Otto Frank, the sole family survivor, have, since his death, been available in paperback under the title *Tales From the Secret Annex* (Washington Square Press, 1982).

The unsigned epilogue to the *Diary* states: "Apart from a very few passages of little interest to the reader, the original text has been printed." These "few passages" amount to over 150 paperback pages and amplify the reader's sense of Anne Frank's imagination. However, it is aesthetically understandable that their presence would have diluted the initial impact of *The Diary of a Young Girl.*

That memorial diaries will survive editorial vandals is demonstrated by the publishing history of the writings of Marjory Fleming, who died in her ninth year in Scotland in 1811. Nearly half a century later, H.B. Farnie, a literary hack, obtained access to her journals and published them under the title *Pet Marjorie*, a sobriquet of his own invention. Farnie cleaned up Marjory's charmingly creative spelling and excised language of which he didn't approve. A still later edition republished this version, adding a syrupy layer of commentary and inventing a friendship between the child and Sir Walter Scott, for which there is no evidence. In 1934, Sidgwick and Jackson published a facsimile of the original journals, letters and verses, and at last Marjory Fleming speaks for herself.

Since 1963, when the first volume of Anaïs Nin's *Diary* was published, there seems to have developed a feeling that the purpose of writing a diary is to get it published. This is diametrically opposed to the older idea that a diary was a private document, one which was frequently hidden away with instructions that it be burnt upon the death of the author. Well, I for one, am very glad that many such instructions were ignored and that a host of wonderful diaries have been published. But I agree with Ochs that publication should not, in many cases cannot, be the goal. She takes a hard look at this issue in her article which was first published in WOMEN'S DIARIES, A *Quarterly Newsletter, vol.* 3, no. 1 (Spring 1985).

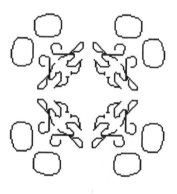

TAKING WOMEN'S DIARIES SERIOUSLY

by Vanessa L. Ochs

I teach a course on writers' journals at a humanistic studies center. My students, usually women in their thirties and forties, are more often interested in journal writing than in writers' journals. The areas of their interests are varied. Some want to know why they are obsessed with writing down their lives. Some want justification for having spent so much time keeping a diary. Some want me to guarantee that their diaries will assure them immortality. Some want me to look at their journals and judge if their lives have made sense. Often they ask me whether their journals reveal talent: either a gift for writing or a gift for living.

As their teacher, I am reluctant to answer these questions that concern the diarist and not the diary. I do feel obliged, though, to answer the questions my students ask that concern the diary as a literary genre. Certain students, women who have always kept diaries and who know that diary keeping is personally useful, want to know if their diaries can be read as literature. Other students who have never written before, but now have the time and desire to do so, want to know if the diary form which seems accessible and appealing, is a sound place for them to begin.

Is the diary the appropriate format for students who wish to write seriously and want to have their writing taken seriously?

I am not sure if I can, in good conscience, say to them: work hard, write your diary, and if it is good, and if some publisher recognizes that it is good, it will become a public document and you will be recognized publicly as a writer. Most of my students were taught that there were rewards for devoting oneself singlemindedly to one's husband and children. They tell me they want to do something in the world, now, something they say "counts." That is one reason I care whether or not diaries count. I fear creating another myth that can lead to disillusionment.

And so, while considering the literary status of the diary, like working through a hard crossword puzzle or anticipating the outcome of a mystery novel, would in itself be satisfying to me, I am undertaking the task because I am concerned about respectability.

Consider this analogous situation: If you are in a position to advise a woman who wants to pursue a career which requires an academic degree, a student for whom you hope and expect power, status, achievement and happiness, do you counsel her to enroll in a traditional Ph.D. program in an Ivy League school and earn a degree that can go anywhere, like a polyester travelling dress? Or do you suggest she enroll in a new, experimental, non-restrictive and non-accredited institution with a program that seems perfect. I would dare suggest the latter only if the student were extraordinarily gifted, that rare person who can proclaim her status without naming her affiliation.

There is no question that diaries are good for our souls. They are therapeutic, they teach discipline, they teach us to convert our experiences into words and to confront ourselves. The writing itself is often its own reward. But when we create excellent diaries, will we get the kind of external approval that feeds our egos? Or does the diary act subversively as a kitchen for fancy cooking, but always in the end, still a kitchen?

When I was first learning to write, I kept a journal. I stopped keeping the journal for two reasons. First, the subject matter was becoming more eccentric and the language more introverted. This went beyond the process of discovering my voice. I couldn't understand passages I had written earlier without reconstructing my state of mind or recollecting the experience upon which the entry was based. I was becoming oblivious to my solipsism and imprisoned by it, a writer wearing earmuffs and blinders.

The second reason for stopping the journal seemed more pressing at the time. I wanted to get out of the diary and into the world I recognized that my earliest apprenticeship was ending. It was time to make my writing available to an audience and face the consequences.

Last week a student asked me, "Isn't it true that you're not a real writer until you've been published?" A glance at what has gotten published quickly refutes that but try to tell an aspiring writer that publication is meaningless and that it doesn't offer a kind of certification. It's a rare writer who can sustain her ego without the gratification of appearing in print.

To return to my students who would choose diaries, I think they risk postponing or eliminating the ego satisfaction that comes from publication, either because their diaries are too private (I'm not referring to decorum, bur rather to a self-referential quality that is impenetrable), or, if they are published, because their diaries will not be given serious consideration.

This problem obliges us to look at arguments for and against the validity of the diary as a literary genre. Critics who would have us see diaries as art begin by asking us to give up our preconceptions about the boundaries between fiction and autobiography. We are asked to recognize the laws by which we write, read and judge diaries in order to define our set of expectations.

Peter Boerner, in his article "The Significance of the Diary in Modern Literature," *Yearbook of Comparative and General Literature*, No. 21 1972)) and more extensively in *Tagbuch* (Stuttgart: J. B. Metzler, 1969), proposes we begin to reveal the status of the diary by recognizing five recurrent traits in modern diaries. They are that:

1. individual entries are typically summaries of objective observations, based on actual occurrence;

2. each entry represents a new confrontation, a possible change of perspective (Boerner calls the individual entry "the center of tension");

3. the diary serves as a platform for public dialogue (by this, Boerner means the diary is especially accessible because it lacks poetic distortion and engages the sympathy of readers, who are themselves familiar with diary keeping);

4. the diarist uses the diary to provide personal orientation and to serve as a vehicle for obtaining self-knowledge; and

5. the diary allows the diarist to explore and record the fragmentary.

Boerner summarizes the possibilities the modern diary offers us: it is hospitable to roughly formulated ideas, "partial views and disparate reflections," and it is free of plot and composition.

On the other hand, let us consider the opposition. The diary has been called the "alibi of scatterbrains," a "home for monomaniacal introspections," the work of writers unable to master other forms and nothing but an artifice requiring no literary skill.

That brings us back to women and diaries and fragmentation. If we accept the fact that the diary is, as Boerner says, expressive of "the same process of disintegration which in modern painting has been defined as the loss of center," then we can call the diary the literary form which best reflects the fragmentation of our century. There's still a big difference between those who choose the diary as their vehicle to express fragmentation (and we might note that all the diaries that Boerner refers to in his study—Gide, Kafka, Camus, Frisch, etc.—are not only by men, but by men who had previously established themselves in more conventional genres) and those who choose the diary form because it adapts to the fragmentary nature of their lives.

Beatrice Dedier, in *Le journal intime* (Presses Universitaires de France, 1976), observes that "the journal has long been a refuge for female creativity, when deprived of other modes of expression." Mary Jane Moffat, in her foreword to *Revelations: Diaries of Women* (Random House, 1974), writes: "The form has been an important outlet for women partly because it is an analogue to their lives— emotional, fragmentary, interrupted, modest, not to be taken seriously, private, restricted, daily, trivial, formless, concerned with self and endless as their tasks."

We cannot help but register concern when we observe that the form which best expresses a world which has lost its center also happens to be the literary form that seems most available to women. If we were to accept that there were male and female sensibilities, then we might accept that different genres are better suited as vehicles for those sensibilities. It seems, though, that female sensibility is not the issue; rather it is the female situation.

Let us follow another path of argument and consider the possibility that the diary will supplant the novel.

If, compared to the romance, the modern novel moves toward creating the illusion of being true to individual experience, then compared to the novel, the diary moves beyond both the illusion of experience and the illusion of the individual. Just as novels in diary form (such as Rilke's *Notebooks of Malte Laurids Brigge* and Lessing's *The Golden Notebook*) give us the illusion that we are reading a real diary by a real person, literary diaries (that is, private diaries which are written with the possibility of publication always in mind) give us the illusion that these reconstructions of the diarists' experiences make us privy to the writers' personal lives.

Any diarist must go through the steps of perceiving, articulating and giving form. Better writers simply do a better job of converting "the private matter of the writer's personal life into the subject matter of art," as Alex Kurczaba states in *Gombrowicz and Frisch, Aspects of the Literary Diary* (Bonn: Bouvier Verlag, 1980).

Most arguments against the dairy rest on the axiom that if the components of a story are true (as opposed to imagined characters and imagined events which reveal truths), then the work doesn't count as art; it is autobiography.

Whereas the novel wrestles with love, God, truth or something equally austere and weighty, the diary wrestles with the mystery of subjectivity.

We could conclude that the diary is most coy and self-effacing when it declares: "this is how I see the world. Moreover, the way I perceive today is different from the way I perceived yesterday, my perceptions being tempered more or less by joy or melancholy, a headache or confusion. My only intention in writing is to register my perceptions for my own clarification and for my readers' curiosity."

We could just as readily conclude (and I would prefer to) that we live and write in a time when the *only* certainty we have is a clearly articulated subjective perception, and even the certainty of our perception is subject to constant revision, refinement and extension. If so, the diary, which comes from life, but is not life—whose hallmark is subjective accuracy—is the most viable genre to articulate a contemporary sensibility.

One myth emerges most prominently from the diary. It is, as both Anaïs Nin and Virginia Woolf would agree, that by recording one's experiences, by getting a hold on the sausage and haddock of one's life by writing them down, by naming them, one validates one's life, holds it, and makes it endure.

The fact that many women are beginning to write now and are naturally turning to diaries is perhaps a sign that they will use their diaries simultaneously to name their lives and write their stories. I can only say to them, proceed at your own risk. As indicated above, the only diaries that are being taken seriously as potential literature are those of writers established in other genres. There are exceptions, but they are rare: the diaries of Anaïs Nin and Anne Frank come to mind. I wonder, though, if consideration of these diaries is not dependent, in Nin's case on her life, in Frank's case on her death.

Diarists should know that critics are not championing the cause of diaries with much force; their language is particularly tentative.

Also, the serious diarist should not fail to recognize that when critics determine that some novels are better and some are worse, the worse ones are at least worse novels; that is, they have the status of belonging to a serious group. Critics determine that some diaries are tedious or pedestrian and others are literary or enlightening. The better diaries have a shot at counting. That is, they might aspire to at least the equivalent status of the worst novel.

These are bad odds for diarists who want to be taken seriously as writers, but I think it is worth the risk for those who are compelled to make the attempt.

PART II

In Particular

Two foreign locales that were centers of expatriate gatherings also proved to be vital hotbeds of creativity. One was the Paris of he 1920s; the other was turn-of-the-century Florence. With Bernard Berenson at the center, Florence became a center for art history. It also fostered a flowering of minor literary efforts. Two American writers who went to Florence in search of fertile ground for their literary creativity were Hutchins Hapgood and his wife Neith Boyce.

This article is a slightly revised version of the one originally published in *WOMEN'S DIARIES, A Quarterly Newsletter*, vol. 2, no.4 (Winter 1984). Subsequently, Langworthy located the original, holograph version of Boyce's 1903 Italian diary, and this is now the basis for her edition of the Neith Boyce memoirs, *The Modern World of Neith Boyce*, which is currently in press with the University of New Mexico Press. An NEH Travel to Collections grant enabled her to do research on the "Diary" at the Harvard University Center for Italian Renaissance Studies at *I Tatti*, outside Florence, Italy. The manuscript for her book recently won a title subsidy grant from the Minnesota Humanities Commission. Permission to quote from the holograph manuscript is granted by the Beinecke Rare Book and Manuscript Library, Yale University Library, New Haven, CT.

THE DIARY OF NEITH BOYCE, A CONSIDERATION

by Carol Rolloff Langworthy

> *Grandma recommends me to write a few sketches*
> *of travel for my own pleasure, says she has sev-*
> *eral trunksfull of her own . . .*
>
> —*"Diary," 1903*

*I*n 1903 "Grandma" King, a woman Neith Boyce had met on board the *S.S. Sardegna* enroute to Italy, recommended that the young writer keep a travel diary, ". . . a few sketches of travel for my own pleasure, says she has several trunks full of her own..."
Neith Boyce took the recommendation to heart. She entered the advice on the first page of her "Diary—Italy 1903" and began keeping a daily record of what was to be a half-year in Italy with her husband, writer Hutchins Hapgood, and their two-year-old son. Both journalists, the Hapgoods were seeking a freer way of life, European culture, inexpensive living, foreign experiences, and time to complete books. Both did complete a book: Hapgood's *The Autobiography of a Thief*, a new literary form called the "human document," was published that same year; Boyce's first novel, *The Forerunner*, came out in early 1904.
Although she and her husband now have been largely forgotten, both were well-known writers in the American Greenwich Village scene of 1895 to 1930. Neith Boyce (1872-1951) was a journalist, playwright, novelist and short story writer of the Progressive Era. Along with her husband she was a member of several Greenwich

Village groups and is one of the few Greenwich Villagers whose memoirs have not yet been published. She published seven naturalistic novels between 1897 and 1923, and five plays, including the first play produced by the Provincetown Players. (It was staged in their living room at Provincetown.) Another, written with her husband, was possibly the first play produced on radio. She was also successful as a short story writer publishing in *The Chap-Book, Vogue, Bookman, Lippincott's, American Magazine, Scribner's, McClure's, Forum, Good Housekeeping, Harper's Weekly,* and *Collier's*—a virtual dictionary of the magazines through which a revolution in cultural tastes and attitudes occurred in a pre-World War I America. She was in almost all senses a "Modernist."

Writing in a ledger book, Boyce created a 120-page holograph diary. She revised and typed it as a 70-page typescript sometime between 1936 and 39, when she wrote her "Autobiography," a 179-page manuscript recounting her colorful childhood in California and coming of age in turn-of-the-century Greenwich Village. According to a letter found by her daughters, this writing and editing occurred about the time she was assisting her husband with his autobiography, *A Victorian in the Modern World* (1939). Intellectual historian Robert Allen Skotheim has called Hapgood's memoirs the one work necessary to an understanding of pre-World War I America. In this author's opinion, Neith Boyce's memoirs are just as significant.

The 1903 trip was Boyce's first time abroad, although her husband had previously spent a year studying in Germany and was an experienced round-the-world traveler. The couple landed in Naples and was met by Mary Berenson, wife of Bernard Berenson, the American art critic and connoisseur who influenced so much turn-of-the-century decorating and revived the status of *trecento* and *quattrocento* painting. As Boyce wrote, "only H. [Hutch] had known them before, but I was raw, fresh from America." Hapgood had met Mary and Bernard Berenson in Munich in 1893, while he was on a grand tour as a break in graduate education at Harvard. Berenson had been a friend of Hapgood's elder brother, Norman Hapgood, when they were at Harvard.

Sometime in the late 1930s Boyce put her "Diary" and "Autobiography" together to form a consistent memoir. They are contiguous in pagination and were obviously meant to be published together. Also among her papers at Yale University's Beinecke Rare Book and Manuscript Room is her "War Diary." This 20-page typed manuscript is another travel diary— of an ill-fated trip she took to Italy with two of her children, Mable Dodge and Mabel's son John, and music critic Carl Van Vechten in 1914. Unlike the other two documents, as prepared by Boyce for publication, this manuscript names names and tells definite dates. No holograph version has been found at the Beinecke, but it is likely that it, too, was taken down by hand and typed during the 1930s. It is an interesting chronicle of the outbreak of World War I and the ensuing social chaos in Italy.

All three of these are interesting documents, but this author finds the "Diary" most fascinating because, in the holograph version, it is the least self-conscious. The first trip to Europe has become almost standard as part of the coming-of-age of literary Americans.

There are many intriguing aspects to the Neith Boyce memoirs. Perhaps the most interesting and the most difficult for the editor is the question of why, during the 1930s, she deliberately obscured the names and/or identities of nearly every person mentioned. In the "Autobiography," only her mother, Mary Smith Boyce, is referred to by actual name—and then only her first name. Even Boyce herself has a pseudonym: "Iras Carolan." The "Autobiography" is written in the third person, with an omniscient narrator who looks down on all of the forces converging on the Boyce ("Carolan") family as they move from coast to coast and suffer the slings and arrows of economic misfortunes and other catastrophes. Indeed, one of the main characters is Fate, whom the young girl recognizes early as a god that needs to be placated. No simple girlhood pieties of on-the-spot diaries here!

As Boyce typed her revision of the "Diary," names were changed or shortened to initials. Nonetheless, the document retains its fresh outlook and less retrospective approach. The diarist does not know the outcome of this trip. Daily entries form the basis of its style— although some of the longer essays on the Anglo-Florentine community, for instance, indicate that she was not enslaved to the format. The holograph version contains rough drafts of articles on such things as Italian farming and synopses of ideas and plots for short stories and novels, mainly based on people just encountered and scenes recently witnessed. Boyce deleted all such items from the typed version. In preparing the documents for publication, however, this author is replacing most such deletions in keeping with current theory and practice of documentary editing.

Her 1930s version also deleted her notations in the ledger's margins. These notations indicate prices of travel and food in francs, the currency used in Italy at that time, people's addresses, as well as occasional drawings. Her sketch of the 1903 house and garden plan of *I Tatti* is a useful record of the original villa before the Berensons began their significant modifications.

In both versions, days are skipped, occasionally, and events then summarized. The tale is told in the present and simple past tenses, with an eye-witness approach. Boyce was adept in avoiding overuse of the personal pronoun, often simply deleting herself in the writing, as: "Cathedral not imposing and the Leaning Tower looks like the little wax models of it, but the Baptistery and Campo Santo perfect . . ."

What makes this travel diary unusual from that of many others, is the people they met. Their first ten days in Italy were spent at Villa *I Tatti*, the exquisite home of Bernard and Mary Berenson, through whom they were introduced to the leading intellectuals and artists of Florence's expatriate and Italian community. They spent the hot summer months at Bagni di Lucca, an old watering-spot famous from the time of the Caesars. The Brownings, Heine, Montaigne, Goethe, and hosts of other writers had also spent time there.

In the typescript revision, Boyce disguises the identities of many expatriates and native Florentines who lived exotic lives. She uses simply first initials or the phrase "An American writer," for instance, when relating stories about Edith Wharton in Tuscany. She herself did not meet Wharton there—merely related some of the juicier gossip.

Indeed, gossip is perhaps what Boyce was attempting to avoid in her 1930s revisions. For all her belonging to the more avant-garde of the Greenwich Village group of "rebels" who effected a revolution in American cultural attitudes in the early part of this century, it appears that she was enough of a Victorian to consider it rude to tell tales out of school. One suspects that her earlier skepticism of Gerturde Stein had ripened into a major friendship. (Both of the Hapgoods worked to get Stein published during a later stay in Italy, 1906-9. In fact, one publisher suggested to Stein that, should "Mrs. Hapgood" write an introduction to one of Stein's books, its chances for publication might be enhanced, as she was so much better known than Stein.) One also speculates that Stein's fame made Boyce wish to soften her earlier remarks.

Which brings up the fact that Neith Boyce's major calling was that of novelist. The tales of the "Diary" are presented with wit, a lack of sentimentality, and a minimum of moral judgments—perhaps unusual in the reactions of an American innocent. Her "Autobiography," however, reflects much more of the novel form, where only the author knows the outcome. Boyce is obviously true to the reality of her life in all her documents, but the "Autobiography," with its 1930s viewpoint, presents a more consistent view of reality. For her, that reality was a naturalistic universe with little hope given and only Art and aestheticism as comfort.

Boyce's novelistic/autobiographical skills combine with her diarist/journalistic skills, however, in her 1930s conclusion of the "Diary" for publication. In late fall, 1903, she receives word that her father has been killed in a trolley-car accident in New York. In the original version of the document, the entry is simply:

16 - The Cablegram.

The following day's entry:

17th - Left Florence for Paris

Subsequent entries describe the French countryside and Paris, including witty and slightly cutting portraits of Leo and Gertrude

Stein: "The Steins came to see us—without manners but interesting as usual." Her descriptions seem rather flat compared to the lively sketches of Italy, and one senses that the writer is forcing herself to document scenery rather than describe her feelings. The handwritten document concludes with dreary descriptions of a dreadful voyage home: "worst trip in boat's history. More than a day late at New York." There is no mention of the death.

In preparing the 1930s version, however, she has her "character" Neith revert to the third-person "Autobiography" pseudonym to convey the crashing in of Fate on her life once again:

> The diary of Iras ended here.
>
> H. [Hutchins] had gone down one morning to Cook's to get the mail. He came back with a cablegram. Sitting down beside Iras, looking very grave, he said, "There is bad news—your father—"
>
> Iras looked at him and said, "He is dead."
>
> "Yes."
>
> "I must go back at once."
>
> "I thought you would feel so."
>
> The cablegram gave only the bare fact. H. went away to send a cable, "Sailing at once," and to take passage on the first boat. Iras began to pack. She was too stunned to weep or to feel much then. Only she thought, I shall never see him again, that day when he saw us off on the boat, that was the last time, when he kissed his little grandson goodbye and turned away. .
>
> They left Florence the next day.

Both versions of the "Diary" are "true." The challenge for the documentary editor is to present them in a form intelligible to readers and historically accurate at the same time. For such work, having an original, holograph version provides the touchstone between a diarist's at-the-minute reality and recollected reality. Since all diarists invent their pasts as well as their "presents" in the making of diaries, documentary evidence can be a way for readers, and history, to make judgments on those realities.

Our impression of early nineteenth century women is that they tend to be pious homebodies, more concerned with fulfilling their Christian duty, as defined by their menfolk, rather than enjoying life or even truly understanding the self. This is due to the fact that the published diaries, letters, journals and memoirs of women of this period tend to be "pious memoirs." What a delight it is to find evidence that all women did not fit this tiresome mold! Caroline Matilda Clements Brown is one. This heretofore unpublished short diary gives a picture of a young women, not so concerned with Christian duty as that she could not find fault with her in-laws. She seems a most human young wife, and this delightful glimpse into her life and thoughts provides a balance to those others who suffered under such a load of guilt.

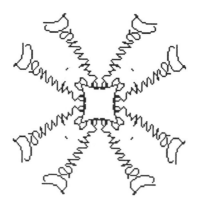

THE DIARY OF CAROLINE MATILDA CLEMENTS BROWN 1833-1837

Edited by Catherine Denning

The manuscript diary of Caroline Matilda Clements Brown is in the possession of the Annmary Brown Memorial, Brown University. This library, devoted mainly to the collection of fifteenth-century printed books assembled by General Rush C. Hawkins (1831-1920), is dedicated to the memory of his late wife, the diarist's daughter. In editing it, I have tried as far as possible to retain the spelling and punctuation of the original.

Surprisingly little can be learned about Mrs. Brown's life outside of her diary. She was apparently born about 1815, and married the widowed Nicholas Brown III (1792-1859), a member of a leading Rhode Island family in 1831. She is said to have been from New Hampshire, but speaks of herself in her diary as an "Englishwoman." She bore her husband five children: Alfred Nicholas (1832-1864); Annmary (1835-1837); Annmary (1837-1903), wife of General Rush Hawkins; John Carter (1840-1907); Caroline Matilda (1841-1892), wife of the Chevalier Paul Bajnotti of Turin; and Robert Grenville (1846-1896).

At the time Mrs. Brown was keeping this diary, which apparently commences in the autumn of 1833, the family was living in Piermont, near Tappan, New York. In 1845, Nicholas Brown was appointed American Consul General to Rome, and the family resided for some time in Italy. The 1850's found them returned to the Brown family seat in Rhode Island. After her husband's death in 1859, Mrs. Brown lived at 21 Brown Street, Providence, now the site of her daughter's Memorial. She died on 9 July 1879.

The Diary

A cold morning stoves would not light cold breakfast. Mr.
... scolded because he had to go to the City wished to be
in my grave. Mr. ... went to the Landing boat could not
go because so much ice in the river. Tried to get wood, no one
would sell. Very fine all this; one of those days in which every thing
goes wrong.

November 23rd   Dined at Govenour .... [1] was met at the door by
His Excellency, a tall well made man with peper =& salt, hair & ush-
ered without ceremony up a pair of stairs into a cold room to make
my toilet alone (or rather unbonneted) and find my way to the
parlour. The dinner which was served or pitched on soon after my
arrival was a fair specimen of American disorder & Irish filth. The
lady presided over a dish of *soup maigre.* & the Govr. himself over a
half cold turkey. The plate (for there was plate) was fairly bronzed.
O for a joint of good old English beef out of a pewter plater instead
of a shabby genteel [gentell?] dinner.

Novr 24th.   Dined at Mr. ... A Lady played the piano whose performance they called brilliant. If I should criticise her playing it was
one grand flourish without time or tune sould or feeling and yet she
is a prodigy here.

June 1 1834. Went to see Fanny Keemble *[sic]*. Heaven defend my
bad taste but I was sadly disappointed. The pleasure I felt from her
fathers fine acting quite repaid me for the inconvenience I suffered

[1] The Governor of New York at the time was William L. Marcy.

from a hot damp dirty house. Considering the rain the house was well filled and there were a great many well dressed woomen [sic] which is ill–advised as the dress which is worn there is not fit to wear again for the men are constantly pacing the cushions & spitting until they are dirty as the street. A light silk in which I had decked myself was handsomely figured with mud & tobacco spittle: thanks to the public for an addition to my wardrobe.

Speaking the other day with a Lady on the subject of Religion I found her very severe on the Catholicks, she said we have a great many here, it is dreadful she added with a sigh we are doing every thing to root them out. I said I thought they should have Toleration with the other sects "Oh no" she said "you would not have a Religion which will not allow the Bible to be read by their Parish." And yet I replied "you countenance the Slave–holders in keeping the Bible from their Slaves surely they might be as much improved by it as any other people "There now she said rather sharply I never knew an English wooman yet who would not stand up for a "Nigger." They would as lief have a "Nigger" for a husband as a white–man." I did not reply but let the mistake pass.

The last [?] day of summer: the morning really dreadful. Rode out over a horrid road through a wood over stumps & logs & mire to our hearts content, got out to walk & pulled up sundry little trees to transplant. Tulips Maples Catalpas & Sycamores are all natives & beautiful as ornamental trees. The foliage is not so thick as ours[2] but there is a variety in them at all seasons unknown to us which in the Autumn beggars all description. The trees never make arms but run up with a great deal of under–brush. I saw one Tulip–tree which seemed to me two hundred feet high without a single arm of many size its trunk was gigantic.

Rode on horse–back over a delightful road with a stream on one side & a wood on the other. The twilight lasted but a moment but the clear cold Moon & transparent sky was heavenly. What would a Nobleman give for this gurgling stream over a ledge of rocks if he

[2] ours (in England?)

could have it on his domain, what would he do to improve it yet here it glides away unobserved & perhaps is owned by some one who would give a little if it were on any one's ground but his.

June 28. Read a part of O'Connel's speech in which he attacks D'Isreli in the harshest & most unparliamentary language. Where was the Speaker to allow this. Oh England how have thy children fallen. These Reformers would bring thy King to the Block thy Nobles to the Gallows that they might get into power themselves. The words "Reform" "Liberty" & "Equality" are words used to deceive mankind. Your Milkman will tell you he is your equal & to make you think so he is a[s] rude & rough as a Bear. This same man will not sit down with your boot–black.

To show how much stress these people lay on station in Society you must know that the Wall–street set think themselves above the Whole–sale Merchants, the Wholesale Merchants above the Retail dealers & the Retail dealers above the Grocers & these last above the Market–woomen & the Market–woomen above the Devil!!

June 13th.

Went down to breakfast, heard two men one a Whig and the other a Tory in a warm argument the Whig said ..... was a great "scoundrel" the Tory said cooly he knew him not personally & newspaper accounts he never read. It surprises me to see how two friends will quarrel about a man who would not nod to them if he passed them. The fact is you may tear a man's wife or daughter's character to atoms with impunity if he is of politics opposite to your own.

June 14th

Went on the Harleam [?] Railroad. The car ran over a dirt cart & broke our shafts waited for them to get another one man very much alarmed. We rode through a ledge of rocks which were divided like the Red–Sea. They seemed ready to close on us again In another place we passed through a sand bank in which the rain had made sad gullies. I should like to ride here in one of our first rate showers & see the rain come tumbling like chaos.

June 16

Rode today against a Dutchman's waggon he would not move out of the track - sat still & heard the men wrangle awhile then got out took the horse by the head & backed him so as to clear the wheels. The day was heavenly bright.

June 20th.

Rode out almost frozen by a keen north–west wind. finished working cap set out some Accasia shoots gathered Orange–blossoms commenced putting scraps on my Music box mended husbands old stockings made some rusk & salted some butter.

June 22 Planted cabbages & Evergreens Drew a patern to embroider my reticule made a Port-folio worked on a cape coughed all the morning. Three ducks died made trimming for white dress.

June 24th Went to the Boat with a friend. read Fanny Kembles journal saw but little in it besides her saying that a gentleman told her the impure state of morals in this country prevented woomen from being as free in their manners towards men as is the case in the old world. She did not say how many woomen travel in this country alone without incivility from any one. The fact is this work has made too much noise.

June 27 The kitten has destroyed two of my pages what a loss to the public. I have been confined to my room with an eruption on my face the Doctor calls it an Erysypelas.

1835 [1836?] July 8th

I arrived in time today to keep an engagement to dinner at four o'clock and dressed myself as American–like as I could (or at least as unEnglishlike) & set off for Mr. ... a merchant of considerable wealth. I was usherd into a room on the ground floor to adjust my dress & then mounted a pair of stairs & entered a door on the landing which opened into two spatious rooms connected by folding doors. The rooms were handsomely furnished & at the further end of one of them sat three or four Ladies huddled together. They all turned their eyes on me & kept their countenances religiously serious until I had walked quite to them & they had heard my name. They then rose with a half curtsey & again seated themselves in the same little corner. Presently four or five gentlemen entered & walked stiffly up the long rooms In a moment a door opened directly opposite to where we sat & dinner was announced. The table was well set with plate & white China but the dinner was jumbled on in strange manner. The guests eat roast-beef roast duck & beef-a-la-mode on the same plate; a great deal of fruit followed but there were no finger glasses. Bye the bye this house & furniture is a good specimen of American houses. The floors were covered with rich Brussels carpeting. The chimney-pieces & tables were of fine marble. There were also large glases rich chairs & sofas a piano & two or three pictures. The two last articles are not so common as the others. The ladies had their heads frizzed & bowed untill they looked like knots of ribbon. They were dressed in figured silks & white dresses Their faces were pretty & their figures slight without any bust. Little or no conversation passed during dinner. One tall exquisite informed me he had been in England & his air & manner was a bad immitation of an English gentleman. He said he had been "home" three years & tho' he thought London a fine City & he thought New York more striking to a Stranger-"don't you think so Madam"? I evaded the question by saying I had had no opportunity of judging as yet. An American always adds Sir or Madam at the beginning or conclusion of his sentence.

August 1 1835

After our arrival we called a Hackney Coach which was much inferiour to those of New York. We drove to several Hotels but they were all full. At last we went to the Indian Queen where we were so fortunate as to be admitted. The house was old & low in the ceiling badly furnished & on the whole a forlorn looking house. My bed-room was still more dreary as it had but one window & that very high. The sheets were not damp as is usually the complaint: they had not seen water in a month nor had the quilts in twelve. I asked for a better room & was told there was none but after awhile I got another which had a clean quilt at least. The table was good, the food well cooked but we were annoyed three times by strangers being bro't in & put down at the same table with us. The apology being that they had no other room in which to put these guests.

And now for the bill! for myself $2 pr day for table private means not at the table d'hote for private it was not, $1,25cts for sundries ie one glass of pepermint & water for my nerves.

Decr 17. Heard of my kind friend & mother's[3] death; I thought she would have outlived me. I grieve for the friends she has left behind & not for her

Decr 25th This is the season of rejoicing & I have always a kind of excitement at the time which makes it a happy season
. My little boy & girl enjoy it extremely I never saw their faces so bright & happy. May they see many more.

Jany 1837. A happy new year to my little children how happy they are with their toys how little it takes to make them happy when no cloud of sorrow has passed over them. May their days be always unclouded.

Decr 11

Feby 11th. 1837. My little girl compleats her second year today I have taken some pains to surprise her with birth-day presents. I may not make her another. In a year many things may take place.

I yesterday came near being killed by a plank which fell from a window.

Feb 14th Suffered great anxiety on account of my little Girl who was very ill yesterday: Tho' today she is very bright.

[3] Perhaps her mother-in-law, Mary Bowen Stelle Brown, who died 12 December 1836.

The diary ends here. Her little girl, Annmary, died on 22 March 1837, a little more than a month after the last entry., In the meantime, Mrs. Brown bore a second daughter on 9 March, who was named Annmary after her elder sister. It was this Annmary Brown who, in 1860, married Rush C. Hawkins, Civil War hero and rare book collector; on her death in 1903, he established the Annmary Brown Memorial in her honor.

The following are copies of letters Mrs. Brown wrote to a friend and placed in her diary. They are included because in their descriptions of her in-laws and her feelings toward them, they serve as a background to, and illumination of, her diary.

Copy of a Letter to S I returned after her death

Sept — 1833

My dear Susette

You desired me to let your know how I liked "my new relatives" - I really don't know! I'll try to give you some idea of my reception and the impression the inter-view with them gave me-

Surely it was not fear or joy or contempt and I am quite certain it was not love nor a very exalted opinion of their dignified position in truth they seem like old Merchant families you read of in a novel that are called "very respectable" - I cannot for the life of me associate gentlefolks with Puritans

I arrived about nine o'clock Saturday. We drove from the boat across lots to a large wooden house painted white with green blinds I[t] stands in the middle of a square plot three streets are shut out by a garden where every kind of shrub and flower is crowded together in admire able confusion - We entered by a back door into a hall and then into an old fashioned furnished room where I was presented to the Misstress of the house in the most formal manner - my Husband calling her Mrs Brown - I saw he was agitated and thought he had made a mistake - and had said this, when he should say - "My Mother[4]" - not at all - he always addresses her thus! - A moment after I heard a heavy tramp along the hall, and a man entered with

94

heavy boots gray yarn stockings - black Breeches a loose coat with large pokets - His hair was white as snow and light in quantity his head large his features marked and manly but with a somewhat austere expression - He wore a white cravat ruffle shirt both having a tumbled slovenly look - His manner was rough talked loud and rapid - and seemed in a great hurry I don't remember what he said except - "Very pleased to see you Ma'm!" This was the Father[5] and also called Mr B! The lady is cold, sacasstic [sacarstic?] and prudish, and betrays a little spice of jealousy in the turn of that deep blue eye - Tho handsome enough in general, it at the same time, betrays an intreaging disposition - There were several persons in the house, but all seemed how unlove able they can be, and as set and determined in their thought, and feeling, as if each had to defend his or her power, with an iron rule - Surely the Godess of discord has thrown the apple into their fireside, and they are all struggling with themselves, not to yield an iota, untill Paris shall decide the point, -which he is not in a hurry to do!

An hour elapesed then came the Brother[6], him you have seen, and so have I - and it was a relief to think there was yet one face I had seen before, to break this ice- but alas! he wore a visage so stern - that I wished he had left me longer in anticipation- He also called My Husband Mr B- and welcomed us to Prov - with a set speach, that sounded like - "I wish you were any where but here"- However this cold stern manner is given to every body in the house, and returned- Indeed there appears to have been a terrible quarrel, and each has agreed to treat the other with this ceremonious politeness to prevent a like occurence -

[4] She was in fact his stepmother, Mary Bowen Stelle Brown (1770?-1836).

[5] Nicholas Brown II (1769-1841), for whom Brown University is named.

[6] John Carter Brown (1797-1874).

They call Alfred[7] handsome tho' I never believe people when they call a child pretty to its Mother- He is too young to feel all this unbending politeness (that they throw around me) fortunately- He plays about showing his legs with as little cerimony [sic] , as if they had no eyes- They look shocked at me- I remained at first unmoved as I never dreamed untill now, that any woman could have her modesty disturbed, at the sight of a Naked Baby!

Four pages and from me! are you not weary? If so save it for tomorrow, as I often do a long ditty-

Yours truly Mat

Prov Sept 18 1833

Dear Susette

To continue my discription if as you say, "it amuses you" The dinner hour here is at two oclock (Gentlefolks in other places dine at three and four) Sunday at one- That surprised me- the dinner, was a cold cut from yesterday- A puritan Sunday!! What a novelty- Breakfast at eight a chapter in the bible then dress "to go to Meeting"- as they call Church- When I returned I was asked how I liked the Sermon- I am sure I never heard a word of it- the sound of the preacher s voice was like Acton's no other word passed at table at least I didnot speak as all this stiffness stifles me- When this repass ended all except the old gentleman, and the children- retired hastily to their chambers to sleep away the tedius [tidious?] hours between one and six o'clock then they have tea Then comes on a long dismal evening- no Book no Papers except the Christian Watchman- which I find on Monday, in a certain place! Every body creeps about with a noisless tread as if a sound would break the Sabbath I stole Col.. Hamilton's new work and hid away in the third story to laugh at his bitterness I wish he had passed the Sunday here and discribed it-

There is a pretty Girl here a sort of adopted child of the House- for

---

[7] Her firstborn son, Alfred Nicholas Brown (1832-1864).

96

no one seems to claim her in particular- She is going to be married and this event seemes to occupy them more than I do- She is about my size very delicate looking, a sort of animated roseleaf- She is treated by the cold austere Misstress, and Master, as a house pet, that is to be well fed, and well clothed, and that she needs nothing more- The same way they treat me- and I for one dont mean to give more odoures to the gales, than they waft back, if they dont understand me, I do them!

The next member of the house, is a little delicate looking child-about ten years old. I call her Lilly of the Vally - like that flower, she is obliged to shrink from the ice and storms beneathe the strong green leaves of prudence! its strange to see a thing so youthful, obliged to throw off the charms of childhood, and put on a worldly garb so soon- I am lectured every day, for want of worldly wisdom, be sure I shall get it, by the time I am twenty- tho I am told to pass for twenty tow - more allowances would be made for me, if they knew my real age- You always said I was a shallow pate- and I believe you!!

The next personage that I have not yet named is one every-body calls Aunty- She is large enough to be aunty, to all the world, and has a heart for it- but then her head often abuses her heart- by litting fly a shaft of irony, a bitter sarcasm, that wounds to the quick, and makes the victim shrink from her with dread, against which I have to (sic) power to contend- tho I feel the sting, too irritating, to be bourn patiently-

[Text breaks off here; there is a fragment of a third letter:]

voice without further explaination, I have told you before that their deity is always clothed in terror. The word awful is often used by preachers- that his listener may feel a dread of his name- This I do not comprehend- How a people that insist on a great goodness, great virtues- the only examples worthy imitation should clothe their God in a robe of terror! I dare not attempt to analize the character of their divine maker as they term him for "He is a jealous God"! punishing the Father, son, grandson, "to the forth generation"

Yet jealousy, and vengence, are crimes in their moral coad that they eschew! I don't think they mean to say that God is wrong/ they only dont wish to emulate Him!

[Text breaks off]

Käthe Kollwitz is now considered one of the most important artists of the twentieth century. It is therefore easy for those who do not know the story of her life to be unaware of the difficulties she had to overcome in order to practice her art. Although her husband was sympathetic to her needs, the times were not, and she had to fulfill her duties as wife and mother before trying to carve out space for her artistic work. Also her choice of subject matter, the working class women among whom she lived, was not popular. It is only now that her work is almost as prized for its documentary evidence as for its articulate power. Her anti-war sentiments, a result of the death of her younger son in World War I, were considered subversive to the growing Nazi power of the 1930s, and she was deprived of hard-won artistic recognition. The remarkable thing is that the artist was able to create an equally powerful written record of her thoughts and feelings in the diary and letters that survive.

Käthe Kollwitz was one of the women diarists included in the radio series "A Private Space: The Personal Diaries of Women," aired nationally over National Public Radio Playhouse. The series was co-authored by Metta Winter, and the Kollwitz segment was narrated by Glenn Close. This article was originally published in WOMEN'S DIARIES, A Quarterly Newsletter, vol. 3. no. 2 (Summer 1985).

KÄTHE KOLLWITZ: ARTIST AND DIARIST

by Metta L. Winter

*K*äthe Kollwitz was forty-two years old when she wrote the first entry in *The Diary and Letters of Käthe Kollwitz,* edited by her son Hans (Chicago: H. Regnery, 1955). She had kept a diary covering the early years of her marriage and some of her travels but, for reasons we do not know, it was burned. It is remarkable that any of Kollwitz' writing ever survived World War II. On November 23, 1943, her home in a working class section of Berlin, where she had lived for fifty-two years, was destroyed by an American bombing raid. All her letters, family mementos, and much of her work was lost.

In his introduction to the published diary, Hans Kollwitz states that he had urged his mother to write an account of her life. She resisted, arguing that if anything in her life was important it was her work. Eventually, she recanted and in her 50's she wrote a short essay describing her early years. At the age of seventy-four, she wrote another, a retrospective of her life. At the end of the war, these two essays along with a sampling of her letters, and notes on her last days written by a granddaughter, were published together with excerpts from her diary. It was not until 1955 that this volume was translated into English. The entries included in both editions were chosen by Hans Kollwitz.

For the English edition, he omitted the more intimate letters and diary entries. It should be kept in mind that the English edition of Kollwitz' diary is two steps removed from the original, first in the amount of material omitted, and second in the subtle distortion that is bound to exist in a translation. Other primary sources on her life, including sixty years of correspondence with her closest friend, Beate Bonus-Jeep, have been published in Germany, but not in English translation.

Nowhere in the thirty-four years covered by the English edition of her diary does Kollwitz state why she kept it. Unlike other artists' diaries, there are no sketches. Writing seemed to serve as an emotional release from the stress she experienced as an artist. The diary was a place where she could write about, and thereby obtain some distance from, the struggle that accompanied each new piece of work. Years of experience, an ever clearer vision of what she wanted her work to be, and the attainment of consummate skill did not make the creative process any easier.

Not only was her work a cause of internal struggle, but Kollwitz also vacillated between long months of depression and much shorter periods of productivity. These mood swings were to cause her much anguish. Like many other diary writers who use their diaries to keep track of emotional changes, Kollwitz tried several times to graph these periods in her journal with the hope that she could determine their course in advance, but to no avail.

Kollwitz was a very private person reserved even among the closest members of her family. She rarely showed her feelings, let alone spoke of them. The diary was that one place where she could express to herself what she could not express to others. Her son Hans commented, "To outsiders my mother gave the impression of being impregnable; only in her diaries can you see how she struggled with the antagonist within herself and how essential that struggle was to her development."

There are a few happy entries in Kollwitz' published diary. It was her family, not her art, that she described as bringing joy into her life. Perhaps the most unexpected surprise of all was the growing intimacy she came to feel toward her husband. Married young, over the opposition of her father and her art school colleagues, Kollwitz accepted the proposal of a man she respected and who she knew loved her deeply. As a a woman artist at the turn of the century, her decision to marry was a pragmatic one; it was the only way to secure both her financial and social freedom. While there were many serious and productive women artists working in Europe and Russia at that time, it was difficult if not impossible for any of them to actually make a living at it. Kollwitz' first commitment was always to her art, yet with a certain amount of wonder she records in her diary the steady growth of the relationship with her husband. As the years went by it was to provide the emotional support she increasingly came to need in order to work.

It was remarkable enough for a woman artist to receive serious recognition at the turn of the century, but Kollwitz achieved even more than that. She did what her art student friends at the Munich Academy of Art had declared impossible: she married, became a mother, and still continued with her art. For although she bemoans in her diary of "wretchedly little working time" when her two sons, Hans and Peter, were small, it was in those years that she created "The Revolt of the Weavers."

That marriage did not end her career, as it had for many of her talented contemporaries, is owed in part to the man she chose to marry. Karl Kollwitz was an ardent socialist who, for more than fifty years, served the working class as an insurance doctor in a Berlin tenement district. From the beginning he had known that above all else Käthe Kollwitz was an artist.

Like other diarists who have lived in times of social upheaval, Kollwitz used the diary to discuss with herself intellectual and moral questions, seeking answers to them. She also used it to cultivate an on-going relationship with her son Peter after he was killed. It is not uncommon for diary writers to work through the grieving process by writing in their diaries to the person who is dead, nor is it uncommon that this act of writing can bring a feeling of comfort and closeness. Kollwitz had what today would be called a strong mystical bent which was evidenced most dramatically in her relationship with Peter. In her diary she summoned his presence to help her in her work. Her commitment to keep faith with him and his lost generation formed the driving force behind the main body of Kollwitz' art.

For a period of time, just after Peter was killed, Kollwitz could do no art at all, having lost her direction. It was only when she read the words of the poet Goethe, "seed for the planting must not be ground" that she knew wherein her future work lay. Peter and all the young men who had died in the war were the seed for the planting, the youth who would have brought forth the future. That they should not have been ground in the machinery of war, that no children's lives would ever again be wasted in such a way became the focus of her work. In spite of the years of technical struggles, she always knew that she had talent, but knew also that it only flourished when it was used to express her deepest feelings. "It always comes back to this," she was later to write, "that only one's inner feelings represent the truth. I have never done any work cold, I have always worked with my blood, so to speak."

This metaphor had become literally true. Peter had been her own flesh and blood, and after his blood was shed, this grieving mother looked with different eyes on the children about her. She took upon herself the obligation to use her talents in their behalf, to portray in visual form the fragility and inestimable preciousness of their lives, that they might never again be squandered in war.

Contemporary art critics judge Kollwitz to be one of the four or five major graphic artists of the twentieth century. It is not for innovation in technique that she will be remembered; Kollwitz was firmly rooted in the German graphic tradition. She saw her task not as experimenting with new techniques but rather mastering the traditional ones, reducing and simplifying them to produce spare, stark images of extraordinary power. Interestingly, this aspect of her work is strongly influencing a new generation of post-Revolutionary Chinese painters.

It is the content of Kollwitz' images that leaves her mark on art history. The central image is almost always a woman, frequently pictured with young children. Kollwitz drew women differently than their timeworn image as passive, primarily sexual beings. Her women have strong peasant bodies, bodies that work hard in order to survive. They are physical rather than sexual beings, drawn with the fierce affection she felt toward working class women.

Kollwitz always depicted these women as strong and loving even while portraying in their forms the disastrous consequences of poverty, homelessness, servitude, sexual abuse, widowhood, a husband's unemployment, or a child's hunger. While men occasionally appear in her prints as fathers and husbands, they are only background figures. The focus is on the women who heroically carry the burden of social conditions they are powerless to change. Although Kollwitz was born into an educated, upper middle-class family, beginning with the drawings of her Koenigsberg childhood, it was working class people she found most visually appealing.

But it is not only the physical image of women that is different in her work. Kollwitz gave women positive inner traits: intelligence, courage, dignity, and compassion. Even in the days when feminist socialism was in the air, she projected an unfamiliar, affirmative view of women as persons of character and mental ability, responsive to the full range of human feelings.

What's more, much of her work depicts events from a woman's point of view. "Raped," the second in her print series entitled "The Peasant War," is one of the earliest pictures in Western art to depict a female victim of sexual violence sympathetically and from the victim's point of view. But all her women were not helpless victims. In the print "Outbreak," also part of the larger "The Peasant War" series, Kollwitz depicted Back Anna, a lone woman who incited a revolution. No other artist had ever created such a powerful image of a self-determined woman before. The main body of her work deals with how women and children were affected by, and actively responsive to, the social and political events of her life-time.

From the beginning Kollwitz' art was strongly political in content as well as in point of view. She was one of many political artists who contributed to the cultural ferment of early 20th century Germany. Poets, playwrights, and prose writers, as well as visual artists, were influencing each other's work. She was probably the only woman among the founding members of The Secession, a group of young socialist artists who opposed the establishment artists of the 1890s. Twenty years later, there were twelve women out of a roster of 228 members. Among them was the innovative colorist Paula Modersohn-Becker, whose diaries have recently been translated into English for the second time.

Yet the position of women members of The Secession remained marginal, a fact of which Kollwitz was only too well aware. Although she was well known throughout Europe, soon to be the first woman elected a member of the Prussian Academy of Arts, and later to become the director of its graphic arts department, The Secession board appointed her the organization's secretary. A job she detested.

Kollwitz never formally joined any political organization. Raised in a household strongly committed to socialism, she, like other intellectuals, supported the social democrats before World War I. After the end of the war and the German Revolution of November 1918, she declared her impatience with the unwillingness of the Socialist-dominated government to improve more profoundly the lot of Germany's working class. She was deeply affected by the murder of Karl Leibknecht and Rosa Luxemburg, two leaders of the German far-left. Her pacifisms made her an opponent of violent revolution, but she continued to support the cases of the German worker's movement as a humanitarian independent socialist.

In 1936, with Hitler firmly in power, the Nazis threatened to break up the entire Prussian Academy of Fine Arts unless Kollwitz resigned from her post as head of the graphics department, a position that she had held for eight years. She was thus deprived of the only regular income she had ever received. Not long after, her more than 1,200 drawings and 270 prints were banned from public display. The ban remained in effect until after the war; she would not live to see it lifted.

On April 22, 1945, Käthe Kollwitz died, penniless and homeless after having taken shelter from the saturation bombings of Berlin in the rural home of a wealthy art collector.

Today, the prints and sculptures of Käthe Kollwitz are shown throughout the world and she is honored as one of the outstanding artists of the twentieth century. Her goal was to be an effective artist, to portray with force and clarity fundamental human truths as she saw them. The accolades her work has received from art critics are one way of judging her success. But of equal importance are responses such as this one, recorded in the Belgian cemetery visitor's book on September 22, 1966: "God bless you, Käthe. And all your children. We carry on what you have wished." It is signed: "A former enemy."

Diaries, at the adolescent level, seem to be written mostly by girls. Certainly it is a fact that there are fewer published boys' diaries than published girls' diaries. It seems to be a matter of socialization. Men view writing as instrumental, whereas women view it as expressive, and this point of view is formed in adolescence. Boys are sent out to participate actively in work or sports. But society has long defined the female sphere as that of the home and family. Women thus have the right to forge the links of communications that hold families together, links which include extensive correspondence as well as the keeping of diaries and memoirs, which frequently serve as genealogical and historical records for the family. Also, the tradition well into the nineteenth century was to educate the girls at home. Since they were not allowed out into the world, what were they to write about but the affairs of their daily lives and the romantic dreams and yearnings they experienced as they grew from girlhood to womanhood? For both the reasons cited, it has always been "all right" for girls to sit quietly and scribble in a book.

Patricia Pendergraft's appreciation of the diaries of high school senior Eleanor Lathrop was originally published in *WOMEN'S DIARIES, A Quarterly Newsletter*, vol. 4, no. 3 (Fall 1986).

THE ADOLESCEDNT DIARY OF ELEANOR LATHROP, AN APPRECIATION

by Patricia Pendergraft

*O*nly two Eleanor Lathrop diaries are known to exist. They were found on the dirt floor of a dilapidated old barn that was being torn down to make way for new apartment buildings. The diaries, dated 1931 and 1933, record two years of a young girl's school life. The "lost" year, 1932, is like a broken thread. What happened in that year of 1932? Eleanor undoubtedly entered the University of California at Berkeley and excelled in her studies as we know from the first diary (1931) that she had always done. She probably continued the round of parties and other social events and practiced her piano with that seemingly boundless energy and enthusiasm for life that is immediately apparent from reading the first diary. In 1933, the thread is picked up, retied, and Eleanor Lathrop's life begins again.

Both diaries are physically in excellent condition. The blue ink is as bright and clear as though, only yesterday, the young Eleanor lay across her bed making notations and putting excited exclamation points at the endings of her sentences. At the bottom of the diary pages Eleanor has placed her initials "E.L.", validating each page as her own.

"Rah for the new year !!! " wrote sixteen year old Eleanor Lathrop in her diary on January 1, 1931. It started out with a burst of activity. That day Eleanor played tennis, ping-pong, and bridge, and danced at the Berkeley Tennis Club Open House. She also bought a new "piece" to play on the piano, *I Am Only The Words, You Are The Melody*. Eleanor, apparently an accomplished pianist, practiced

109

faithfully and often with her friend, Ed, who played the saxophone. Ed's name is mentioned throughout both of the diaries. "Ed called for me in the Duesenberg" and "Ed phoned and we talked for hours" are frequent notations.

To judge from the diaries, Eleanor's family enjoyed considerable wealth. There was a servant, a neat, comfortable home on a good upperclass street in Berkeley, California, a room of her own and lovely clothes to wear. Her father was a professional man, though it is never clear just what his profession was. Notations in the diaries mention his catching the train with briefcase in hand and returning home in the evenings. Eleanor's mother led a busy social life, often giving formal dinner parties and teas. Of one such party for twenty-eight, Eleanor wrote: "The house is all decorated so prettily and the seven card tables are all up. . .At seven the guests began to arrive. There were two caterers. . .All the men wore tuxedos and I wore my organdy." A man came to take moving pictures, she wrote, and she didn't get to bed until after one a.m.

Eleanor frequently drove the family car and the clear impression in reading the diaries is that the Lathrop's and all their friends drove to and from theater parties, private club dances and dinners, luncheons and tennis matches in their Pierce Arrows, Duesenberg Roadsters, Packards and Auburns. There were plays to attend, frequent sprees into San Francisco and always the feverish whirl of parties.

On January 3rd, Eleanor wrote: "Tonight Ella's dance. it surely was a pack of fun. There were ninety there. . . and the boys kept cutting and tagging." A few nights later she wrote: "Ed sent me flowers for tonight. . .they are gorgeous. . .we went to Flora's for dinner and it certainly was fun. We all sat at one big table and the service and food was lovely. . .I had on my pink dress, mother's fur coat, and long white gloves. The dance was keen." That night Ed gave Eleanor his frat pin to wear. "It is his Phi Alpha Omega," she added in writing about it. But Eleanor accepted the pin as a gesture of friendship and nothing more. There were too many interesting boys around for her to give her heart away to one. There is, however, a strong undercurrent throughout the both diaries that Eleanor was attracted to a handsome boy named George, and it was about

110

this boy that Ed, in a mood of despair, wrote to her in the summer of 1931 from a vacation spot: "You were dancing with some goodlooking boy and he [the person who had related the story to Ed] thought you were married the way you were dancing with him and looking into his eyes. It must have been George because you always look into his eyes when you dance with him and you also go into a trance." Eleanor must have read the letter with amusement for Ed was, after all, a close friend and she enjoyed teasing him from time to time.

Although Eleanor was a popular girl and spent much of her time attending social functions, she was a serious student who studied hard and was always proud and excited when she received good grades. She could also become upset if she had put in long hours studying and received only a mediocre grade for her efforts. Keeping good grades was extremely important to this exuberant, enthusiastic girl. There are many notations in the diaries such as: "Studied hours on Physics!". . ."Studied most of the afternoon". . . Physics exam today. It was terrible! Afterward found out my English mark is an A-minus. Throap said it was a perfect paper!". . . "We received our character studies back in English and I got an A on Palonius. Rah!". . ."I studied hard this afternoon and was so sleepy I had to lie down and *sleep* for an hour."

On January 4th, Eleanor wrote: "This review business certainly is strenuous! I studied most of the afternoon and all tonight." A few days later there was a reprieve from studying and Eleanor wrote that "Ed came over and brought his sax and we played together. Some pieces we could play quite well. . ." That night she listened to the radio and noted: "Einstein talked. . .his thery [sic] was explained and I understood a little."

The next few days were filled with more studies for Finals. But on the 23rd, perhaps as a small celebration to let off steam after an exhausting week of Finals, Eleanor and some of her girlfriends took off for San Francisco to see a Marie Dressler movie, *"Reducing"*. "Then," Eleanor wrote, "the orchestra gave selections from Faust while they showed scenes from it on the stage. It was perfect. . .we had a dandy time."

Not only was Eleanor Lathrop an ambitious student and a talented pianist, she excelled in dramatics as well. She took acting lessons and appeared in several high school plays. When she got the main part in *Elizabeth Refuses* she wrote: "I am Elizabeth!" infusing the words with her excitement. "It was great fun and I was sorry when it was over! Everyone said I did very well, excellent, clever, etc., and so I guess I was all right." At this time there was a 20th Century Costume Ball which she attended as a Spanish senorita. "I had a black shawl with red flowers wound around me, then a big red rose in my hair and big black earrings."

Eleanor, according to her own words, was "greatly pleased" with her appearance. Her hair was "curly, fluffy, goes up nicely and looks fine." She was a petite five feet tall, slender, dark-eyed and dark-haired and quite obviously attractive. But one soon discovers in reading the diaries that it was not only Eleanor's looks that made her appealing. Her friendly, vivacious, and enthusiastic personality drew boys and girls alike in her direction.

Early into the new year of 1931, Eleanor made a "startling discovery" that "there are to be *ten* dances at the Junior-Senior Formal instead of eight!! We got our programs for the Formals and they are darling. They are fixed so you can use them as card cases after the dance!"

In her senior year of high school Eleanor began to be "courted" by some of the university sororities. "Naomi Smith called and invited me to her sorority for dinner tonight!" she wrote with her usual exuberant exclamation mark. The next night she wrote: "Tonight I went to dinner at the Zeta Tau Alpha House. . .met all the girls and they seemed quite nice. We danced, ate and talked. I wore my blue satin."

There was also time to attend a movie with Ed. It was *The Blue Angel* with Emil Jennings and Marlene Dietrich. And, at this time, she was reading *Ariel*, the life of Shelly by André Maurois.

By the 25th of the month, all of Eleanor's grades were in. "Received. . .A in English, A in Physics, and B, nearly A, in French!! Rah!! I have *first* honors!! Only five out of the whole school were on. . .I received ten dollars for my report card. . ."

On February 3rd, Eleanor wrote: "A man came to visit our History class and we thought he was also going to visit Physics, so Miss Hoffman got agitated and came to us at recess to say that we would talk about review work, for *she* was not capable of talking about steam engines! That shows," Eleanor added in a little note of sarcasm, "what a good teacher she is!! She doesn't even know what it's all about!"

The next day there was a lecture at school by the Deputations Committee from Cal telling the seniors about the university. That night, Eleanor went to a horse show and sat in a front box where she could see everything. "It was perfect," she wrote. "The Governor of California, Rolph, was there and went around in a chariot, then made a speech and sat in a box on the opposite side. He made a break in his speech saying Henry VIII said, 'My kingdom for a horse . . .'" But the quick-minded, alert Eleanor noted: "It was really Richard III!" And she added: "The horses were wonderful and there were three little horses that jumped hurdles all by themselves. They were darling."

That night Eleanor studied late for a Physics exam. The next day she wrote in her diary: "It was terrible!! She asked us things we hadn't had, and the whole class agreed that it was terribly unfair and so hard we could hardly answer some questions." And on a sad note she added: "Startling news! When I arrived at school, I heard that the stables and all those beautiful horses were burned last night! It seems horrible!! Only a few horse saved and millions of dollars, horses and four men lost!"

On the 6th of February, Eleanor wrote in a grumpy mood: "In Physics exam I got a C which was a great injustice! She has it in for me somehow, for I should have gotten much higher. I was good and mad!"

To make herself feel better perhaps she bought a new dress. "It is a luscious shade of sort of tomato red, white fur on the sleeves, a cowl neck, a peplum, and a full skirt. It is darling and I am crazy about it." She also "bought some pretty white kid shoes for eight dollars and fifty cents and a rhinestone buckle for my dress. . ." She was now reading *Comus* by Milton and had bought a book, *She*

Stoops To Conquer at a sale for five cents.

On Valentine's Day Eleanor went to the Berkeley Junior Assemblies with Ed and wore her red dress. "George Heath was there," she added and, somehow, it is clear that George is to be very important in the young Eleanor's life. The next day she bought a "piece" called *I Surrender, Dear* and, that night, she was at another party.

The ten days that followed found Eleanor engrossed in her studies once again. She received an A on her History exam "and there were no corrections at all!" There was another French exam and the teacher "told me at recess that I was the only A in the class." Between studies Eleanor went to the theater to see a Lawrence Tibbet movie *New Moon*. ". . .L. Tibbet has a marvelous voice!" Eleanor noted enthusiastically.

On February 16th, Eleanor wrote: "I took the streetcar to school this morning. We made blue prints in Physics of the fields force of magnetic filings. It was fun. . .Miss Throap was trying to spell *onomatopoeia* today in class and after looking it up twice she admitted that the way I said it in the beginning and stuck to was right." And, as a gossipy little tidbit, Eleanor penned: "I hear a lot of scandal about Miss Throap, how she smokes all the time and etc."

There was a play in the French Club and Eleanor performed as "a weeping widow all dressed in black, which brought forth many laughs." On her father's birthday, the family attended an auto show in San Francisco and Eleanor wrote: "There were Duesenbergs, Cords, Packards, Rolls Royces, Cadillacs and Lincolns, etc. Nothing less than seven thousand dollars and most about fifteen or twenty thousand dollars."

Report cards were given out and Eleanor wrote: "I got an A in everything except a B in Physics, which pains me." She added that day that Ed had a "new cuckoo horn on his car." And the next day she was elated because "I received second prize in a literary contest!! Rah! I was quite thrilled."

Like many teenagers, then and now, Eleanor did not always see eye to eye with her parents. With her father especially. "I had a terrible row with Dad tonight about going to the Palace Sat. night and after saying I absolutely could not go and raging for hours, he finally came around later and said I could go, but he didn't want me to!" For the event, her mother had "lengthened my school skirt and tightened it around the waist, so that it feels keen now." Although Eleanor was fond of social life, she always managed to get back to her studies and make up for lost time. At one time she was working on no fewer than five reports at once and, miraculously, completed them all in a very short period of time.

In March, Eleanor wrote that she had received "the highest English mark in senior class, the only good A!!! Throap raved in every class about it, how I wrote on every page, and that everything was right, it showed clear thinking and that it *could* be done!! Rah!!!"

Eleanor attended an Alpha Chi Omega Sorority House dinner, and read *Ethan Frome* by Edith Wharton. There were bookclub meetings to attend, shopping trips, and attention to be paid to all the incoming invitations from the Sorority Houses. Friends driving their Pierce Arrows, Duesenbergs and assorted expensive cars called on her. Judging from Eleanor's diaries, life was wonderful, exciting and thrilling. There was never a lack of friends, places to go, or things to do. Every day seemed to be a new awakening for this intelligent, creative and talented girl.

At the end of March, report cards came out again and Eleanor wrote: "I got an A in everything except a B in French, at which I am furious for I certainly deserve an A in that of all things!" And she added with indignation and determination: "It is ridiculous and looks like insidious proceedings. I went to Miss Jones but she wasn't home, but I *will* see her!" The next day, cornering Miss Jones, Eleanor spoke to her "about my B and she would give me no satisfaction."

But, to help salve her wound over the French grade, another sorority invitation arrived. This time from Alpha Xi Delta. The following days were filled with Glee Club rehearsals, play rehearsals, a Nods and Beck staff meeting and going to the Junior Assemblies with Ed. "The minute I got in the door, the boys began asking me to dance," Eleanor wrote and she named several of the boys she refused, then added George Heath's name "whom I danced with." And in perhaps sympathetic amusement, she added, "Poor Ed!" But Ed's ruffled feathers were soon smoothed for the next night he was escorting Eleanor to another dance.

"At five," Eleanor wrote, "my corsage came from Ed and it was gorgeous. Gardenias and baby roses and forget-me-nots!!" Ed wore his tuxedo and hat and "looked very nice," Eleanor thought. The dance was at the Berkeley Country Club and she arrived home after two a.m. "It was a perfect time and a dandy dance."

On April first, Eleanor's diary page shouted: "APRIL FOOLS!" That night she went to a dinner with Ed, and on Easter Sunday she found "a basket near my bed with a bunny in it and a few eggs, then I had an Easter egg hunt!! They were hidden around the house and I got a lot of fancy ones, chickens, nests, etc." The next day she was studying again for an exam in Physics and reported later that she had gotten an A and B, only missing part of one problem.

On the twelfth, Eleanor attended an Alpha Xi Delta house dinner, and wore her "flame" dress and her mother's straw hat. The next day she went shopping and brought home "a pretty straw hat for six dollars and seventy-five cents and a darling Panama from Magnins for ten dollars. I tried them on with all my dresses and it is a problem. I think I like the Panama best. It is smart." And, mentioning Ed, she wrote: "I had more fun teasing him. It was a scream, and he was frantic!"

There was more shopping. "I bought some darling spectator pumps in brown and white for seven dollars and fifty cents." The next day her father apparently disapproved of the shoes for Eleanor wrote: "I phoned Dad and finally convinced him into letting me keep the shoes so I wore them with my new hat and my cord dress."

One bright spring day Eleanor and Ed drove into San Francisco and she wrote: "We talked a lot about *my* boyfriends and Ed teased me about George and I said, 'Oh that's right, I did have a couple of dances with him. . .'" George was beginning to appear more and more interesting to Eleanor's young eyes.

On the twentieth, at Senior meeting at recess "We talked about names on diplomas, graduation dress, etc." Ed came that night and teased her again about George. The next day she took the streetcar to school and learned that Ed had been arrested for going thirty-five miles per hour! "He may have his license taken away for thirty days, and if he does, he says he will let me use his car!!!"

The next day Eleanor wrote: "We got our programs for the Senior Formal and they are pretty. Green with a gold crest." That night she attended a Phi Alpha Omega dance, Ed's fraternity. "It was a big kick." On the twenty-fifth, Eleanor placed three X marks on the top of the diary page and wrote: "This is the day of the Heads formal!!! My corsage from Ed came, and when I opened the box, it was an orchid!!!!" Her four exclamation marks are an indication of her excitement. "I was thrilled," she continued, "the first time for that!" [an orchid] "What a dear boy Ed is. It is a gorgeous lavender orchid with lilies of the valley. Ed came at six-thirty in his tux and he looked so handsome. The girls at the party were as excited as I was and said, 'You certainly must rate!'" In reading the diary one is aware of the enormous pleasure and excitement Eleanor Lathrop obviously felt on the April night of 1931.

From the first formal, they continued to another Senior-Junior Formal (there were ten in all) and "the last dance was at the Head's. I had a good time and didn't leave until late, so I arrived home at three-thirty! The latest ever, but this was an eventful night." The next morning Eleanor set her orchid on the fireplace mantle and observed: "My orchid is as fresh as can be and looks wonderful." But, in a darker mood she wrote: "Had a terrible row with Dad. He is the most unreasonable and tyrannical person there ever was!!" It is easy to envision a concerned father trying to harness a rather headstrong, young daughter who balks at every turn and wants only to go on with her youthful merriment and fun.

Ed was over the next day with a new piece called *Stardust* and after trying it out, they went for a walk to Ed's grandmother's house. There they strolled through her beautiful garden and perhaps talked of the events of the day and night before.

Report card time came again and Eleanor received A's in English, French, and Physics, and a B in History. "I thought that was a gyp for I had an A in my exam and A's for practically all recitations. It looks like a put-up job," she ended sourly.

There were more and more parties and excursions on the Oakland ferry to San Francisco. There were luncheons and teas and drives in the expensive and showy automobiles of the upper class; shopping sprees and long talks on the telephone at night with her friends. All the while, Eleanor continued to study seemingly fearful of her grades dropping below that shining A she so desired and revered. From time to time, there were arguments with her father. "I had rather a row with Dad, but went ahead and did what I wanted to anyhow - for once!" she wrote in May. And after hours of study, she added: "This end of school is terrible!"

There was another senior meeting "to decide on our flowers for graduation day. A man was there with different floral pieces, and Miss Wilson just railroads everybody into everything! She wouldn't let us talk or express any opinions at all! I wanted a stunning piece, a yellow flower in the shape of a basket with a rose coming out of it..." But a hat was chosen instead, but Miss Wilson apparently. Eleanor described it as being "filled with flowers of different colors."

The next day Eleanor and a friend were off to San Francisco to shop for graduation dresses and she confirmed that "Ed had his license taken away for thirty days." At this time Eleanor was reading *The Forsythe Saga* and wrote: "I hope to finish it someday!"

At another senior meeting, "the girls decided on stockings" and later in the day, Eleanor "dashed to Oakland and bought a darling fur jacket, real light, for twenty-nine dollars and fifty cents! It's adorable! It is my graduation present." On the twelfth of May the senior pictures came. She had some good times driving Ed around since his license had been revoked. She "studied hard, especially on History and I finished the book." That same week Eleanor found her graduation dress for "eighteen dollars and seventy-five cents" which she described as "a darling white chiffon with a full skirt with pin tucks in it."

A few days later Eleanor "read for hours on Galsworthy then started writing my term paper for English on him. After working steadily for six hours, I stopped for dinner then I worked for two more and finally finished the first copy of it - a 'masterpiece' of one thousand seven hundred and twenty-five words - five typewritten pages. It was really rather fun writing it though."

Eleanor was chosen with ten other girls from her class to go on an excursion to an all-girls school in Pebble Beach. There was swimming and horseback riding, tennis playing, and bunking in the dormitory where they "talked all night." One morning there was a game of musical chairs played on horseback. "I didn't want to enter," Eleanor wrote, "but Dick said, 'Oh, Yes, Eleanor, it's easy.' So I tried and the horse started jumping around and I fell off!! Dick (he is so adorable, so handsome and cute) came running up, but I was all right and he rode on the horse with me!!! The girls were all excited about it and never finished talking about it. I heard afterwards that Mrs. Douglas said, 'That's just like Dick to do something original like holding that girl on the horse!'" When the trip was over, it was back to studies as usual for Eleanor. There was an A for her History term paper, a hundred on a spelling exam, and an A for an English term paper.

On a Sunday evening at the end of May, Eleanor donned her brown dress, hat, shoes and fur jacket. Deciding it "made a stunning outfit" she went with her family to attend the baccalaureate service at St.John's . . . all the senior class was there," she reported. On the first of June, after a Physics final, she went to buy her stockings for commencement. "They're terrible." she wrote. "So long and heavy so we [several of the girls] went to Miss Wilson and told her we didn't like them. It did little good! We burst out laughing and acted dumb. Lucille said she couldn't wear a garter belt because it would show through her dress and Miss Wilson said, 'Well, we'll have no *display* like that on commencement day - you'd better wear underclothes!' She thought it was terrible that we *rolled* our stockings!"

Three days later, Eleanor was picked up by a friend in a new Packard automobile and driven to school for the commencement rehearsal. After going through the performance several times "we dispersed to go to the senior luncheon at the Claremont Country Club. It was such fun having the whole senior class together . . . we heard the class will, then Miss Wilson asked how many were gong to college. Forty out of fifty-two! And how many were engaged? None!"

That night Eleanor "dressed in my pink formal for the alumna dinner . . . all the seniors sat together at one big table in the center and the alumna all around us. It was very impressive and thrilling!!! There were songs and speeches, entertainment and dinner. We're almost graduated!" Ed had given her a "darling white leather bag for graduation and his mother sent me a lovely bottle of French perfume."

June fifth was a red letter day. "Graduation Day!!!" Eleanor wrote at the top of her diary page using exclamation points to show her excitement. "It's really here!" All morning long she was kept busy answering the doorbell and telephone. Flowers came, roses and gardenias and three enormous orchids from friends. There were congratulatory cards, a telegram from her older brother living in the east. And her father gave her a bank book with a deposit of seven hundred and eight-one cents in it as a "starter for college." Eleanor, dressed in her white chiffon graduation dress, arrived at school for "the great occasion. We got our flowers - hats filled with pretty flowers of all kinds." And at two p.m. the line formed in the auditorium and the procession down the aisle started toward the stage. "It was a very exciting and *some* moment," Eleanor wrote. "We sang, had a speech and rec'd our diplomas. After the ceremony, with the auditorium filled, we went through the garden accompanied by the juniors to the porch where we sang our senior song and were showered with rose petals. We all laughed when these things hit our heads, neck, nose, and all over. We had our picture taken, then stood on the lawn and watched the many dancers and finally dispersed for refreshments. I saw everyone I knew and talked with all of them. After eating and talking for hours, we finally left, saying good-bye to all the teachers. . .it was such a gala day!"

Katherine Mansfield as a person has remained endlessly fascinating, even though her writings have gone in and out of fashion. Considered by some to have had a genius for friendship but a talent for hatred, Mansfield's personality also certainly had a devious and deceitful bent. In spite of the fact that she left a journal and numerous letters, her reputation for many years after her death was at the mercy of her husband John Middleton Murry, who heavily edited both before publishing them. Still, the writings remain, and the journal, with its deletions restored, must serve as a foundation for any biography of this greatly talented writer. McLaughlin explores this facet of her journal in the following article which was first published in *WOMEN'S DIARIES, A Quarterly Newsletter*, vol.2, no.3 (Fall 1984). It was originally presented as a paper at the 1981 MLA Convention.

KATHERINE MANSFIELD'S JOURNAL, AN EXAMPLE OF THE JOURNAL AS GENRE,

by Ann L. McLaughlin

*K*atherine Mansfield, the brilliant New Zealand short story writer who died in 1923 at the age of thirty-four, knew that journal writing was crucial to her creative process. "Queer this habit of mine of being garrulous," she says, referring to the journal. "Nothing affords me the same relief. What happens as a rule is if I go on long enough I *break through*. Yes, it's rather like tossing very large, flat stones into the stream." Mansfield felt that the act of journal writing helped her to break through the stillness of self-consciousness and doubt and allowed her to plunge down to the level of real work.

Mansfield used her *Journal* as a kind of stew pot for bits of description, dialogue, and ideas, which appear in her work in different forms. She also recorded personal events in her *Journal* and used it to examine her feelings about them. Mansfield's journal writing was, in fact, a way of rinsing the concerns of self from her mind for a time so that she could turn to her stories with a clearer, more transcendent vision.

Mansfield's *Journal* is actually not a complete on-going diary, but an edition of journal scraps, notes for stories, and unfinished letters, which her husband, John Middleton Murry compiled after her death. Although Mansfield once referred to her *Journal* as "my huge complaining diaries," she guarded them fiercely, keeping them with her through her many moves, aware that they were an essential piece of her life.

123

In *Metaphors of Self: The Meaning of Autobiography* (Princeton University Press, 1972), James Olney says the central question of autobiographers and journalists is: "How shall I live?" Mansfield adds a second vital question: "How shall I work?" She examines her work habits repeatedly in her *Journal* and scolds herself for lapses in discipline. But frequently the act of writing out her guilts and goals seems to help her break through to her story writing. "I have failed very badly these last few days and the evening was a 'comble,'" she confesses on April 2, 1918, but resolves, "Now, Katherine, here goes for tomorrow. Keep it up, my girl." Interestingly, she terms April 3rd "a good day," and begins a story in her *Journal*.

Since Mansfield was seriously ill with tuberculosis for more than five years before she died, her *Journal* includes many interior monologues concerning pain, depression, and her terror of dying young.

> I woke up early this morning. . . opened the shutters
> . . . and bounded back to bed. The bound made me
> cough—I spat—it tasted strange—It was bright red
> blood. . . Oh yes, of course, I am frightened. . . I
> don't want to find this real consumption, perhaps,
> it's going to gallop—who knows?—and I shan't
> have any work written. That's what matters. How
> unbearable it would be to die—leaving "scraps"
> "bits". . . . nothing real finished.

The tone of despair that Mansfield allows herself in her *Journal* contrasts markedly with the cheerful front she presents in her letters to Murry. "I'm better today," she writes, "fever gone, but weak as a blutterfly [sic] and thin as a match. All well except I can't bear you should be troubled with all this.' Shortly afterward, however, she confides in her *Journal*:

> I cough and cough, and at each breath a dragging,
> boiling, bubbling sound is heard. I feel that my
> whole chest is boiling. I sip water, spit, sip, spit. . .
> Life is getting a new breath. Nothing else counts.

The next line in the *Journal* shows a remarkable transposition from the personal record to a fictional beginning. "Can't you help me?" asks a fictional character in the same situation, and Mansfield, the writer, adds: "But even while she asked him she smiled, as if it didn't matter so much whether he could or couldn't." Although this fragment does not appear in any of Mansfield's published stories, it is another example of the way her journal writing helped her to move from the personal record into the world of fiction.

Mansfield's *Journal* reveals her swing of feelings about her mother. In her early rebellious years in New Zealand, she wrote angrily about her mother and siblings. "Damn my family. . . . What bores they are: I detest them all heartily. . . . Even when I am alone in my room, they come outside and call to each other, discuss the butcher's orders or the soiled linen and—I feel—wreck my life."

After a long separation from her mother, Mansfield wrote about her very differently. "Six o'clock. I am sitting in my own room thinking of Mother. I think of *our* house, *our* garden, *us* children— the lawn, the gate, and Mother coming in. 'Children! Children!' I really only ask for time to write it all. . . ."

When Mansfield created Linda Burnell, the mother of her fictional New Zealand family, she blended her early anger with her later nostalgia to produce a strange, vivid young woman, caught in ambivalence.

Sitting beside her new baby boy, Linda thinks,

> It was all very well to say it was the common lot of women to bear children. It wasn't true. She, for one, could prove that wrong. She was broken, made weak, her courage was gone, through childbearing. And what made it doubly hard to bear was, she did not love her children. . . The boy had turned over. He lay facing her, and he was no longer asleep.
>
> "I'm here!" [his] happy smile seemed to say. "Why don't you like me?"
>
> There was something so quaint, so unexpected about that smile that Linda smiled herself. But she

checked herself and said to the boy coldly, "I don't like babies."

Like Linda's feelings about her children, Mansfield's feelings about New Zealand, which she expressed frequently in her *Journal*, were ambivalent and deep. As a young woman restless to leave for England, New Zealand seemed ugly to her. "Oh, this monotonous, terrible rain. The dull, steady, hopeless sound of it. . . the narrow, sodden, mean bedraggled wooden houses." But later, when she was in London, a visit from her beloved brother evoked vivid memories of their childhood. When he was killed in France, Mansfield conceived that her duty to him was to write of their childhood and its island setting.

> Yes, I want to write about my own country till I simply exhaust my store. . . it is a 'sacred debt' that I pay to my country because my brother and I were born there; Oh, I want for one moment to make our undiscovered country leap into the eyes of the Old World. It must be mysterious, as though floating. It must take the breath. It must be "one of those islands. . ." I shall tell everything, even of how the laundry basket squeaked at 75."

In "At the Bay," another of Mansfield's famous long short stories about New Zealand, she reveals some of this 'mystery' in the opening paragraph, so that her 'undiscovered country' seems indeed to 'leap' before our eyes.

> Very early morning. The sun was not yet risen, and the whole of Crescent Bay was hidden under a white sea-mist. . . . A heavy dew had fallen. The grass was blue. Big drops hung on the bushes and just did not fall; the silvery fluffy toi-toi was limp on its long stalks. . . . It looked as though the sea had beaten up softly in the darkness, as though one immense wave had come rippling—how far?

Mansfield never returned to New Zealand, but she continued to record thoughts of it in her *Journal.* Toward the end of her life she wrote, "A long typical boat dream. I was, as usual, going to New Zealand."

Since Mansfield's New Zealand stories are largely autobiographical, we can ask what differentiates them from her *Journal.* In the stories, impressionistic as they seem, events and moods are carefully selected and the whole is very consciously formed. In Mansfield's *Journal,* on the other hand, on-going events are told to the self unselfconsciously, and its openendedness creates a far looser form. Mansfield's *Journal* might be considered a "sub-species" of her autobiographical stories, but, without it, her stories might not exist. Like the tossing of those large, flat stones into the stream, Mansfield's journal writing broke the still surface of inhibition and unease, and helped her to produce those luminous and memorable stories that are among the finest in our language.

John Middleton Murry edited Katherine Mansfield's *Journal* in 1927, and in 1954, he edited a second "definitive" journal. Since the first edition is easier for American readers to obtain, it is quoted throughout, except for the early section that Murry added in the second edition. (*The Journal of Katherine Mansfield,* edited by J. Middleton Murry, Knopf, 1927)

In his edition of Mansfield's *The Urewera Notebook,* Professor Ian Gordon, a Mansfield scholar and a New Zealander, describes Murry's editing as "utterly unreliable, because [without recourse to the documents from which they have been drawn] one cannot be certain on any page that it has been accurately transcribed, or that what one reads is the whole of what KM wrote, or that what is presented is presented in a sequence that KM herself would have determined. . . ." This author agrees with Prof. Gordon that the *Journal* is an insecure basis for biography, but thinks it casts light on the journal genre.

The earliest travel diaries were written by men, who were the explorers. Women stayed at home. It is not until the seventeenth century that we get a Celia Fiennes, who traveled around England on sidesaddle - and kept a journal of her journeys. In America, the intrepid Madame Knight, who rode from Boston to New York on horseback in 1704, seems to have been the first to have felt travel was an adventure worth recording. Since the nineteenth century, however, women have led more mobile and more adventurous lives. They have traveled, and still travel, for pleasure as well as for knowledge. And they keep travel journals. Following are selections from the travel journals of two contemporary women: Marcia Miller, who looks for the challenge, and is not afraid to step off the beaten track; and Augusta Molnar, who studies the people in Third World countries, recording and analyzing her finds in order to discover methods for improving the lives of the peoples she studies.

Those of us who are average travelers simply want to bring back the sights and sounds, no matter how civilized, of that special trip we have dreamed of making for years.

These two articles were first published in *WOMEN'S DIARIES, A Quarterly Newsletter*, vol. 4, no. 2 (Summer 1986).

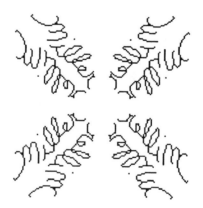

ASIAN EXPERIENCES, FROM A JOURNAL

by Marcia Miller

*M*arcia Miller, of New York City, began traveling in 1967 and has usually traveled alone.

As she approached middle age, her life was shattered by a series of severe personal illnesses: mycoplasmic pneumonia, cancer, and a "terrible two-year grinding depression." The last was the worst. It required drastic action. For Miller, that took the form of "survival" trips — to parts of the world not cushioned by the comforts of Western civilization, using local means of transportation only. In this way, she learned that "to be challenged is to know you are alive."

Although she must still travel with her two bags—one containing the hundreds of pills required for her physical well being and the other containing two changes of clothing—Miller continues to follow her own prescription for good health.

These excerpts are from a journal she kept of a trip she took in the summer of 1983, a journal which she is shaping into a book. Her co-traveler was another woman whom she had met on a previous trip to Indonesia. They discovered that they were compatible traveling companions and planned this journey to Thailand and Malaysia together.

Thailand. August 19. - We had planned to push on south after an overnight stay in Surat Thani. But, after seven hours of cramped bus travel, as we neared the port of BanDon, we spontaneously decided to get off and take the night ferry to Koh Samui, an island in the Gulf of Siam, which was supposed to be an undeveloped dream. At the bus stop, we each engaged a *trishaw*.[2] We used our fingers to bargain with the men who pedalled us to the pier after agreeing with each other and us about the fare. There we bought tickets for the boat trip. Margaret was thrilled for me, knowing how much I favor boats. But this was not quite my idea of an overnight ferry trip. In fact, when I saw how and where we would sleep, I lay down and insisted that she take a picture, as I knew no one at home would believe this story. We had paid for first class, fifty *baht*[2] each, which meant that we were on the top of the two decks. We had a semi-clean, sheet-covered, foam rubber pad to sleep on. The pads were double size, laid in two rows the length of the boat; each ticket, carefully numbered, entitled the ticket holder to a side of a pad. The ceiling was too low for me to walk upright, so I kind of crawled along, knocking over the brass chamber pots. I wondered, am I really going to be able to do this; sleep with fifty-eight strangers in one room on a boat? Mostly, I was terrified that one of my bags would "disappear" and with it a good portion of my essential medicine. Well, I placed as much as I could in my handbag and hoped for the best. We left our larger bags and went out to look for food, as we had not eaten a proper meal since breakfast. From a stall, we selected rice cooked with bright orange duck eggs and several vegetables, the only one of which I recognized being scallions. This food was prepared by a pregnant woman, who looked ready to deliver twins that evening, and served to us by her two naked children.

Sitting at a rickety table overlooking the sea, I tried to calm down by observing the ambience around us—blinking colored lights, a tin

[2] *trishaw* - a three-wheeled conveyance similar to a rickshaw, but pedalled.

[3] *baht* - Thai money; $1 equals approximately 20B.

roof, patched and with many holes, ear-shattering Thai rock music, soldiers on motorcycles, pedicabs, Mercedes-Benz buses, flying balloons, a children's carnival, *klong*[4] life, ferries plying to and fro across the black river. We bought fruit and nuts, not knowing when our next meal would be. I had my thermos filled with tea and we walked back to the boat. The lights were on in second class; we could see that the ceilings were even lower than ours. Straw mats covered the floor. Their tickets were good for the passage only and did not guarantee a specific place. Upstairs, in "luxury," we tried to read amid the din of many languages—the Thais, so reserved on one side of the boat, and the Westerners, mostly German and British students, on the other, large and loud, carrying enormous backpacks. The boat left promptly at 11 p.m.

This is the flip side of my life. I am as far away from American urban life as I can be. Questions: 1) why are Margaret and I always the oldest travelers? 2) where are all the women?

August 20, Saturday. - We are well-situated now, but this has been a very difficult time. We arrived at 4 a.m., in pitch blackness. The lights on the boat had failed because the generator was down, and there never were any lights on the pier. With my small bag on one shoulder and the larger bag on the other, I stood at the edge of the vigorously rocking boat, trying to find the ladder attached to the pier. I could not see my hand in front of me. I could hear and feel the water, but ominously, I could not see it. This was one of the times in my life when I nearly faltered. I thought, I will not be able to do this. But aware that I was holding up people behind me, I steeled myself and somehow grasped the wet metal ladder. Splashed with water, I climbed seven steep steps up to land. *Bemos*[5] lined the pier; but we waited thirty minutes before we could board one. Because we had slept little and were somewhat rattled by the whole experience, we violated our hard and fast rule of never accept-

[4] *klong* -a canal.
[5] *bemo* - a converted pick-up truck used as a taxi in Southeast Asia.

ing any unseen accommodation at night by agreeing to an unsolicited offer of a "dream seaside bungalow." Finally, after another confusing wait, the driver took off. Several people were dropped off as we wound our way over one dirt road after another. The horn blasted constantly, waking everyone from a sound sleep, until we arrived at our "dream." We were both tired and shaken, ready to lie down anywhere, but even in the darkness, we looked despairingly at the tiny woven-wood hut, no larger than my clothing closet at home, with an open roof, slatted floor, filthy sheet, and ten million mosquitoes. We tried to console each other, spread insect repellent, and resolved to sleep an hour until daybreak, when we would try to find something else. In the sunlight, of course, everything looked better and a bit of our natural resilience surfaced. We ate an egg with fresh tea and, walking along the road, found beautiful quarters just ten minutes away.

So we are lodgd for a few days in a large, private cottage with a terrace overlooking the sea, and apparently the owner is a sensational cook. The menu is interesting and extensive. All the tension seeped out of us. We swam, washed ourselves and our clothes, and took a long walk to the sacred shrine of Big Buddha. This is a wonderfully unspoiled island, utterly silent, not as lush as Bali. The only problem is the sand flea, who is attracted to my legs and ankles by the hundreds. My "Moskol" is completely ineffective against them, so we save that for the ants, which it demolishes. Instead, I use Margaret's "Rid." Thus, we have the perfect system. We read, and treated ourselves to a wonderful meal—poached fresh fish and banana flambe. The owner, who cannot possibly weigh more than eighty pounds, manages this entire operation with grace and calmness, aided part-time by her son and a neighbor.

Malaya. August 30. - Frequently, the bus by which we were traveling was forced to crawl behind tree-laden trucks as the road was too narrow for passing; we had to wait patiently until they turned off into a saw mill with their priceless, chained and cumbersome load. The trunks of the cut trees were huge—I judged eighteen inches in diameter. Each truck carried three or four sections of the never-to-be-replaced, vanishing trees.

There was continuous village life along that road—a few shops, a few houses—bordered by plantations and mills. Then, more houses and more shops. People had been leaving the bus intermittently; it was half-empty by the time we arrived at Mara, a small junction.

There, a group of ten—different from any other people we had ever seen—ran onto the bus and made for the back. Unlike all the other passengers, they did not pay the driver. They were small-boned, muscular, dark-skinned and short—the grownups about four feet, eight inches—with tight curly hair. They resembled pictures I had seen of the people who inhabit the Kalahari Desert. It was obvious that the group was cohesive and interdependent, and that the adults enjoyed each other's company and were bonded by mutual respect and good-will. They spoke to each other constantly and in a language which sounded completely different from Malay. Once they selected seats, they did not remain in them but shifted around, often jumping up and down.

We did not know who they were, but noticed immediately that almost every other person in the bus reacted unfavorably to their presence. A few women drew in their skirts and pulled their children closer. Several men reading newspapers raised them high to hide their faces. We witnessed two teenagers reach up and remove their bags from the luggage rack to place them on the empty adjacent seats.

Clearly, these newcomers were despised by the Malays.

I nudged Margaret. "They're the Orang Asli, the Malay aborigines. The Semais. And they're probably moving. I bet they will get off in a deserted spot and just walk into the forest."

For the next hour, Margaret and I, the only Westerners in the bus, sat quietly, observing the aborigines around us. I especially watched the small family nearest us. The man was jittery, unable to sit still for more than the moment it took to roll cigarettes, some of which he would hand to the woman beside him. Each would puff three or four times in quick succession and throw the butts on the floor. Alternately, they picked from a newspaper parcel full of *rambutans*,[6]

[6]*rambutan* - a red and green Asian fruit with thick, prickly skin.

which the man shared eagerly with the other members of the group. They peeled the fruit quickly, threw the skins on the floor, and ate voraciously, shoving the meat into their mouths. I have never seen people who moved like them; there was a jerkiness to their movements, like marionettes or monkeys.

They were dressed in old, threadbare Malay sarongs or cast-off, threadbare Western clothes. The man wore skin-tight purple pants ripped at the knee and two plaid Levi shirts; the woman wore three tee-shirts of varying sleeve lengths and colors, and two sarongs, one which hung to the floor and one which was draped around her hips. Their young son wore two shirts and shorts, cut out at the sides to fit. No one wore shoes.

The boy was sick. He lay on the seat in front of his parents whining pitifully. His eyes were bloodshot and half-closed from fever. Pus ran from his right ear. He half-heartedly scratched at the sores on his legs.

The driver stopped to pick up other passengers. But, before driving on, he walked back to the group and demanded money for their fares. The other members paid in coins which were wrapped and knotted in cloth and which they extracted from deep within their clothing.

By the time the driver reached the little family, the aborigine man looked as though he would explode. He clutched his money tightly in his hand. I had watched him count it—all bills, six of them, six ringgits,[7] three American dollars. He had fingered each bill carefully. He held out three of those bills to the driver who insisted that it was not enough and pointed to the boy. The father held up three fingers to indicate the child's age—that meant a free fare. But the driver shook his head angrily and held up six fingers. The tortured father sat rigidly on the edge of his seat, holding out the three bills in front of him. Every person on the bus was watching. No one said a word. Finally, the driver grimaced, grabbed the bills and resumed his driving.

[7]*ringgit* - Malay money; $1 equals 2 ringgits.

At last, I understood—that those other three *ringgits* were all the money this family had. That was their total worth. I also understood that the two sarong-covered, oddly shaped packages, which lay on the floor among the cigarette butts and rambutan skins and which the man often moved and patted, contained all their possessions. They were obviously wearing all their clothing. That was it— total money, total possessions, total clothing.

The mother had kept beside her what I thought was another small package, covered in a torn, faded, blue-print sarong. It was not until I had been riding next to them for thirty minutes that an almost imperceptible movement caught my eye and I realized a baby was wrapped in that material. I never did see the baby's face. Once only the mother lifted the cloth, peeked in and recovered it immediately. Neither the mother nor the father offered the child any food or held it in their arms. Meanwhile, the whining cries of their older child grew louder, more insistent.

Suddenly, the group stirred as one. I looked outside. We were driving on a particularly narrow part of the road. The forest was dense and overhanging branches scraped against the roof of the bus. There were no dwellings, no sign of human life. The family prepared to leave the bus: the mother draped the sarong with the baby inside over her chest, the father carried his whimpering son. Each parent picked up a cloth-wrapped package and followed the seven other members of their tribe off the bus.

My last impression of that group of Orang Asli, as the bus sped off, was their looking happy and relieved, pointing their fingers and their heads in their characteristic jerky manner, first in one direction, then in another, trying to choose the best place to enter the forest and to erect their next homes.

"DOCTORING" IN NEPAL

by Augusta Molnar

ugusta Molnar is a cultural anthropologist. In 1976, she went to a tiny village in Nepal to carry out the required field work for her doctoral dissertation. On the advice of fellow scholars, she made plans to study the Magar tribe and spent two years living in the remote primitive village of Mema. To get to Mema, she set out from Kathmandu, the capital city, and headed west traveling by bus. The journey had to be completed on foot with a guide. She "struggled up hills and fell into streams and at last came to Mema, a clump of rough houses piled up against a mountain." There, she stayed in a small room in a stone house run by an "opinionated, compassionate, cheerful matriarch named Nana."

Molnar has written an as yet unpublished book about her life in Mema and the Magar villagers who became her friends. This is a selection from the book, which is based on material taken from a journal she kept while there and from field notes which supplement gaps in the journal. It shows just how it was that things never went as she expected. When she innocently offered her knowledge of first aid to villagers who were miles from a doctor, she soon found that she was operating a full-time infirmary.

I made two trips to Kathmandu from Mema in the next year; one in August, shortly after the summer festival in the high pastures, and another in January. A few days before the second trip, a woman came into my room, looking frantic.

"Little Sister, are you home?"

"What can I do for you?"

"You must come to the house immediately. Bring some medicine.

My eldest son cut his foot chopping wood today, and his brothers brought him down from the shepherd's hut where they are staying. You must come quickly."

I gathered up what I thought was adequate: disinfectant, gauze, bandages, an antibiotic ointment, cotton for cleaning, scissors and tweezers. When we got to the house, I found the son and his wife in a room on the lower floor, where they lived.

The son was in his mid-twenties and had that strong, stocky, Magar, central Asian build. I knew him fairly well as he sometimes substituted for the local postman.

"What did you do to yourself, Elder Brother?" I asked, using the respectful form of greeting, unsure which of us was older.

"I was chopping up a log and the axe slipped. It seems to have cut sort of deep." He was in obvious pain as he said this.

I unwrapped the foot, which was done up in a dirty strip of cloth, a piece of someone's old clothing or a food sack. It was a gaping wound, but not deep, and he seemed to have severed some tendons in the foot. It was definitely something that needed professional care.

"You will have to take this to a real doctor. You should have someone carry you to the district clinic. Someone heat me water, so I can clean it."

"I can't go to the clinic; it is too far. Who would carry me all that way?"

"But look at this. If I just disinfect it, that will not help the tendons grow together properly. You must see someone professionally if you want to be able to walk normally."

"Can't you do something yourself, Elder Sister?"

"I don't have the *gyan* (knowledge) for that sort of thing. I have no idea how to sew it up, or if it should be sewn up. You must go to the clinic."

"You took care of Raji's knee!"

"But that was a different type of cut. That was fine with just a bandage." I had put a butterly-style adhesive on the knee and wrapped it so he could not bend it. Amazingly, it had healed properly. This was very different. I started to clean the wound. It was not infected, fortunately. It did need some attention if the son were

138

going to walk properly when it healed, however, and I tried again to convince them of it.

But they were adamant, and persisted in harping on Raji's knee, implying that I could really help if I chose to. It was hard to convince a villager that my knowledge was limited. The clear-cut cases that I treated led patients like this one to believe I was playing favorites, treating Raji, but not this woodcutter. The mother, the son's wife, and the son all had that look. 'You treated Raji, why won't you treat us?' They obviously thought me unkind.

I didn't seem to have much choice. My treatment for wounds came directly from page 78 of my first aid manual, and it did not tell me how to repair tendons. I was going to Kathmandu in a few days, anyway, and to try some bizarre treatment meant I would have to stay in the village to make sure he was all right. Better keep it clean and disinfected and let it heal. To be on the safe side, I left the son some additional antiseptic solution and some clean bandages to replace the ones I had supplied. I gave him careful instructions on how to keep it clean and dry and left him, concerned only that he would lose the use of some tendons.

I barely got home from treating the wounded foot when another villager came to see me about another patient.

"Little Sister White Lady. My mother is sick. You must come and see her."

"What is the matter?"

"You will see. It is a wound. She is very feverish. Come with me and I will show you. Don't forget your medicine."

"She is too sick to come here?" I asked, tired from the last house call.

"No, you must come."

I went to the woman's house and found her mother lying on a mat by the fire, obviously quite sick. She sat up with help and showed me a horrible looking gouged wound in her forearm. It was infected, and her arm was swollen to three times its normal size. I was overwhelmed. Was this *my* problem? Was I the person responsible for healing this old woman? I felt like running right back out the door.

"What happened? When did she do this?"

"Four or five days ago. My mother was sitting by the fire spinning. She had apparently put the small sickle we use to harvest barley in that rack over the fire, but not very securely. It fell out and cut her arm. I don't know why it fell so sharply. It has gotten much worse."

With my limited experience, I was certain that the woman would never recover no matter what anyone did for her, because she had a high fever and was aged. I gave her aspirin, cleaned the wound, applied an antibiotic powder to the infected area, and, after testing her for a reaction, gave her a penicillin shot because she seemed in such desperate straits. I hated to give penicillin shots,, even in extreme cases, because I was always afraid the person would have an allergic reaction. The test was supposed to be indicative, but I also kept adrenaline on hand, which was supposed to alleviate a reaction, according to page 109 of my manual. I really did not want to find out if it were true or not.

"You should take her to a professional. This is a serious wound." I told the daughter out of the mother's hearing. "She could easily die. You should have sought Western care as soon as it happened. Have you seen a *shaman*?"

"Yes. He was not very positive either, but he put this poultice of herbs on the wound."

"Well, leave the poultice on." What harm could it do? Maybe it had more power to draw out the infection than my antibiotics. What did I know? "But take her to a doctor!"

"You *are* a doctor."

"I most certainly am not!"

"Suppose she dies along the way?" the daughter continued. "What can the health post do that you have not yet done? You have given her an injection." (To a Magar an injection is a magical source of all-powerful medicine, when compared to simple oral medication.)

I was unable to convince her. I returned once to give the woman another shot, after rereading the brief section on wounds in my manual. When I left for Kathmandu, the woman looked no better.

Neither the *shaman* nor I felt very confident.

When I returned from Kathmandu, I asked almost immediately about the state of these two patients. I was surprised and shocked by the answers. The woodcutter, whose wound I had thought would heal without much trouble, had died, apparently of gangrene. Gangrene was something I had always associated in my mind with swampy, steaming jungles, not mountainous Nepal, home of Everest and abominable snowman. This violently brought home to me the dangers of complications from a wound, even if it is initially cleaned and disinfected. I reluctantly asked about the old woman, dreading the answer.

"Oh," Nana told me cheerfully, "she is fine. She is even walking around these days. She came by to give you a bottle of homemade wine and some home-brewed beer, but you were still not back. Her arm is as good as new." By all logic, she should have been the one to die, not the young man with a much less serious wound.

I went up to my room that night terribly upset. How had I come to be 'dabbling' so intensively in 'doctoring'? 'Dabbling' so much that I had brought a whole supply of drugs and bandages on this trip—much more than the basic store of bandages, ointments, asprin, cold medicine, and stomach remedies I had brought the first time to use when I might need to treat myself; self-treatment that had originally consisted entirely of following the advice from my two manuals, one on first aid, the other on mountaineering. Neither was meant to be used on the premise that after the initial treatment, the patient would never go near a trained doctor.

I realized that my 'dabbling' went back to the beginning. When I first came to Mema I occasionally treated members of my landlord's household or other villagers for minor problems, such as round-worms or pink eye. If Mun Maya or Nana cut their fingers cooking, I applied antiseptic and bandaged them up. If, in the course of conducting interviews, I found a child that had burnt itself on a hot pan, I went home and got ointment for the burn.

Then, not long after I started living in the village, I met a Gurkha solder home on five-months' leave; he had worked for sixteen years in India as a medical practitioner. I figured he had more practical experience than any doctor I knew, given the range of Indian diseases. He practiced medicine informally during this leave, and I often accompanied him to help and to learn from him. I wanted to compare the way his patients responded to Western treatments with the way they responded to the remedies and supernatural cures effected by the local *shamans*, or witch doctors. Local attitudes to modern medicine were mixed. People had a varying degree of exposure to it and knowledge about it. In general, no one was averse to Western medicine, but they relied mostly on local treatment—on *shamans* for serious cases and on themselves for minor ailments. They were reluctant to travel to a distant medical center where they had no assurance that a cure would be found and where government-supplied medicine was in short supply. Such a trip was expensive and few villagers relished the thought of dying so far from home.

I learned a lot from the soldier, and had no lack of opportunity to use my growing knowledge. After he left, people I had helped once came back again later. They also sent their friends and the friends sent more distant friends. The list of ailments I was asked to treat grew more diverse as my patients increased in numbers. I was glad to help when I could. Without realizing what was happening, I began to be considered the 'doctor' in the village. And 'doctor' was the last thing I saw myself to be. The role gave me mixed feelings and not a few reservations. As a product of a highly specialized industrialized society, I was used to highly trained doctors and other medical personnel. 'Dabblers' were prosecuted, and here I was devoting major chunks of my time to my acquired profession, often to the detriment of my field work. I felt morally wrong because I lacked the necessary training to make decisions about some one else's health. Peace corps volunteers stationed in the country were strictly forbidden to treat local people for any but the most minor medical problems. I felt that ethically I should follow the same advice. But the patients continued to come.

Once, Nana's half brother came to me at her suggestion with a broken finger. It had slipped out of joint and he was afraid it would heal at an angle. Following my manual (page and illustration 27), I reset it and splinted it with bam-boo, Magar-American style. I had no idea if it would work. Treating it left me shaky and scared. Had I helped or made the finger worse? Would his own relatives have done a better job with their traditional use of bamboo splints? Would they have treated it better if I had stayed out of it? By some miracle the finger healed properly. That it did gave me no new confidence, however. And the brother made me feel worse by presenting me with a precious bottle of his mother's best wine and four eggs, a real treat. I would have welcomed being paid for my expertise, but felt bad accepting tribute for what I knew were just good intentions. And the faithful continued to come, presents and all, with every kind of external and internal ailment. It never ceased to amaze me.

The eighteenth century explosion of personal religious writings is credited to John Wesley, who mandated it for his followers in the English evangelical reform movement. By then, it was no longer unusual for women to appear in print. During that century spiritual journals began to be crystallized into a form combining autobiography, chronicle, and aspects of the curriculum vitae. They were written in the first person and replicated the standard pattern of religious stages. Gillespie calls these works, specifically by women but edited after their death by husbands or children, "pious memoirs."

This is a revised version of the article published in WOMEN'S DIARIES, A Quarterly Newsletter, vol. 4, no. 4 (Winter 1986). An earlier version was presented at a conference on Autobiography and Gender at Stanford University. A forthcoming study of Martha Ramsy's crisis will appear in the William and Mary Quarterly under the title "1795: Dark Night of the Soul for Martha Laurens Ramsay."

MARTHA LAURENS RAMSAY, A CASE STUDY OF DIARY AS AUTOBIOGRAPHY

by Joanna Bowen Gillespie

*M*artha Laurens was born in 1759 in Charleston, South Carolina, to a wealthy family of French Huguenot descent. Her father, Henry Laurens, built his fortune in the slave trade although his increasing ambivalence about the morality of such "odious business" led him to give it up shortly before the Revolutionary War. In the early 1770s, Martha lived with a childless uncle and aunt after her mother's death while her father took her brothers to England for schooling. In 1775, Martha, too, went to England with the uncle's household because of the uncle's failing health, at the very time her father returned home to join cause with the American Revolutionary patriots. In 1778, Henry Laurens served as President of the Continental Congress, the only Southerner elected to that office, and in 1780, went to Europe on urgent financial business for the nation. Captured at sea by the British and jailed in the Tower of London, he was released at the beginning of 1782 and later appointed one of the three signers of the Preliminary Treaty of Paris. Martha, also still in Europe, served as her father's diplomatic hostess and secretary. In 1785, she returned to Charleston with her father and the few surviving family members. At age 27, she married Dr. David Ramsay, and gave birth to eleven children, eight of whom were living when she died in 1811, at 52 years of age.

Martha Ramsay began keeping a diary in 1791, the year she had to cope with the first major tragedy in her married life—the death of an infant daughter, Frances. Martha's diary, the centerpiece of a posthumously-published two-hundred-page memoir compiled by her husband, exemplifies the truism that diaries served to help their writers cope with tragedy and trauma rather than triumphs. In typical autobiographical reflection, her diary recorded an individual woman's struggle to make sense of her life in the midst of griefs, disappointed dreams, and painful maturing. The chaotic economy of Charleston in the 1870s and -90s, the writing and ratifying of the federal constitution (of which her husband was a prominent supporter), the diminished importance of family fortune and reputation, her own evolving understanding of citizenship in the new nation—these were the context, but not the focus, of her diary. Twentieth-century readers have to assemble a mosaic of facts and information about her actual day-to-day existence from the Laurens Papers, at the University of South Carolina, and from various collected papers of her historian-husband, David Ramsay, in order to reinhabit the entries in her diary.

Nevertheless, a second-hand (i.e., edited) document such as the *Memoirs of the Life of Martha Laurens Ramsey* by Dr. David Ramsay constitutes a special type of eighteenth-century "autobiography" at least in part because it is all we have. Memoirs of varying composition and content, nearly always including diary/autobiographical material, were the only publications preserving the lives of a substantial proportion of influential, educated women in the early nationhood period. More important, however, is the personal voice—the essence of autobiography—that speaks to us from aging print, even if stylistically foreign to the autobiographical form and style we today take for granted.

Martha's diary is today labelled "a religious diary" because we read it with a mind-set that (unlike hers) firmly separates out religion from secular, emotional, and psychological themes. For her it was a diary whose analytic language, the only one she had at hand, was religious. Through her religious language and metaphor, however, it displays the essential elements of autobiography (Janet Varner Gunn's *The Poetics of Autobiography*): the autobiographical impulse, her need to locate emotions and events in time, by writing them down under a date; the autobiographical response, her own ethics of interpretation, in Martha's care the perspective of a believing Protestant Christian and the perspective of one of Charleston's 'first families' plagued by the unexpected twists of life; and the autobiographical perspective which led her to ponder in agony the searching question 'where do I fit? How does all this locate me, in this world (as well as in the next)?' As with many diarists whose primary language for self-construction and self-management was religious, equal effort to fit one's self into this life and the next was a given; keeping the other-worldly perspective in balance with an earthly existence was crucial to the mental and emotional balance of the didactic-Enlightenment mind-set (see Henry May's *The Enlightenment in America* for a definition of that type of mentality).

Some of Martha's religious writings other than the diary were also incorporated in the *Memoir* by her husband. According to Dr. Ramsay, the existence of the diary itself was unknown until a few days before her death, when she revealed where she had hidden them all those years. Perhaps, faced with the end of her earthly existence and unconsciously following the model of other women diarists, Martha longed for the earthly immortality of having her words in print. She could count on her husband's burning desire to contribute to his country (and personal reputation) by writing and publishing books. The dying woman merely requested that her writings be preserved "as a common book of the family," a narrative about life and spiritual triumph for her children. Her husband's turning it into a public Memoir indicated that his editorial, husbandly hand would also be visible, his own agenda traceable in her words.

David Ramsay, born into a humble but high-minded Pennsylvania farm family, had migrated to Charleston after graduating from the Philadelphia medical school in 1770; there he expected to find a ripe field for medical practice and financial self-improvement, even if on principle he opposed the institution of slavery and was a restless Northerner by temperament. Eager to be a leading citizen, and married into one of the city's most honored pre-War families, Dr. Ramsay envisioned promoting his wife's spiritual mode of coping with disasters in a book that would set a standard for her fellow countrywomen; he also needed to transform his grief into a public service. Today we may wonder if his haste to idealize his wife and to insert a woman into the new nation's pantheon of heroes—he published the memoir only six weeks after the funeral—blinded him to the diary's implicit focus on *his* feet of clay. Or, perhaps all too cognizant of his financial mismanagement as a central factor in her psychic struggle (though she only hinted at it in the diary), the *Memoir* at one level could have been an expiation of his guilt.

The woman David Ramsay intended to honor had been a triumphant mother-of-the-Republic, a metaphor of twentieth-century historian Linda Kerber's but clearly an image embraced by Mrs. Ramsay herself and enlarged by her husband. She had been the educated woman who "read Mary Wollstonecraft's *Rights of Women*," was intellectually *au courant* with modern views about women's independence, who chose, *on principle,* the Biblical "standard of faith and practice" as her domestic ideal. He proudly presented her, in his biographical introduction to the *Memoir,* as the type of wife who did not challenge traditional male leadership in either domestic or civic and religious circles, though she was fully capable of so doing. He vastly admired her discharge of "relative duties"—the woman's role as shaper of citizens in the new Republic, using the most modern version of enlightened religious citizenship either of them could imagine. Not for her any fashionable contention for female autonomy; she, Martha, would persuade by her own superior example. Dr. Ramsay's memorial profered her as exemplar of the new American woman, just as he—ambitious, upwardly mobile and a published contributor to the cultural fabric of his new nation—envisioned himself as "the new American."

Her first diary entry evoked the agony of a parent over the death of an infant. Martha used the device that was part of her psychic strategy for coping: balancing a trauma to her heart with a challenge to her soul, a phrase about the child with a phrase about her own sinfulness. Somehow a logic of debits and credits, costs and accounts, was essential. Attaching her terrible grief to a sense of personal 'just desserts' brought balance to the wounded self, horrifying as it sounds today. It was her unconscious means of staying at least partially in control. "Oh my God," she wrote July 20, 1791, "how lately hath thine afflictive Providence been wringing my heart with a two-fold anguish: the loss of my sweet baby, and the consideration of those sins which required this chastisement." A week later she wrote, "The two last days have been days of mournful walking. O how does the remembrance of my sweet Fanny press upon my memory." Then , from her perspective, she had to add, "How good is God that though [I am] cast down, yet my heart is kept from murmuring, and aches more for my sorrow-causing sins than for the sorrow itself."

Grieving autobiographical reflections would today be viewed as an understandable lament for a dead baby, but Martha reminded herself that there was indeed "a heaven purchased for us where we will all be without sin, and of course without sorrow." By the end of that year (1791), already pregnant with the next child and using the religious and psychic tools she had at hand, Martha had wrestled her emotions into a bearable state. "I thank thee that thou art a God that givest as well as takest. I praise thee that I have one child in heaven. Lord have mercy on those who remain on earth." The larger world's problems were non-existent in her secret musings, only her own anxiety and distress.

In 1794, the yellow fever epidemic raging in Charleston was no excuse for her uneasiness. "The reigning disorder is said to be confined to strangers or people who live irregularly," she comforted herself. The problem identified in her diary was her"easily besetting sin." Today we would speculate about something physical, such as exhaustion, lack of calcium or even post-partum psychosis. Instead, in typical Calvinist self-scrutiny, she began her quest for peace of mind through internal dialogue with her diary.

It seemed that an Achilles' heel in her self-evaluation was drawing her into the vortex of dismay: *"I cannot perceive an increase in my sanctification, according to my desire."* Her own ambition for spiritual achievement was the key to diary-conversation about the never-specified "easily besetting sin" In a long footnote her editor-husband took pains to explain that the term "easily besetting sin" was code for some character flaw, rather than an act she'd committed.

He himself had no clue as to what kind of sin his wife so repeatedly "confessed and resolved against in her diary," he assured his readers; she was never angry but "meek to a fault"—a view hardly confirmed by the fierceness and self-determination we today see in her diary. But in his eyes she had been a model mother "with an excess of love, tenderness and anxiety for the comfort and happiness of her husband and children, ... making too large sacrifices of her own enjoyments for their accommodation."

One interpretation of her "easily besetting sin" suggests it may have been something as mild (to us, but insidious and destructive to her) as disappointment—disappointment that the version of partnership she had envisioned between herself and her husband, between herself and God, wasn't measuring up to her expectations. In Martha's social and religious cosmos, it was wrong to feel the slightest disloyalty to either God or husband; disappointment in either anchor for her life could qualify as a character flaw, even if one could not acknowledge the anger and sense of betrayal underneath it. The diary traces her progression from disappointment to despair and depression, and out the other side to a religiously-constructed acceptance and resolution.

Martha entered 1795 in deep psychic distress. Her diary that year began with the psalmist's cry of anguish: "Out of the depths have I cried unto thee, O Lord. I am in straits, trials and perplexities of soul and of body. My outward affairs can only be helped by thy providence, my spiritual troubles by thy grace." A few days later she wrote, "Calm, O Lord, the tumult of my thoughts; compose my disturbed mind, and make me...resigned before thee," adding the requisite afterthought, "as becomes so great a sinner."

By the end of March she was tracing her soul-sickness chronologically: "Since the 27th of January my mind has been more exercised from both outward pressure and inward conflict than I can ever recollect it to have been, since I gave myself to be the Lord's." The 14th of April was so bad she feared "heart and flesh" were both going to fail, though she could not blame any "bodily indisposition." "Only God could know what I endured that day," she declared in the diary, then temporizing: "Wo [sic] is me for fear I have I have sinned away God's mercy."

Next day there was a momentary "lifting up, and tokens for good vouchsafed." If God was powerful enough to stop the sun in its daily round for Joshua, she reasoned in her diary, he could certainly bring about *her* heart's desires "which I believe the Lord will grant me, though the favor has been deferred." Again she shifted to auto-biographic interpretation: "Alas, alas, I have not waited as one so suffering ought to have waited. I have left off to walk so softly before the Lord as I had done before this aid was granted me...now I am in a plunge again.

In June, 1795, a third-person pleading registered the function of diary-keeping in her psyche: "If I may not record that the Lord hath heard and granted my request," she wrote ironically, "at least let me know and record that he hath given me brokenness of heart!" and "the frowns of his Providence." Though she had three beautiful daughters and a four-month-old infant son, David Ramsay, Jr., they were not visible in her diary at this point. Nor were the money troubles distressing the Ramsay household (and many middle-class and poor families) in the galloping inflation of the 1790s. She begged only for spiritual assistance in "notic[ing] God's providential deal-ings. . .especially those remarkable incidents that happened in the past three years." Obliquely she acknowledged (without naming) their failed investments, the forced sale of houses and properties, the endless lawsuits, by writing, "God is leading me by a way that I know not, but I am persuaded it will be the right way." In the midst of terrible inner turmoil, she mused: "I am waiting upon God for a mercy which I have sought so long and so earnestly that I cannot but think God has drawn me to pray for it. . . .Many a thought [has been] sent thither in the course of every hour while at the necessary avocations of my situation."

Martha's "necessary avocations," secondary to her spiritual an-guish, are enumerated in her husband's adulatory introduction: running the family 'school' and writing her own curricula for her pupils, caring for her own and extended family members, educating the children of slaves and various paying guests. She also assisted her physician-husband with both his diagnostic research and his historical writings, carried out the charitable works expected of all important white Christians in the community, and conducted her own numerous intellectual spiritual exercises. During this same troubled period her husband, a member of the South Carolina legislature, was often away in the new capitol city of Columbia, South Carolina. The one real complaint against God that was allowed to surface in the diary focused on herself, not the economy, her husband, or other painful circumstance: "I have been many years a professor [believer]. . .instead of having just life enough to be grieved at sin, I *ought to have made great advances in sanctification and to have been eminently pious,* instead of being saved as it were by fire (emphasis added)."

The end of July she suggested a bargain. "If the Lord would grant me a certain favor," she vowed to set aside "two days of thanksgiving in every year, on each day giving to the poor $30," a considerable sum in 1795, and one that defied their financial condition. Additionally, she promised to "keep two days of humiliation in every year, on set days," dedicated to removing the cloud of "darkness" (her word for depression) separating her from God. In September for the first time, Martha named, and numbered systematically, the things destroying her spiritual equanimity. "First, . . .my easily besetting sin [sh]ould receive its death wound." Second *she* wanted desperately to be agent of "the thorough conversion of a very near and dear friend," and third, she wanted "her dear husband...preserved from worldly entanglements and enabled to so manage his earthly affairs that they don't interfere with his heavenly business." Fears of "loss of reputation, dearest relations, some threatened stroke" were a nightmare. Balancing these were three vows emerging from her autobiographical analysis: she would "avoid even the occasions of the easily besetting sin" so it couldn't enter her conscious mind; she would "walk" in her own family in such a "holy and uprightly" manner that nothing attributable to her would "hinder those who love me from entering on a religious life;" and third, since "I lived less frugally in the first years after my marriage than I should have done," extreme economies would be undertaken to prevent additional demands on her dear David.

152

At the beginning of 1796, she inscribed the significance diary-keeping had assumed for her. "Let me not receive especial favor of the Lord, and fail, as I have too often done, to record it." Finally, early in January, she experienced an epiphany. Christ made himself "known [to her] in the breaking of the bread" at a Sunday church service during Holy Communion. A religious experience at the depths of her misery transformed her perspective. Gradually the entries in the diary became less frequent, and less agonized. Her daily meditations began to include more events of household and family—fire in the neighborhood, funerals, a woman's prayer group being formed, the payment of a long-due bill—and less of "the easily besetting sin." The tone changed, calmed, retaining an undertone of sadness (she would have called it hard-earned wisdom): "I will even now praise him[God] for whether he gives or takes, he is still my God."

In 1803, writing in her diary remained a healing ritual. "Let this favor never be obliterated from my heart; let me record it to thy glory, and when I look back on my last [most recent] writing, and on this, see that truly God is good." In 1805, she mused, "None that trust in thee shall be desolate. If this is so, why then are my hopes faint, and my spirit cast down within me?" She listed the realities of her situation. . . ."The grave covers most of those with whom I kept up much intimacy; and various providences have changed the hearts of some who yet remain. [My] conflict with affliction is very great. My husband is under trials and straits which make my heart ache for him, and for myself. . . My children, though in many respects sources of great delight, cause me. . . much anxiety for their souls, and for their future temporal welfare." But she summarized that entry with her standard method of coping, the lifelong struggle to be cheerful, loving, and faithful in an uncertain life: "Chase away my sinful anxieties."

Her last diary entry in 1808 reflected declining physical heath, and of course concern for her family. "My anxiety is not so much for myself as for those connected with me..." Perhaps her diary had served its purpose and was no longer an essential psychic balance-wheel. Martha Laurens Ramsay was able, her husband reported, to die the classic "beautiful death" toward which she had always striven, her leave-taking witnessed by surrounding mourners and family. Her diary had served its function as confidante and battlefield for a soul struggling to find its placd in a troubling, diminished personal world—the brash, unsettling nineteenth century nation. The beginnings of America as experienced by Mrs. Dr. Ramsay in Charleston, South Carolina, were both cradle and crucible for her "autobiography," a pious memoir.

Journal keeping seems to be an almost instinctive reaction to being imprisoned. The urge to try and tell "how it is" plus the need to escape from unpleasant or horrible reality outwits the most zealous guards who try to keep writing materials away from the inmates. There does seem to be a difference in content between diaries kept when one is cut off from normal life, such as that of Anne Frank, diaries that are written as a form of protest for being incarcerated, which is itself a form of protest, such as Barbara Deming's *Prison Notes*, and the compulsive notes written in desperation and defiance by those being held in hostile imprisonment, such as war internees. Bloom first got involved with internment diaries when she edited Natalie Crouter's *Forbidden Diary*. This let to a flood of mail from other internees who had also kept written accounts of their ordeal. Now, Bloom has edited a second internment diary. This article is adapted from her "Introduction" to *Forbidden Family: Margaret Sam's Memoir of Wartime Internment, 1941-1945,* is reprinted with permission of the University of Wisconsin Press.

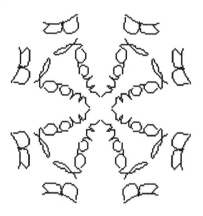

FORBIDDEN FAMILY: MARGARET SAM'S TALE OF WARTIME INTERNMENT

by Lynn Z. Bloom

*W*hat we talk about when we talk about love in an internment camp is fear and food and raids and radios. Margaret Sam's account of her three years in the Japanese internment camps of Santo Tomas and Los Banos in the Philippines throughout World War II is a love story, a confession, and an apologia. Narrated with the simple eloquence of a born storyteller, *Forbidden Family*, edited by Lynn Z. Bloom, will be published by the University of Wisconsin Press in 1989.

Margaret Coalson, born in 1916 near Cordell, Oklahoma, was the daughter and granddaughter of pioneer homesteaders. She was reared in the small, quiet town of Beaumont, California, and typical of her era, she acknowledges, "I simply wanted to be a nice wife for someone, have a nice home, nice children, and a nice husband." But atypical was her unquenched wanderlust, "I also wanted to see the world."

That her college boyfriend, Bob Sherk, shared this wanderlust was part of the attractiveness of this tall, dark, blue-eyed engineering student. Bob had been "insatiably" eager to see the Philippine Islands because of enticing accounts from an uncle who had been a soldier in Manila during World War I and remained to prosper. During the Depression the Philippines, until 1935 an American protectorate, was a place where adventurous, hard-working white men could make money rapidly in far better jobs than they could have held in the States. Bob went there in January, 1936, to become a

157

mine-shifter, "a white man who supervised the work of several dozen perspiring Filipinos who blasted, dug, and hauled the ore to the surface." His letters were alluring, "full of strange words and echoes of strange sights and sounds." Within months he was able to send Margaret enough money to join him, she booked steamship passage immediately, and they were married in Manila on the night she arrived.

Books and adventure became an inextricable part of Margaret's new life, in an isolated mining camp at Nyac, high in the mountains above Suyoc, 150 miles north of Manila. The only white woman in a community of diverse Filipino tribes that ranged "from the peace loving Benguets to the head-hunting Bontocs," Margaret learned to accommodate to a variety of cultures markedly different from the safe, predictable middle-class life of rural California. With the help of Velasco, a Filipino boy-of-all-work, Margaret transformed a primitive mountain dwelling into a home, painting the walls, making curtains, baking bread. She set up a small clinic among the Igorots. Big boxes of books, sent from the States, became the principal recreation for the isolated newlyweds. Margaret learned, for the first time, the meaning not of fear (only "cowards" would be afraid of native uprisings), but of horrendous loneliness, and bore a child, David, in April, 1938, to solve that problem.

Margaret's prewar life in itself would have made a fascinating story to one with her narrative gift. But a more dramatic tale was yet to come, with the advent of World War II. The mines closed; the mountain trails were blown up. Bob Sherk joined the Army and went off to Bataan on New Year's Eve, 1942. Margaret never saw him again. After three years in Cabanatuan, the "death camp" where survivors of the Bataan Death March were incarcerated, Bob died in December, 1944, aboard a Japanese prison ship enroute to Japan to work in the mines. Margaret and David, along with 5000 other American and British civilians, were incarcerated in Santo Tomas, a Japanese civilian internment camp in Manila. The natural drama of the situation intensified; in the making was a significant story that was to become a watershed experience in Margaret's life. Nothing would be the same after internment, after she met Jerry

Sams, after the war.

"I felt as if I were a widow [at 25]," wrote Margaret, "though I was not to become one in fact for almost three years. I was already on my own, with no one on earth to protect David and me." In Santo Tomas, Margaret mended library books at twelve and a half cents apiece, enough to provide David's nursery school and supplementary food. She learned how to defend her few square inches of territory, keeping at bay predatory men and thieving roommates. She became skilled at trading and bartering. But as a single parent with a small child, she could never overcome the long hours of standing in line (a task couples shared) "to get your food, to wash your hair, to take a shower, to get soap—when they had any." David spilled everything he tried to carry—precious food—so Margaret could entrust him with nothing. For the first nine months of the war she remained especially vulnerable psychologically, desperately isolated amidst the hordes. "I thought no one on earth cared enough about David and me to be interested enough to even write us a note."

September, 1943, came "with no change in anything except that we were all just a little hungrier and a little more concerned with nothing in the world except our own immediate problems." But on September 13, came also her chance meeting with Jerry Sams, a casual comment while watching a ballgame (What's the score?") with cataclysmic consequences. Margaret thought him "one of the most handsome men I had ever met." His photograph, taken at the time with his clandestine camera—one of the countless contraband items with which he delighted in violating the rules—shows a handsome man indeed, sensual eyes agleam in a sullen, enigmatic face. And everything changed.

Jerry, 31, an electronics engineer employed before the war as a troubleshooter for the Navy in Manila (his wife remained in Albuquerque), was an operator, a risk-taker, not content to accept a passive role in a rigid system. He connived and concocted a privileged existence in camp, shared with a few, envied by many less resourceful, less insouciant than he. He gradually bestowed some of these benefits on Margaret, cooking clandestine meals over bunsen burners in a former chemistry laboratory, inviting her to sit on the first real chair she'd occupied in eight months. With contraband tools ("the walls were alive with contraband") he built her a washboard from scrap iron, a board, and a tin can (I'd have killed for a washboard—David wet the bed every night throughout the whole war and every morning I had to wash his sheets and mattress pad by hand." He made a partitioned tin pail so David could carry his food without spilling it—utilitarian gifts of courtship.

"I most likely would have fallen in love with the devil himself if he had offered me help and food. When I had sympathy and understanding as well, it was inevitable," said Margaret. Such a love was bound to generate risks, in addition to the inevitable guilt that Margaret felt as a married woman: "Marriage was for life, divorce was the work of the devil," adultery was unthinkable. Such a love would also generate an extraordinary tale, for although many people had affairs in internment camps, few wrote about them; a love story is very unusual in prison literature. And it was unusual to play for keeps.

A confession is even more unusual in such literature. That Margaret, a thoroughly nice, wholeheartedly middle-class wife and mother, became pregnant and chose to have a baby under these circumstances (an abortion would have been possible, though Margaret never contemplated this) was explosive for the time and the context, however commonplace it may be today. After Jerry had been transferred, virtually incommunicado, to another camp, Los Banos, Margaret chose to risk her life to bear and keep the baby.

To my knowledge, this apologia, *Forbidden Family's* account of extra-marital pregnancy and maternity, is unique in internment literature. Margaret (and Jerry, too, though the perspective is hers throughout *Forbidden Family*, which he read for the first time some forty years after Margaret wrote it, both risk-takers extraordinaire), chose to violate the mores of the time, as well as the prohibition of internment camp. Although their behavior was punishable by imprisonment (yes, even within the prison itself), for every additional mouth to feed during a time of privation further strained the system, neither was officially penalized. When Margaret arranged for a transfer to Los Banos—against the advice of Jerry's skeptical friends—and arrived with 6-year-old David and three-month-old Gerry Ann, Jerry as the guilty father was removed from his camp job, broadcasting records, that carried with it the perk of a semi-private barracks room. And Margaret, hypersensitive from a perpetual sense of guilt at being, as she calls herself, "a fallen woman," "a scarlet woman," suffered slurs from some internees and ostracism from others—while at the same time enjoying the moral and material support of a host of newfound friends.

As Margaret and Jerry worked to become reacquainted ("I did not know an intimate thing about him. Was he happy before breakfast? Did he sing in the shower?") and gradually to become a family, the focal point of much of their activity became Jerry's clandestine radio. Indeed, the radio assumes the role of a major character in the third section of *Forbidden Family*. To possess a short wave radio was punishable by death, for, concealed in a sewing box or in a canteen ("the screw cap provided the tuning"), the radio provided the only access available to uncensored news from the outer world. The radio gave its possessor—Jerry—the power to leak the truth gradually to other internees, to control moods, to provide an antidote to Japanese-controlled news and propaganda. The radio gave Margaret continuous anxiety, ranging from mild uneasiness to sheer terror: "I look at Gerry Ann and wonder why she isn't a nervous wreck, simply from having nursed from such a shaky bag of bones for so long."

Forbidden Family talks about war when it talks about love, with a candid mixture of pride and guilt, defiance and fear, remorse but not regret. At the end of this most remarkable narrative, the "Prodigal Daughter," *de facto* wife and new mother, on release from internment brings her forbidden family to California to meet her relatives and her fate, "as eager, as reluctant, as hesitant as a virgin on her marriage night."

May Sarton is quite a different kind of diary keeper than Anaïs Nin. For one thing, she does not seem to have begun as early. She became a writer first, then began to keep journals of certain specific periods or events in her life. For another, she seems more self-contained in her journal writing than Nin ever was. It is as if Sarton knows she is writing for an audience, whereas, in the beginning, Nin did not. This does not invalidate Sarton's journals by any means. It merely puts them on a different level, and indicates that the reader should approach them in a different way. Schwartz, who has met Sarton and conducted a workshop on journal keeping at which the writer was the guest of honor, takes a look at Sarton the journal keeper in this article, published here for the first time.

MAY SARTON AS JOURNAL KEEPER

by Patricia Roth Schwartz

*M*ay Sarton, a poet and novelist who is also a consummate journal keeper, gives us no more nor less than the whole of her self. The opus of her five published journals reveals that self in all of its glories, rages, imperfections, struggles, moments of despair, glimpses of transcendence. The journals, as well as the rest of Sarton's writing, the fifteen volumes of poetry, the seventeen novels, shimmer with the "quality of transparency," as she calls it. All of it gives to us as readers a clear view, deep through many layers, of a complete life.

Plant Dreaming Deep presents a homespun portrait of a placid, middle-aged writer nestled in the bosom of a quaint New England town, complete with endearingly eccentric neighbors and a benign landscape. Sarton could have stopped there and found a niche as a writer of pleasing reminiscences, yet something within her that constantly pushes upward toward light and truth would not long permit such a fraud, such an incomplete and misleading version of her self.

Journal of a Solitude, the continuing saga of her sojourn in Nelson, New Hampshire, tells of her decision to leave for York, on the coast of Maine. It stands as a work of sheer personal courage as well as literary effort. This journal chronicles storms, wild bouts of wind, weather, and the dark—both in the material world, and the inner world. In this volume, Sarton emerges as artist, woman, lover. The writer lets us know fully the struggle of the creative woman who needs to live alone, and attempts to balance passion in love with passion for the work.

She states her reasons for self-revelation:

> How one lives as a private person is intimately
> bound into the work . . . as human being and as
> artist . . . we have to be willing to go naked . . .

As much of her self as was bared in *Journal of a Solitude*, Sarton had yet more to reveal. Here, the lover in question, the one with whom she battles over time, space and energy, is called "X." Just as Sarton had already "come out" as a woman who has known anger, despair, and loneliness, she comes out again in subsequent journals, as a woman whose primary erotic and affectional ties are to other women. "X" becomes "she," even though the journals never expose the privacy of individuals. Sarton's desire, beyond her belief in truth-telling as necessity, is to reveal the wellspring of her creativity. As she tells us in her novel, *Mrs. Stevens Hears the Mermaids Singing,* for her, "the must. .is she. ."

In *House by the Sea*, the next volume of Sarton's journals, the storms have calmed. The reader senses the deep progress that Sarton, the artist, as well as Sarton, the woman, has made in taming demons without sacrificing vital energy. She writes:

> The sea has erased the pain. I have never been so
> happy as I am here . . . Peace does not mean an end
> to tension, the good tensions, of waste. It means
> being centered.

In *Recovering*, the journal which follows, Sarton endures a mastectomy and begins a season of healing, both physical and spiritual. In *At Seventy*, her last published journal to date, ripeness is all. This volume alone, even if a reader has not discovered the joys of the others, brings a sense of a soul having travelled full circle. The fruition of a lifetime of dedication to one's muse, despite consistently vicious critical reviews, is present now. Love and acclaim come from a diverse readership of all ages, all over the world. In the private realm, which often intersects with the public, friendships of long-standing still flourish, new ones appear. The garden continually blooms. This is one of the rarest chronicles we have: a woman in old age, yet at full strength, an inspiration for us all.

A close attention to the particularities of each day creates the special quality of a Sarton journal. The reader experiences the soaring of the soul, the plunging of the emotions, the forging of a poem at white heat. All the while the car is being repaired, a diet is attempted, a raccoon decimates the daffodils. We learn the cast of the poet's mind and heart, as well as how light falls across a room full of music and flowers. We learn about transcendence—and humanity. Sarton gives us the whole of herself—and in the so doing allows us all the more clearly to see ourselves.

How can women use their diaries to understand their dreams, and bring their dreaming-lives into harmony with their waking-lives is the question that Whitehill asked herself some years ago. She was inspired to use the method of dream interpretation Baldwin outlined in her book. Baldwin offers five basic questions to ask about any dream, then, if you wish to proceed further, she suggests going through the dream symbol by symbol, asking each one to explain itself. Baldwin writes that she uses the "empty chair" Gestalt technique for this exercise, but Whitehill, being a committed diarist, decided to take this technique one step further and write it out in her journal.

After a marathon session with her journal, electrified by the results of using this method, she wrote the following essay. She describes it as a personal narrative that takes the reader step by step through her dialogue with dream characters and symbols. It concludes with the idea that dreams function as psychic barometers, keeping us in touch with our deepest feelings and perceptions as women in a patriarchal culture. It was first published in *WOMEN'S DIARIES, A Quarterly Newsletter*, vol. 3, no. 3 (Fall 1985).

VOICES FROM THE NIGHT, FROM A DREAM JOURNAL

by Sharon Whitehill

*L*ast winter I had a dream that wouldn't let me go. It surprised me. Other dreams have been more provocative, more emotional, more extraordinary in their imagery. Yet this one clung to me, like the invisible filaments of a spider's web, even after I had written it down. What, I wondered, was it trying to tell me?

I had recently expanded my journal to include a record of my dreams, and was using the method suggested by Christian Baldwin in *One to One: Self Understanding through Journal Writing* (New York: M. Evans and Company, 1977) with the most puzzling or provocative of them. I had begun to question the reliability of the conventional and superficial dream analysis I'd been using. This essay grows out of my desire to share that dream and the meanings I discovered with other diarists.

We must begin with the dream itself:

> *I am with a female companion, both of us dressed in lovely, long flower-print dresses, walking on a blacktop path in the woods. On both sides are deep ravines. As we step off the path to explore, we tumble down into a ravine. Struggling, we look up to see that we have rolled under a foot-bridge, and that on it is a crowd of people staring down on us and jabbering in a foreign tongue. From their gestures it is clear that they are wondering who we are.*

167

Though they don't appear to be hostile or threatening, they take us prisoner and lock us in the bedroom of an elegant mansion.

I realize that my companion is my lesbian friend Mary. She sits on the bed and examines her nylon-stockinged thigh through a slit in the tight silk dress, saying to me, "You should always wear clothes like this." I am surprised, because Mary is very althetic and seldom wears anything but blue jeans. I notice that her face is covered with scabs.

Once every day, Mary and I are taken from the beautiful bedroom which is our prison to swim in an ornate, circular pool. Often the pretty daughter of the mansion's owner swims with us. One day the three of us are planning our escape when a convoy of long black limousines drives slowly by outside. Through the window we see this entourage which consists of politicians and ambassadors dressed in black suits, arriving to visit the owner of the mansion.

I turn away from the window to find that Mary has transformed into a black-haired and handsome young man floating in a small barge in the middle of the pool. It is covered with transparent plastic, like an oxygen tent, and the young man is sleeping as he drifts. The owner's daughter seems amused and delighted at this, pointing to the young man with a tinkling laugh. I smile, too, soaping myself meanwhile as I stand waist-deep in the warm blue water. I am startled to find my own body young and slim and small-breasted, and disappointed in the soap I'm using because it has no scent.

In the next scene I have made my escape—not with Mary or the young man, but with the beautiful daughter of the lord of the manor. We enter a shabby motel room, our first hiding place. Somehow I have become a male and am feeling both protective and amorous. She now seems smaller, slimmer, and more shy than previously. She feels *petite and childlike in my arms. As I embrace her she whispers, "Oh, no," in a small, sad voice; "I've just started my period,"she explains. Gallantly I reply that it doesn't matter, and we lie down on the bed and begin to make love.*

During the love making we have a mutual mental image of a single androgynous sex organ: either a small penis or a large clitoris. As we have oral sex, I am thinking, "This is taking a long time, but it's what women require. Be patient." And when she finally has a climax, I feel it, too, as if we are the same person. Active and passive roles have blurred along with male and female anatomy. I notice some blood on the sheet, but it doesn't matter because the sheet is plastic.

In the final scene my lover is dressed in clean but faded jeans. I notice her small rounded rump and the stiffness of her walk. She stands on a landing by some stairs, and someone tells her there is a message for her. This seems to take her mind off the fact that she is walking awkwardly.

Why am I dreaming this dream now? I ask myself, turning to a fresh page in my journal. "My dream is full of women," I wrote after a moment's thought, "and full of female imagery—silk dresses,nylon stockings, and fairytale motifs like princesses and castles." Many symbols seemed obvious: the silk dresses as the restrictions of traditional femininity; the circular pool as the perfect containment of the womb; the oxygen-tent barge as an image of suspension and unconsciousness perhaps associated with my recent surgery (a real-life event that probably gave rise to the dream blood on the sheets, too).

Was the dream suggesting that I ought to turn away from men, and toward women, for emotional and physical gratification? This seemed the easiest interpretation, but perhaps it was *too* obvious. I sat for a moment nibbling my pen, still feeling unsatisfied. Then I turned to Baldwin's book. Proceed through the dream symbol by symbol, she suggests, asking each one to explain itself. "I do this in Gestalt form," she writes, "using what is called the'empty chair' technique. 'I' sit in one chair or on a pillow, and 'place' each symbol on an opposite chair or pillow. After asking the symbol my question, I switch pillows and assume the place and consciousness of the symbol and answer from the symbol's point of view."

I'll try it, I thought, and I began to list the dream symbols one by one. Then, taking several deep breaths with my eyes closed, I turned to a clean page in my journal and began to write, rapidly and continuously. Words, sentences, paragraphs flowed from my pen without conscious effort, almost as if they had bypassed my brain.

ME: Female Companion, who are you and what are you doing in my dream?

FEMALE COMPANION: I am those resources within you that will always be there, that you can always rely on. I accompany you wherever you go.

ME: Silk Dresses, who are you and what are you doing in my dream?

SILK DRESSES: We are those "feminine" fetters, those clinging stereotypes in your mind that trip you up. We keep you from moving freely.

ME: Footpath, who are you and what are you doing in my dream?

FOOTPATH: I am the road that you follow when you adapt and conform. I am necessary, and I will take you to prescribed destinations. But to follow me slavishly is to miss a great deal.

ME: Ravine, who are you and what are you doing in my dream?

RAVINE: I am excitement and risk. I am that dangerous but real gulf in you, full of brambles and snares. I exist. Use me, but keep moving.

ME: Foreigners, who are you and what are you doing in my dream?

FOREIGNERS: We are the foreign selves who people your unconscious. We are strangers to you, but we are not hostile. Learn our tongue; make friends with us. We will teach you much. We will help you laugh at yourself in some of your ridiculous predicaments.

ME: Elegant Bedroom, who are you and what are you doing in my dream?

ELEGANT BEDROOM: I am the place where you are now, in the mansion of yourself. I am attractive, comfortable, pleasant. But if you stay here, you will be a prisoner.

ME: Mary, who are you and what are you doing in my dream?

MARY: I am your sister self. Trust me. I am your androgynous potential.

ME: Mary's Scabs, who are you and what are you doing in my dream?

MARY'S SCABS: We are the unattractive aspects of lesbianism. We mar the ideal in your mind. We represent sickness—but also healing. We blemish the lesbian face today, but tomorrow we will fall off and leave no scars.

ME: Mary's Instructions ("always wear clothes like that") who are you and what are you doing in my dream?

MARY'S INSTRUCTIONS: We are the "shoulds" that burden you. Lesbians do not have all the answers. Listen to your own voices, not to others'.

ME: Circular Pool, who are you and what are you doing in my dream?

CIRCULAR POOL; I am the perfection you seek in the house of yourself. I am Woman; I am Mother; I am Love. Seek for me. I am there.

ME: Sleeping Man, who are you and what are you doing in my dream?

SLEEPING MAN: I am the image that you have of the male: somnolent, unconscious, cut off, out of reach, encased in plastic. I am to be seen and admired, but never awakened and never really contacted. I am the beautiful, smiling, desirable man with my man's body and crisp black hair. I barge into your life, then I drift just out of touch. I am centered only in myself; I smile and drift and dream, handsome but rather boring. I begin as a partner, but I change, detach, drift away once we are imprisoned in this house together. I am not like you. I am not a seeker of *your* dreams, only of my own.

ME: Oxygen-Tent Barge, who are you and what are you doing in my dream?

OXYGEN-TENT BARGE: I am that which is incomprehensible in the male. I move and sustain him, yet he is contained in me; he doesn't need you. I take him away, out of reach. I enable him to sleep alone. He is visible to you, but unattainable. I am independence.

ME: Young Woman, who are you and what are you doing in my dream?

YOUNG WOMAN: I am the image of the ideal. I know that sleeping young men, however beautiful, are merely amusing. I do not need them or their beauty or their attention because I am beautiful and happy in myself.

ME: Tinkling laugh, who are you and what are you doing in my dream?

TINKLING LAUGH: I am joy. I am all the beauty in the world. I am music. I am in you. Discover me.

ME: Unscented Soap, who are you and what are you doing in my dream?

UNSCENTED SOAP: I am that which cleanses you of illusion. I am plain truth; I am honesty. Though I may disappoint you at first, you will learn how delicious I feel. Notice my initials: US!

ME: Small-Breasted Torso, who are you and what are you doing in my dream?

SMALL-BREASTED TORSO: I am your potential. I am all that you are beginning to be, newborn from the water like Venus. Though I feel strange to you at first, I will become familiar.

ME: Black Limousines, who are you and what are you doing in my dream?

BLACK LIMOUSINES: We represent the world of men. We are Wealth and Importance and World Power. We are presidents and businessmen and generals; we are economics and politics; we are wars and strikes and closed meetings. You look out the window as us as we pass by, but we do not even notice you.

ME: Foreign Ambassadors, who are you and what are you doing in my dream?

FOREIGN AMBASSADORS: We have come to speak to the owner of this house. He is Rationality. We do not know (nor does he) that the other inhabitants plan escapes, live lives beyond his awareness. We, in our black suits and self-importance, are very narrow. We speak our own language, and only to each other.

ME: Young Woman Transformed, who are you and what are you doing in my dream?

YOUNG WOMAN TRANSFORMED: I am ideals and goals beginning to be practiced in the real world. I am frightened, so I shrink and become child-like. I, too, am potential; I need nurturing and love.

ME: Shabby Motel Room, who are you and what are you doing in my dream?

SHABBY MOTEL ROOM: I am an aspect of reality and an aspect of you. I am where you end up when you shed old garments and wash off illusions. I am Insecurity, the other side of your confidence and pleasure in yourself. Live in me and you will see that it is what you *do* in me that matters.

ME: young Woman's Period, who are you and what are you doing in my dream?

YOUNG WOMAN'S PERIOD: I am your fear and vulnerability. I cause messes. But I am necessary: I make you a woman; I make you human. Accept me.

ME: Androgynous Sex Organ, who are you and what are you doing in my dream?

ANDROGYNOUS SEX ORGAN: I am union and communion. I am the two-in-one, the paradox, the Yin and Yang. I am the wholeness at the center of life. I unite male and female, outside and inside. I am a vision.

ME: Oral Sex, who are you and what are you doing in my dream?

ORAL SEX: I am forbidden pleasure, and I am one form of the communion that you seek. I am total acceptance of the sexual you. I speak in tongues.

ME: Mutual Double Orgasm, who are you and what are you doing in my dream?

MUTUAL DOUBLE ORGASM: I am pleasure that is found only through effort and honest doubt. I am joy shared. I am mutuality.

ME: Blood on the Sheet, who are you and what are you doing in my dream?

BLOOD ON THE SHEET: I am the memory of trouble and pain that will no longer matter in the larger joy. I wash off.

ME: Rump in Faded Jeans, who are you and what are you doing in my dream?

RUMP IN FADED JEANS: I am satisfaction. I am comfortableness and contentment. I follow from success after struggle. I am those moments of earned smugness when you say to yourself, "I'm pretty good after all." I am the view from behind. I am hindsight.

ME: Awkward Walk, who are you and what are you doing in my dream?

AWKWARD WALK: I am the awkwardness of unaccustomed success.

ME: Landing, who are you and what are you doing in my dream?

LANDING: I am the place you pause to rest before resuming the climb. I am the necessary plateaus in your growth.

ME: Message, who are you and what are you doing in my dream?

MESSAGE: I am the guiding voice of your dream. Hear what I have to say.
ME: Self Transformed to a Man who are and you and what are you doing in my dream?

SELF TRANSFORMED TO A MAN: I am Power. I am confidence and determination to succeed. At the same time I am your capacity for tenderness and nurturing, imaged in the childlike young woman. When the two of us—your Power and your Potential—come together, there is no stopping us. We will give birth to a new, transformed You.

I was finished. I laid down my pen, astonished and awed. It had been time-consuming, to be sure, but I felt unburdened, purged, and in a strange way, exonerated. Gone was my earlier confusion. If my feelings about men and about my place in a patriarchal system were still muddled, that came not from the dream, but from waking reality. At last now I could see how all the pieces fit together.

What I had though was a dream about wishing to be a lesbian had not so much repudiated that wish as revealed itself to be a great deal more. In both dream and dialogue, references to foreign language and to voices and tongues—the instruments of speech—abounded. This was a dream about the need for *communication*. It was my own personal version/vision of Adrienne Rich's "dream of a common language." It was a dream about self-image and self-fulfillment, a dream about the possibilities for continuing growth.

Using, as dreams do, a collage of visual images from everyday life, my dream had thus brought me a message of hope and encouragement. Trust yourself, it had told me. Trust your own process. You are sometimes sustained, sometimes constrained by cultural stereotypes; but at the same time, you possess a dark and fertile inner depth, both dangerous and revitalizing. Become aware of this depth; move with it and through it. The marriage of psychic Power and Potential within the deep place will engender multiple new and evolving selves.

What I learned from this experience is that there is nothing in our dreams that lies. Dreams speak their own language, and they speak true. They are barometers of consciousness, measuring private reactions to pressure from within and without, signaling fluctuations in the emotional weather. If we are wise enough to attend, they will encourage us, guide us, and enrich us. Listen to the language of dreams.

PART III

Applications

Diaries and journals are supposed to be written for the self, with no thought of pleasing an editor or an audience. In spite of this generally accepted convention, the readers of diaries and journals cannot seem to keep from making value judgements about the content of diaries they read, nor can they curb their curiosity about why each particular diary was written. Sometimes, our expectations can color our readings. Then our interpretation is skewed in the wrong direction and we end up with something that is a world apart—our world apart—from the world of the diarist. Is a diary invalid because it is not literary? Is it dishonest if it is more than a strict record keeping? Have we, the modern readers, the right to condemn early religious diaries as boring, when the diarists were writing of something that was extremely important to them? How will the future look at the diaries we are writing today? These are only a few of the questions that scholars must address when dealing with manuscript material, trying to use it as a source for some "lesson of the day," so to speak. Bunkers has some thoughts to share in this area. Her text was first published in *A/B: Auto/Biography Studies*, vol. 2, no. 2 (Summer 1986), and is used with permission.

READING AND INTERPRETING THE UNPUBLISHED DIARIES OF NINETEENTH-CENTURY WOMEN

by Suzanne L. Bunkers

*A*s a woman who has kept a journal for years, I am interested in how my journal functions as an autobiographical text which reflects my purposes for writing, my perceptions of my intended audience, and my uses of speech and silence. As a scholar who has studied scores of unpublished diaries by nineteenth-century Midwestern American women, I have developed a healthy curiosity about each diarist's reasons for writing, the dynamics of my interaction with diarist and text, and the ways in which these diaries function as forms of autobiography.

My research has grown out of an interest shared with scholars who have begun an intensive re-examination of the lives of un-known women. Central to this re-examination is the acknowledge-ment that these women's private writings—their diaries, journals, letters, memoirs—offer one of the most reliable indicators of what their lives were like and of how they saw themselves, both as women and as writers. Women's unpublished diaries in particular provide rich soil for such an exploration because they challenge readers to expand the traditional definition of autobiography to include texts written day by day, many with no editor except the diarist herself, many with no statements about an intended audience or about the form which the completed text might take. Diaries like these are not a retrospective examination and interpretation of a life already lived; they are a commentary on life as it *was* lived, on life as *process*, not *product.* Such diaries, then may well represent the most elemental form of autobiography, for they reflect life as lived experience rather than as carefully shaped, edited text.

For many a Midwestern woman writing during the period 1850 to 1900, a diary served as an essential (and perhaps only) form of autobiography. It represented more than a tiny book where she could record daily events; it also provided her with a safe place where she could generate a sense of self, share thoughts and feelings, contemplate her relationships with others, and comment on institutions and events.

As a twentieth-century reader of these texts, I confess that an autobiographical impulse lies at the heart of my research. My interest in these diaries is based on more than curiosity about what the writers' lives were like; it is also based on my desire to know more about myself and about my reasons for keeping a journal. My journal writing is a source of self-revelation; when I write, I am keenly aware that I am creating a record of my life. My research thus far has borne out my hypothesis that the women whose diaries I have studied wrote with varying degrees of this same self-consciousness.

My research has a second autobiographical component: I approach the reading of another woman's diary with certain assumptions and expectations arising out of my own experience as a woman who keeps a journal. It is essential that I name them and attempt to understand the ways in which they influence my responses to individual diaries and journals. If I assess the value of a given diary according to the amount of introspection it contains, I interfere with the integrity of the diarist and her text. If I try to exert control over a diary by emphasizing certain of its aspects while ignoring others, I run the risk of abusing my power as interpreter of the text. If I fail to recognize the essential subjectivity of my response to a text, I labor under the delusion that an "objective" presentation of the diarist's life and writing is possible and desirable. When I engage myself with the text and its writer, I need to develop a sense of the personality that emerges from the diary's pages; yet I must recognize that, in my interaction with the text, in my interpretation of the significance of what the writer said and didn't say, in my analysis of how the diary functions as a form of autobiography, I am creating my own construct of the diarist, one influenced as much by who I am as by who I perceive the diarist to be.

As a twentieth-century woman, my daily experiences might be quite different from those detailed in diaries by nineteenth-century women, yet my feelings about my experiences (and about writing about them in my own journals) have turned out to be surprisingly similar to those of the women whose lives I have followed by reading their diaries. Like those diarists, I sometimes write quite explicitly about my attitudes and feelings; at other times, however, I cloak my feelings in euphemisms or formal language. Sometimes, particularly when those feelings are very painful, I do not record them at all on the pages of my journal. Sometimes I have a clear sense of who my intended audience is when I write in my journal; at other times, I do not realize until rereading specific journal entries long after having written them who my intended audience might be. Sometimes my vision of intended audience shifts during the course of writing a given journal entry. Sometimes I write with only an indeterminate audience in mind or with the belief that my words are being recorded only for myself.

All of these aspects of my own journal writing help to shape my responses to the diaries which I study. It is essential that I be aware of them before, during, and after my reading process if I am to approach such texts respectfully.

What are my ethical responsibilities when studying unpublished diaries? First, as I have noted, I must be constantly aware that I approach each text from a point of view that is not value-free and that I must take responsibility for my interpretation of the text, just as any reader must do. Second, I must be conscientious about placing a given text, and a given writer's life, into a well-rounded historical and cultural perspective. To do so, I must acknowledge that the form and content of the text are shaped by the diarist's experience of race, ethnicity, class, age, and geography, as well as by her perceptions of purpose and intended audience. Nineteenth-century Midwestern women were far from being a homogeneous group. Although most of the women whose diaries I have studied were caucasian and middle-class, they lived in a variety of settings, sustained a broad range of relationships, and worked at many kind of jobs, both inside and outside the home. Their lives were influenced by factors such as the Civil War, conflicts between Indians and whites, urbanization, industrialization, and periods of economic boom and depression. When I interpret a diarist's text, then, I have an ethical responsibility not only to recognize the biases inherent in myself as a reader but also to consider carefully the ways in which a particular writer's historical and cultural context may have influenced the creation of her text.

The study of such nineteenth-century autobiographical texts is important to twentieth-century readers for several reasons. Diaries and journals document the experiences of Midwestern American women—ordinary women whose daily lives passed unnoticed and whose texts now stand, for the most part, as the only extant records of their lives. These diaries and journals *are* their autobiographies, and our validation of these texts as forms of autobiography gives voice to the silence which has surrounded these women's lives for too long.

Each diary was created in a specific historical, socio-economic, ethnic, and geographical context; by virtue of specificity of context, therefore, no one diary can rightfully be called "typical" of all diaries written by nineteenth-century women. Midwestern women writing during this period did so for a variety of purposes, and they addressed many different intended audiences. Thus, it is crucial that we not compromise the integrity of these women's texts by insisting on excessive categorization according to thematic emphases, writing styles, symbolism, or questions of "literariness" of the text. The value of such unpublished diaries as autobiography does not rest on their designation as literary text; it rests on each diarist's expression of the inner or symbolic truth of her experiences. If we are mindful of the ways in which a diarist's subjective perceptions are woven into the fabric of her diary, we can respect the integrity of the text and appreciate the myriad factors that have contributed to both its creation and its interpretation.

When I read nineteenth-century Midwestern women's diaries as autobiography, then I do so with an awareness that my analysis can yield valuable and satisfying insights into the everyday lives of my foremothers. I do so with the understanding that my own autobiographical impulse as well as my preconceptions influence my responses to a given diary. I do so with the belief that my ethical responsibility is to enter into but not to attempt to control the delicate interaction of diarist, reader, and text. Most importantly, I do so with the knowledge that I bear the continuing responsibility for not violating the diarist's trust by misrepresenting her perceptions, by dismissing her life as unimportant, or by relegating her diary once again to the status of a forgotten text.

When I began this research, I made a distinction between the diary as a form for the recording of events and the journal as a form for the expression of feelings. I have found this to be an artificial distinction, both as the result of my research and as the result of my own journal writing. I now use the terms *diary* and *journal* interchangeably.

Some of the ideas presented here are developed at greater length in two articles. "Midwestern Diaries and Journals: What Women Were [Not] Saying in the Late 1800s" will be included in a forthcoming collection of essays edited by James Olney, *Studies In Autobography*, Oxford University Press, 1988, and based on papers presented at the International Symposium on Autobiography and Autobiography Studies held at Louisiana State University in March 1985. "'Faithful Friend': Nineteenth-Century Midwestern American Women's Unpublished Diaries" appeared in a special issue of *Women's Studies International Forum* , vol. 10, no. 1 (1987), devoted to women's autobiography. Funding for my research has been provided by grants from the National Endowment for the Humanities, the American Council of Learned Societies, and Mankato State University.

In the past few years, studies by psychologists have shown that people who write about their traumatic experiences and their feelings about them in their diaries prove to be healthier than those who only write about superficial events. In fact, using a diary as a place to vent one's strongest emotional feelings seems to strengthen the immune system. For many years, depth psychologist Ira Progoff has advocated his own system, "The Intensive Journal," as a means of using a journal to confront the issues of life and to express one's feelings toward life, work and others. Techniques in the Intensive Journal can stimulate creativity and a sense of inner peace and can be used to enrich one's life in many ways. Harms, a certified Intensive Journal instructor and a long-time Intensive Journal keeper, offers some examples of the ways in which its use has helped her. This article in an expanded version was first published in *BOOK FORUM*, vol. IV, no. 3 (1979); this abridged version was published in *WOMEN'S DIARIES* , *A Quarterly Newsletter*, vol. 1, no. 3 (Fall 1983).

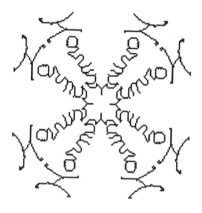

EXPERIENCING THE INTENSIVE JOURNAL METHOD

by Valerie Harms

*T*he "Intensive Journal" is no ordinary diary. It is not a writer's notebook, a naturalist's log, nor just a secret outlet for self-expression. It is none of these but can include all of them. It is a repository of personal experiences; more important, it creates experience.

I have been "working in" ("writing" is not an active enough term) the "Intensive Journal" for years. Like everyone else I live a life of eating, sleeping, working, loving, hating, etc. but I live another life in the Journal. In fact in the Journal I live most intensely, creatively, and productively. The Journal depends on me to feed it experience, of course, which I do faithfully (no fixed schedule though). Then the Journal principles get activated and pretty soon are producing energy, changes, and profound illuminations, which I carry back into my other life. The "Intensive Journal" is far more than a mirror of my life; it is largely the creator of it.

It shapes my life out of the raw material of my existence, just as an artist shapes a work out of raw materials. Progoff has said in *At a Journal Workshop*, "Outward activity propelled from within is the essence of the creative experience. Thus one of the main indications of the strength of creativity in individuals is the degree to which they have brought themselves into connection with the multiple and interrelated movement of the mini-processes in their lives." In making this dynamic connection possible for a person, the "Intensive Journal" makes the whole life an art work. But it is not an art work that can be shaped entirely consciously or according to one's will. The "Intensive Journal" evokes from persons knowledge they did not know they had. It also connects them to that underground stream, the source of life, that flows through all of time. It does this in surprising ways. Every individual's life in this way becomes a unique epic.

Progoff is not easily categorized. He avoids flashy settings and cultishness. He is a psychotherapist who now only works with people in relation to their "Intensive Journal." He is a professor, having from 1959 to 1971 directed the Institute for Research in Depth Psychology at the Drew University Graduate School.

Progoff says that his studies of the lives of creative persons conducted at Drew University became the empirical base for developing the "Intensive Journal." In the 1950s, he studied with C. G. Jung and D. T. Suzuki, whose works influenced the "Intensive Journal" method. In 1966, Progoff formed Dialogue House as his center of business operations. But Progoff himself does not stay put. An independent spirit, he winds his way across country, often to California, to lead "Intensive Journal" workshops.

A fundamental feature of the "Intensive Journal" is that it is a non-analytical or diagnostic form of psychological work. In his book, *Death and Rebirth of Psychology*, Progoff demonstrated the weakness in the analytical approach to psychotherapy and set the basis for the development of an organic depth psychology. His view is part of the wholistic approach to the study of human behavior which seeks to evoke the potentials of persons in order to provide a sense of individual identity and stability. Progoff believes that the next step in the evolution of humanity depends less on intellectual applications than the stimulation of people's growth and creative capacity. Toward this end, Progoff strives to find a structure that will evoke, not analyze or interpret, the inner direction of the individual. Thus, a person's own experiences take the place of an outside authority as the guide to moving around in the Journal format to achieve a re-channeling of energies and new integrations. A person remains open to the way in which his/her psychic future wants to evolve, a process which is assumed to be unpredictable by an observer, including the person him/herself.

The structure of the "Intensive Journal" includes four main parts, each of which is divided into sections. The four parts are called Logs, Depth Dimension, Dialogue Dimension, and Life/Time Dimension. In this space I can barely suggest the cope of each section; I refer the reader to *At a Journal Workshop*, (New York: Dialogue House Library, 1975) which is Progoff's complete text and guide to using the "Intensive Journal."

The Period Log is the section wherein persons begin to draw their life into focus by describing the present phase of their life. The present phase may span several years or just a week. It has a certain feeling tone; it involves relationships, projects, body states, interaction with society. It may be a time of beginning, or turmoil, or ending—whatever comprises the current phase of life one finds oneself in. The Daily Log is for the collection of daily thoughts, feelings, and intimations with respect to the external events of a person's life. It provides the source material for further work in the Journal.

The Depth Dimension includes the Dream Log, Dream Enlargements, Twilight Imagery Log, Imagery Extension, and Inner Wisdom Dialogue. In *At a Journal Workshop* Progoff writes, "The Depth Dimension deals with the nonconscious levels of the psyche from which consciousness comes. Its contents are sleep dreams, waking dreams, and the varieties of intuitions by which we make our direct connections with the implicit wisdom of life." The Dream and Twilight Imaging sections are used in relation to other Journal sections as a means of balancing the process with energies arising from the nonconscious depths. The Inner Wisdom Dialogue is an extended engagement on the depth level wherein persons commune with a figure representing Wisdom . It is in this section where the ultimate truths of existence open out of themselves.

The Dialogue Dimension deals with the person's many relationships. Dialogues with Persons, the Body, Events, Works, and Society enable the individual to establish an ongoing interior connection to these important parts of our lives. As persons grow and change in relations to them, they become aware of mini-processes at work in themselves that are creating their life history. The Dialogue sections enable persons to communicate with the many facets of their life on a deep enlightening level that is simply not possible in other ways.

Working in the "Intensive Journal" I find is both easy and difficult. It is easy in the sense that I need to have a safe refuge from the outer world that can take everything that happens to me. It is difficult because I have to live through frustration and pain and have the tenacity to feed those energies back into the Journal rather than dissipate them in other ways so that the techniques work for me. In a way it is a waste of time to work in the Journal with the expectation of receiving pleasure or pleasing anyone else; it is done more in the spirit of dedication to the requirements of life.

As a complement to "Intensive Journal" work Progoff uses a method of meditation he terms "Process Meditation." It does not use guided imagery nor does it "empty" the mind. It does make use of mantras, not Sanskrit, but arising out of each person's own inner experiences. The mantras correspond with the person's stage of development and become the starting point for the next experience. Progoff's books, *The Well and the Cathedral*, *The Star/Cross*, and *The White Robed Monk*, are not texts but his own meditations which are used by others to enter their own inner depths. Progoff considers Process Meditation a major development of his work, which he intends to enlarge upon, among other things. In workshops, Process Meditation is used to deepen the individual's own atmosphere while working in the Journal sections.

The Life/Time Dimension includes the Life History Log, Steppingstones, Intersections: Roads Taken & Not Taken, and Now: The Open Moment. These sections relate to the chronology of a person's outer life as well as his/her inner timing. In the Life History Log the person's autobiography is gradually built up through an accumulation of memories. In using Steppingstones persons spontaneously and briefly outline the main steps in their lives from birth to the present moment. This can be done many times for subjectively the past is always changing. Steppingstones help persons to realize the underlying thread of their lives despite veering paths. In Intersections: Road Taken & Not Taken, the particular choices persons made or changes they underwent are re-entered to see if other unlived possibilities existed that in the past could not be taken up but could in the present. Through a cumulative process of "time-stretching" avenues to the future manifest themselves. Now: The Open Moment is the place where an entry of hope, a summation, or a new imagery is made as a person stands on the threshold of the future, after having worked in the past and present time frames of the Journal.

The levels of depth attainable in the Journal are astounding. People experience for themselves states of being and wisdom such as they had only heard or read about in the annals of art and religious history. Poetic, artistic, mystical, cosmic conceptual visions are some of the ways that the depth level expresses itself. People communicate directly with divine powers for a prolonged time in a fully awakened state. They move out of their separate selves to merge with the whole universe and literally feel an expansion of consciousness. In this process persons become truly at one with the Unity of Being.

The dynamic effect if the "Intensive Journal" is in its structure which, through the interplay of the multiple energies and mini-processes, has the force to propel the inner self to further levels of expression without being bogged down by details of events and emotions. In "Intensive Journal" work depression is unknown because movement is constant. The "Intensive Journal" captures elusive feelings, states of mind, and emotion even where no inner growth is perceived at all, especially in low, negative cycles. Reading Journal work back to oneself periodically reveals the active process that remained hidden from view. This form of recognition is one aspect of the Feedback the Journal provides, which is beyond the scope of conventional diaries. Feedback occurs as new ideas, recognitions, or feelings. It by and of itself breaks through a person's crust of old habits and psychological barriers and thrusts them into a new stage of life.

The approach does not require verbal facility, nor does it attack problems head-on. One rather floats the problems and opens up other nooks and crannies of his/her life. No area need remain hidden or protected from fear. Working around conflicts dispels fear, leading a person to become sensitive to the opposite within.

Nowadays when people live longer than formerly, making the transition from the death of one phase to the birth of another can be a time of heavy anxiety and self-doubt.

One of the dynamic features of "Intensive Journal" work is that it allows a person's life to grow and achieve wholeness at his/her own tempo. "Intensive Journal" work systematically enriches the inner life creatively and spiritually, as the life is being lived. It provides a way for sustaining contact with one's inner core, which to many people occurs only as a flashing in the woods of intellectualism or the mire of low self-regard. In organic depth psychology, according to Progoff, a person needs to be connected to this inner principle, this "seed of spirituality" or else become stuck in pathology. Herein lies the zen aspect of the "Intensive Journal," which serves to keep persons connected to and in harmony with their inner reality, so that their outer lives flow naturally; when a person is out of sync, everything in the outer life becomes problematical. Life lived in sensitivity to the inner timing of the seed potentials is capable of profound depth and meaning.

At this level the psychological and spiritual paths unite; the Journal Feedback principles of self-balancing and life-integration happen. The self-balancing principle takes place as persons work in the mini-processes of their lives. It is experienced as energy for directions that balance each other as they go along, which can be seen in retrospect as the main thread of a life revealed. One learns to trust that this balancing will take place of its own accord. Overarching the mini-processes and the varied paths on which they take persons is the larger process of life-integration. Life-integration occurs when all the times of joy, despair, hope, anger, crises, conflicts, failures, and successes reveal what they were for. Their goal is seen in a crystallization of wholeness.

There are now more than 60,000 registered "Intensive Journal" holders. They are male, female, young, old, wealthy, poor, intellectual, unlettered, of varied ethnic origin. What are these people seeking? Many become involved with the "Intensive Journal" in times of conflict, transition, and crisis. Or, when life is more relaxed and they want to explore its philosophical aspects. They want to grow in a safe way. They want to discover unknown potentials, evoke new awarenesses, and crystallize decisions. As people catch on paper the multiple transitions in their lives, the flux of feeling and thought, they acquire a disciplined subjectivity in relation to the contents moving in them. They are capable of feeling balanced in the midst of danger or difficulty. They are able to act from the center of themselves rather than in response to outer stimuli. Anxiety become not something to be avoided but the carrier of meaning in its very ambiguity. In the dark labyrinth potentials are found, which show the passage out. But, as in nature everything has its own timing, so in a person's life. People can't be short-changed the fullness of their anxiety; otherwise they are robbed of their possibilities. The Journal is there to catch the contents of a life and keep it moving—as through a transparent cloth.

If a diary is a "book of one's own," should one take lessons in how to keep it? Who taught Maria Whitford or Anaïs Nin? On the other hand, the Quakers certainly instructed their young in the proper way to keep a spiritual diary. Today it is common for writing instructors to assign as home work that "members of the class will keep daily journals." And if many today are asking "How do I keep a diary? How do I start? What do I write in it?" these are questions to be addressed. Lifshin, herself a writer, poet and journal keeper, teaches courses in journal keeping with emphasis on its uses as an outlet for creative expression and as a sourcebook for finished literary works. These excerpts from her diary describe both how she structured her class and how her teaching stimulated her own creativity. An expanded version of this article was originally published in *Sing Heavenly Muse*, and this version was published in *WOMEN'S DIARIES, A Quarterly Newsletter*, vol. 2, no. 2, (Summer 1984).

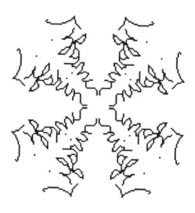

TEACHING A JOURNAL CLASS

by Lyn Lifshin

October 14, 1980
In bed, under a lump of quilts, the cat. Books from the workshop like a moat around the bed. Moat, a word I used earlier today in a drawing exercise in the diary class: I asked everyone to do drawings of their internal self, the self they see and the self others see. I drew a large red jagged circle—not jagged so much as swirling, large and red and big with a little black box inside. The outside lines were red and swirling and inside was straight and cramped. This is what I wrote under it: my external self is bold, vibrant, daring, contained. It's big and it's like a moat really, a wall. Bright. Curvy lines. Suggests something sensuous, splashing, a circle, suggests love, the pattern of a flower, something bisected and separated. What was inside my internal self, is angular, black, in a box, sharp, nothing like a flower. Cramped, more like a maze, barbwire. The two selves don't touch. What's inside is dwarfed, the color of shadows. Isolated. Small. Moat. The things I make a moat of: clothes, flippancy, poems. In class I'm most comfortable with a lectern to stand behind. I wear sunglasses, let my hair blur me. Branches row across the door I don't answer without knowing in advance. Knowing somebody will come. I use plans as a draw-bridge.

For the first exercise, I asked them to suddenly begin writing—I gave no suggestions, no guides, no examples or warnings. Nothing about techniques or subjects. The room, greyish green, non-descript. Not a leaf at the window or a branch banging the glass. Nothing in the room to evoke much. But I was amazed at what came out—a piece beginning (perhaps because I'd brought in a container of coffee) with the longing for a cup of hot coffee developed beautifully into a piece remembering and longing for some man no longer there. A jump, through free flow, that surprised the writer, pleased her and amazed the rest of the class. It was, almost without changes, a moving and striking poem or prose poem. Someone, smelling roses, wrote some sensuous notes for what could be a poem. Another piece on the smell of rosemary and marjoram: herbs picked and in the house after the frost the night before, filling the next morning. Someone wrote about a visit to old friends, a disappointing visit but, in writing it down, felt her feelings were more mixed than she thought at first. An amusing piece about going back to a class reunion, with a pun on the word "corps" and "corpse," like a short essay or article or filler. Each piece has seeds for its own direction: essays, songs, poems, articles.

The next exercise also worked interestingly: with crayons on the table I asked the group to imagine their inner selves—what they see and then their outer selves. What others see. Again some fascinating drawings. Am trying to get the class, and myself, to use, to rely on, to try drawings and doodles, sketches, images. After they had done the drawing, I asked them to go back over what they had told themselves in the drawings. The colors that predominated, shapes, relationships. If the two views or drawings touched or didn't. As I've said, mine intrigued me. And many others were fascinating. One, like a harlequin, suggested an extreme split. Others showed wild crazy lovely jagged busy unique insides surrounded by a simple ordinary outside self. The woman who drew it said she preferred her inner self, felt it was wildly more interesting, creative, funny, alive, than the self others saw and that she liked it more, that she had more to her than others saw. Some drew their outer selves in three parts, or lugging groceries with a halo. And seething inside, The woman who drew that said she was sure something was wrong.

One woman drew in pale yellows as if not wanting to see what she saw. Suddenly time was dissolving. I talked, with too little time, about memory, asked them to remember a childhood memory, but

194

there wasn't time to read what had been written. But I did ask a few to say what they'd written about and suggested several things they ask themselves about this particular aspect of childhood and how it continued to affect them through adulthood. I suggested lists of things they try to remember about their childhood, suggested they pick a date from their childhood, write a diary entry from that point of view. Also suggested they get some photographs of their childhood out and put them around and study and react and relate to them. Have a dialogue with themselves and the child.

Wednesday morning. Early. Cold. Grey. I was too tired to finish this last night. Fell asleep with the TV on and woke to hear Nancy Friday talk about fantasy. Two strange dream slivers (after talking in the workshop about dreams, about how thinking of them can make them stay, happen—

My dreams were that my grandmother dies suddenly, for no reason anyone knows or seems to look for, at sixty. In another part of the dream I go somewhere to look for papers or documents put away. In the middle of looking, a woman looks up, says she smells old roses. I cut her off.

Back to the rest of the journal class. The last, most extensive writing exercise was squashed into the last fifteen minutes. Mutilated as a baby squeezed into the tiniest trunk. Arms and toes and fingers flailing. Chopped off. It's still hard for me to focus on the process rather than what is written. But I suggested so much they could do with the piece they'd begun, and I'll start with talking about what happened with that next time. I had a list of enough suggested diary entries to last for twelve months.

As I'm making the bed, David Lederman is interviewing Studs Terkel, who is talking about the poetry that comes out of common speech, the untapped creativity, sensitivity, awareness of beauty, need for beauty. All this in contrast to what one woman told she suddenly remembered of going to her first creative writing class: some professor glowered in, smirked, stared like a huge angry hawk and bellowed out, "Which one of you is idiotic enough to believe there is anything in your life worthy of being said?"

Another type of diary that can be taught, or at least that is capable of being analyzed for guidelines, is the visual diary or journal. Visual diaries are appealing to look at as well as to read. Artists do not always keep visual journals, but many talented amateur artists do, and many naturalists, as well. We all keep the kind of visual diary that includes tucked in pieces of ephemera, such as post cards, photographs, printed programs and menus, or a newspaper clipping that has captured our interest. McNeil is an artist-teacher who has explored the concept of visual journal keeping for a Master of Arts degree at Goddard College, Vermont. This article is a condensed version of her thesis, and was first published in *WOMEN'S DIARIES, A Quarterly Newsletter*, vol. 3, no. 4 (Winter 1985).

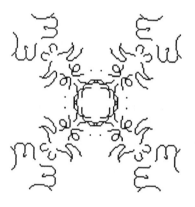

ON KEEPING A VISUAL JOURNAL

by Mary Ann McNeil

*W*ords and images have often been combined, both historically and today, in public and private documents. Some early examples include highly decorated family records, created by itinerant artists in Europe and America. Private documents also sometimes contain beautiful illustrations, such as Van Gogh's letters to his brother Theo. Other historical examples are New England whaling log books, and the old Cheyenne Indian ledger books. Contemporary advertisements, calligraphy, political cartooning, greeting card art, visual poetry, visual notetaking, and most pages of children's books are examples of visual-verbal communication.

Some images are illustrations for written material, and the reader's understanding of the words would not be significantly changed if the illustrations were removed. Others enrich the meaning of the written material, while still other visual images are interlocked with words and have a direct connection with what is written, in such a way that both words and images are needed to complete the meaning in the communication process.

My first experiences with a "visual journal" began twenty years ago while living in New Zealand. Each letter I sent back to the United States contained written descriptions and drawings of places visited, our new baby, and bits of memorabilia about life in a new country. During later visits to Europe, South American, Africa, and Mexico, my letters continued to be full of visual materials.

I have kept visual journals of three kinds: a travel log for our van, a special project journal about soft-sculpture, and a personal private life-tracking journal.

The "van journal" is a five-year record of places visited. It is useful for income tax purposes and as a sentimental family record.

The soft-sculpture journal, which I started when I began to make dolls seven years ago, developed into a personal educational tool. It contains notes from classes and workshops, ideas for designing and constructing dolls, reviews of exhibits, critiques of craft fairs and shops, as well as personal philosophy and observations about doll-making and about being a craftsperson.

My private journal contains day-to-day observations about life, with personal comments, drawings, and memorabilia. In the journal I draw a "Doonsbury," a political cartoon character who philosophizes and comments as an observer on my life.

But what is the definition of a visual journal? A visual journal is one which has a non-verbal content. Typically, it becomes the format for personal artistic expression as well as written expression. Some visual journals contain only pictures, however. The visual journal has the characteristics of the traditional journal; it is a personal, private document, in which each entry is dated. In a visual journal, the artist-author creates a personal book, developing its design and content.

Entries in the visual journal, as in the written journal, are done without thought of publication. The artist-author does not edit or critique the work as it is produced, since it is not finished art work and should not be subject to aesthetic criticism. The images in the visual journal reflect the creator's art-making skills, naive or sophisticated, just as written words reflect the author's writing skills. The visual journal is private and need please only its creator.

The visual journal can come in a variety of forms, such as a notebook of loose pages, a bound book, pages of equal size stored together in a binder or portfolio, a handmade, personally designed book, which can be simple or extremely creative, or an innovative book that reflects the needs of the journal keeper.

A visual journal may develop around a specific goal, project, or idea; in this case the journal becomes a learning tool. It might be used to increase visual and verbal understanding in any subject area. It is only necessary that the words and images interact to promote learning.

As a tool in art education, the visual journal is a place to begin a learning experience in art, or a place to increase one's knowledge of art. It can served as a record of personal reflections after reading about art, attending lectures, and visiting museums, as well as a place to practice drawing and design. Thus the visual journal may become a rich source book for the practicing artist—a place to store ideas, plan, reflect on the intellectual reasons for one's approach to art, and on one's place in the world of art.

For the person keeping a written journal, art-making and visual awareness add a fresh dimension to the journal. For the writer who uses personal journal keeping as source material, a visual approach can offer a new perspective and perhaps a wealth of new material.

As a visual record book, journals are kept by travelers and naturalists. It often contains a daily account of events, places visited, and people met—any of these may be the subject of drawings, watercolor paintings, or photographs. The on-location art making experience provides a unique sense of and an intimate relationship with things seen. After a trip, re-reading the journal becomes a sentimental journey back in time.

For others, the visual journal can become a means of expressing emotions through art making. As a means of self-therapy, the journal is a place to give oneself advice, review life experiences, nourish oneself, organize life's activities, analyze relationships with others, and plan the future. It becomes a visual record of an inner state of mind where emotions and feelings are expressed in words and images. It is a place to explore dreams, fantasies, obstacles, affirmations, loves, tensions, inner conflicts, self-image, personal beliefs, childhood, adulthood, and other intimate states.

How can visual elements be added by those who keep a written journal? First, think of the journal itself as a visually pleasing object and select a "beautiful" book to write in. Or consider the "graphics" of the journal and plan the way words and paragraphs are to be placed on the page. Write in colored inks; change the size and style of writing for emphasis or mood; or create visual interest by adding collage, memorabilia, or drawings.

The visual journal offers the opportunity for using a variety of media in order to create a particular mood, a special affect, or to express a form or idea. Pencil, pen and ink, crayon, gouache, watercolor, collage, or colored pencils may be used alone or in any combination. Add clippings of words, phrases, or pictures to the journal. Photocopy interesting images, textures, or words; cut them up and paste them in alone or in combination with a drawing or painting. Add bits of decorated papers or expressive greeting card images; cut or tear photographs and add them to a page.

Perhaps there will be a recurring image in the journal: a pig, heart, cow, rabbit, or anything that the journal keeper identifies with. Use rubber stamps, drawings, paintings, or gummed stickers. Add found objects: leaves, dried flowers, precious bits of paper, tickets, programs, napkins, or other memorabilia. Use traditional drawing techniques and equipment, rapidograph pens, twigs, bamboo pens; use black inks and colored inks, or watercolor paint. Invent a secret code or color code. Write in circles, heart shapes, or other configurations. Develop a personal iconography. Add captions and balloons; write and draw a story board of events.

How can the visual journal be used as a tool by an artist? It can be a rich source book for the advanced art student or the practicing artist. Here, there is a distinction between an artists's visual journal and the traditional sketchbook into which drawings are placed as a preparation for a larger, formal work, created for exhibition. The artist's visual journal is a gathering place for thoughts, ideas, and art work. It may also be for planning, reflection, and evaluation.

The visual journal is an art form without competition. No critic or censor stands at the artist's side to evaluate the work, nor does a museum or gallery stand by waiting to discover new talent. Journal art is art that is not framed or presented to a public audience. It is personal and private and need not be judged by the standards of others. The artist is the only one to view this solitary work, which is done for personal growth, nourishment, and enjoyment. This type

200

of journal keeping activity is closely related to that of writers, many of whom feel that their most creative and unrestrained work is accomplished in their personal journals. Ideas discovered in the writer's personal journal often become inspirations for more formal work later written for publication. In a similar way, the artist may discover ideas for formal pieces in the visual journal.

How can the visual journal be used to learn the language of art and about art itself? Write a "critique," from a visual standpoint, of a film you have seen. Visit galleries and museums and write, draw, or paint the inspirations based on our visit. Go to the library and "plow" through the shelves of art books; pick out an art object or painting that you like and record the reasons for your choice. Select one that you hate, and analyze your reasons. Search for books that reflect your ethnic heritage. Study them and write about your feelings. Draw or paint, letting your work be influenced by your heritage. Reflect on your consumer choices from an aesthetic point of view. Record your feelings about art, your art experiences in school, your anxieties about making art; theorize about why you grew to accept your beliefs about art. Write about and draw your favorite places—romantic restaurants, shops, beautiful parks, or secret locations that nourish you visually and emotionally. Compare these with places you find less visually pleasing—nursing homes, bus stations, fast food restaurants, and other places that you visit.

How can the visual journal be used as a tool in art education? It can introduce beginning students to art. Since the journal is private, it becomes a "safe place" for a student to begin to draw and develop personal concepts about art.

Traditional assignments both in the classroom and as homework can be done in the visual journal format. There the student can learn about color, line, composition, and other elements of art, as well as how to draw through practice. The journal can also be a space to write about art, including feelings about first art experiences, notes and critiques of readings, and reviews of art works seen in galleries, museums, or reproductions. Since the art work and writing are informal, unedited and unjudged, the student can concentrate on the art.

How can the visual journal be used as a self-instructional tool in art? As a means to study art, the visual journal may be goal or project-oriented. It can provide a format for studies to develop visual awareness and art making skills, to make aesthetic judgements, to develop personal taste through reflection, or to reflect on one's ethnic aesthetic heritage. It can become a tool to overcome the "I can't draw a straight line" syndrome. Some activities to motivate and guide this type of visual journal keeping include: making a checklist of approaches for looking at and evaluating TV films and commercials as visual experiences; creating guides for looking at art exhibits and reproductions, including a list of questions to answer verbally. Do exercises in beginning drawing, and exercises that lead to an understanding of color, line, texture, light and shade, and composition. Make guides to source materials, and list questions for analyzing one's ethnic heritage. Practice exercises to develop skills in observation both in writing and art making.

How can the journal be used a a learning tool for visual awareness by non-artists? One can begin to develop an attitude of awareness to the visual world by becoming conscious of the aesthetic qualities of the physical world. To sharpen senses and sensibilities, explore the meaning of line, color, texture, form, shape, pattern, composition, balance, energy, and rhythm. Stimulate the senses of touch, smell, taste, seeing, and hearing. Go for a walk. Listen to a quiet day, a spring day, a river, a city street; smell them. Touch objects and feel their texture. Relax and get in touch with the environment; draw, paint, or write about the experience.

Fill pages with drawings of your apartment, favorite restaurant, summer cottage, or park. Do the drawings on location or from memory. Write descriptions of the places and about your emotional reactions to each. Spend an afternoon selecting one precious autumn leaf or summer wildflower to put into your journal.

Create a self-portrait once a year on your birthday; use a mirror, camera, or photocopying machine. Draw portraits of your family, friends, acquaintances, and interesting strangers. Draw what you had for breakfast or other interesting meals; or your unmade bed. Express your feelings about them in words or pictures. Draw your pet often; draw or write about its antics. Observe shadows made by the sun, the glow of street lights, the moon, the flickering of candle-light. How does the atmosphere of a specific environment affect your mood? Draw by candlelight.

Use personal experiences and observations to create memory drawings. Take ten minutes to closed your eyes, relax, and remember a place or event. Think about the setting, the weather, who was there, what they looked like, what they were doing and saying. What was the mood of the event; what were your feelings; what other questions cause your memory to stir? Visualize the event and the people involved. Open your eyes and draw pages of line draw-ings about the event. Don't worry about artistic presentation; just let your drawing flow as if you were writing about the same event in detail.

Draw and write about your garden; its flowers, vegetables, insects, and soil. Celebrate its successes and harvests in your journal. Draw about your travels on location; sit in cafes or on the beach. Design inventions, contraptions, or systems to solve real and invented prob-lems. Draw or write your reactions to a poem, story or play you've read or seen; write visual poetry. Keep a journal related to some special aspect of your life, such as a new school, a trip, or a new baby. Keep one for a special area of your life—a hobby, military service, or religious growth. Include clippings, drawings, and writ-ings. Keep a meditation journal and paint or draw after meditating.

These are but a few of the ways of bringing forth emotional re-sponses in the journal, of creating exercises that force one to look at and feel the outside world more carefully, or of developing long lists of possible approaches to art by combining old and new art making techniques.

"Visual journal" is a kind of catch word which is heard differently by each person, who, on hearing it, begins to build a personal defi-nition of the term. It is an adaptable phrase which strikes the imagi-nation, and many who have heard it have developed a"visual jour-nal" of their own. It brings me great pleasure to hear of each new interpretation of the visual journal concept, and to hear of each new visual journal keeper. I feel the visual journal can be a powerful tool in education, artistic development, personal growth, and in the recording of personal history.

Many diarists have used their journals as a source book for creative, literary works. Anaïs Nin was pre-eminent in this regard, and examples abound of how she converted sections of her diaries into her prose works. Virginia Woolf did not, but she did record the progress of her literary works in her diaries. Here, Perkins shows us how she is able to use her journal to write fiction. She had written several short stories by drawing on her journal, then began working on a novel about a woman involved with a troubled Vietnam veteran. Her first draft of over 200 pages was typed up from material she wrote in her journal over several years about her own relationship with such a man. When she wrote all those pages in the journal, she says that it just seemed like "dumping." But years later, the very same passages sprang out as a complete novel. Thus she feels she undergoes a double therapeutic process with her journal, and also finds that her journal is the foundation for creative work. This article was first published in *WOMEN'S DIARIES, A Quarterly Newsletter*, vol. 3, no. 1 (Spring 1985).

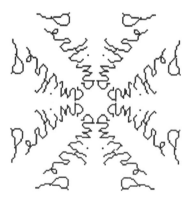

USING MY JOURNAL TO WRITE FICTION

by Dorothy Perkins

One day in the spring of 1972, I rode my bike to the stationery store in my small town and bought a big spiral-bound notebook with lined paper. This notebook was just like the ones I used for my graduate school courses, but it had a special purpose. I was going to start keeping a journal! There was a good reason for my decision that day to begin writing a journal. I had just broken up my bad marriage, freeing myself from a violent husband and taking my life back into my own hands. From that day on, for more than a decade, my journal became my confidante and therapist. At that time, journal keeping was not widely discussed in the popular culture, apart from the diaries of Anaïs Nin, and I had no books (other than Nin's), courses, or other guidance on how to go about it.

I soon realized that two strands were becoming intertwined in my journal. The first was a grand philosophical mission. I wanted to reconcile my life as a woman with the principle of non-attachment that attracted me to the study of Zen Buddhism. I wanted to express myself through my sexuality as a woman and to live freely without the anxiety of wanting to be what I am not and wanting to have what I have not. The second strand was just the opposite, for I found myself obsessing about men and sex. The emotional turmoil which a number of men put me through is right there in my journal.

Men weren't the only thing in my life. I had many close women friends, and I became a feminist who cares strongly about women's issues; I taught college courses, attended cultural events, traveled, protested the Vietnam War. All of these were highly meaningful activities for me. However, in terms of my journal, men seemed to be my dominant problem.

It's not that I was obsessed with men because I felt incomplete. To the contrary, I felt very sure of myself and got involved with men who were troubled. My journal entries about two men in particular often read like psychoanalysis, almost as if they were case studies. I tried to figure out the causes of their problems in order to deal with them in our relationships. Since both men were Catholic, and my field is religion, I engaged in convoluted speculations about the roots of their problems in their Catholic upbringing. At the same time as I was trying to understand these men (several years apart), each in turn began to pull away from me, not because I wanted to make them feel inadequate, but because they felt ashamed of being so disturbed. They shied away from me precisely because they wanted a relationship with me. But they left behind a legacy of words, endless words which fill several big notebooks from the mid 1970s.

While I was writing all of these entries I frequently felt disgusted with myself. What garbage I was writing. How could I waste my time putting down such drivel? I would get depressed and discouraged to find myself sounding like a broken record. Good Lord, I kept asking myself, how many times can I write *that* again?

Later volumes replaced these notebooks as my journal writing progressed. Once in a while I would go back to them for browsing but never did anything more with the material. Then five years ago I suddenly felt a new impulse. I had always been a nonfiction writer, but now I wanted to write fiction. My first story was one that I had been carrying around inside of me since 1972. It tells of my encounter with a Moroccan student in Paris and how I spent Bastille Day with him. The journal I kept while traveling throughout Europe that summer preserved the basic details of the story, and they were enhanced by my memories of the experience, which remain vivid more than a decade later.

Another story that I began (but still haven't finished) was a light comedy about my weekend trip to the Hamptons with a fellow I was dating in New York. This story was just a lot of fun for me. However, it provoked the first harsh reaction to my writing, and I realized that the woman who criticized me was not talking about my writing but about the "immoral" content of my story. Oh well, I thought to myself, there goes all of my fiction. . . .

No, I didn't really think that. I'm not about to change the primary concern of my writing just to make the sexual conservatives happy. Not only did I want to write about sex, I *have* to write about it. By sex I don't simply mean physical intercourse, but the entire spectrum of interaction between women and men on the physical, emotional and spiritual levels. I feel that it's especially important for women to write about this intriguing mystery, because almost no women have done so. We have always been prohibited from writing about sex from our point of view. Erica Jong was able to break through this barrier, but Anaïs Nin kept her material mostly hidden, protected within her journal. Henry Miller and John Updike have received widespread attention for writing about sex; why should not women do the same?

It was just a matter of time before the biggest story would leap out at me from my journal. One of the two Catholic men took hold of my imagination again. He was a Vietnam veteran, and my mind worked over his stories in its usual obsessive way. I went back to those old notebooks again and started typing. Several weeks later I had 250 typed pages which form the rough draft of my first novel. My writing has taken me full circle in a double therapeutic process. The original act of writing in my journal was cathartic; now, with the journal serving as the foundation I have been able to transmute that material into creative art.

This process is therapeutic because I have gained the courage to write in story form about life as I myself experience it. I have learned not only what to put into my fiction, but also what to leave out. I can't use everything. Some things that are really important to me in my journals don't work as fiction, so they have to be carefully trimmed out of the stories. Needless to say, I also have to weed out my philosophizing tendencies. I am learning the hard way that stories are stories, not cerebral exercises.

There's another reason why I can't use everything. Even though the material makes a terrific story, I have to be careful about invasion of privacy. If I give the main character in my novel all the traits of the real man on which he is modelled, I could get both of us in a lot of trouble. Therefore I'm trying very hard to change some details and create a composite character in order to protect my former lover as well as myself.

My biggest problem was whether to write my novel in the first person or the third person. When a story is told from the point of view of "I," the reader can't help assuming that the author really did everything in the story exactly as it's written. The third person hides the author and may also give a story more universality; however, I find that it dilutes my novel's spontaneity and immediacy. I'm inclined to take the risk and write "I." I can't let any worries about how people are going to judge me interfere with telling the story in the way that I want to tell it.

The most valuable thing I have learned is to respect my journal. I no longer view it as the container into which I dumped all the junk of my life. My journal has served me well in preserving experiences, reflections, complaints, questions. I am doubly grateful for the second process of taking what I wrote in journal form and sharing it as stories with other people. Old passages that used to dishearten me have, many years later, enabled me to re-live the deepest experiences of my life in the most intimate way. They make me cry and laugh and feel old desires again. But today these desires are being given a different kind of fulfillment than I dreamed of years ago. Thanks to my journal, I am creating my own self-fulfillment.

Just as creative writing teachers frequently make use of journal writing as a means of getting their students to loosen up and let the ideas and images flow, so therapists in recent years have more and more suggested to their patient that the keeping of a journal would be helpful in learning to express feelings. Many diarists confess that they seemingly resort to their diaries when things are not going well, either with work or with relationships. Writing it out in the diary brings relief. "Troubles shared are troubles halved," according to the old saying, but one is frequently reluctant to share life's deepest troubles with even a best friend. A journal seems to be the perfect confidante. Schwartz is one of many therapists today who encourages journal keeping for some of her patients. This article was first published in WOMEN'S DIARIES, A *Quarterly Newsletter,* vol. 3, no. 4 (Winter 1985).

JOURNEY-COMPANION: THE JOURNAL IN THERAPY

by Patricia Roth Schwartz

*T*he archetypal journey-quest always provides for the questor a companion—Virgil for Dante, Una for the Red Cross Knight, the Good Witch for Dorothy. On the journey that psychotherapy represents, the client and therapist are, of course, co-voyagers. Another kind of companion, one that's at once soul-mate and chronicle, can be the journal.

Psychologists have written about the adolescent diary as a "transitional object" for the passage to adulthood: the notebook into which the young girl pours her heart is a real person to her (as Anne Frank envisioned the "Dear Kitty" to whom she wrote), one that bridges the gap in her life between the parents she's separating from and the adult relationship she will form. I believe in the truth of this view. I also believe that using a journal in this way is not merely a "transitional" experience that one abandons as soon as one is fully "adult".

People of any age may benefit deeply from the experience of journal-keeping; it's especially useful as a tool for growth and change during crises and major life passages. Putting one's thoughts and feelings into the journal, using it as a workbook to map out what happens from here, are all ways of externalizing the internal, getting emotions out and onto the page, and yet a way of keeping them close to home. The journal's absolute privacy (it may or may not be completely shared with a therapist) guarantees that. The fact that writing for the journal is not for publication, for pleasing anybody else, even for having correct spelling or grammar, is an additional benefit.

As a psychotherapist working primarily with adult women from a feminist and holistic perspective, I encourage journal-keeping both in a general and a specific way, whenever appropriate, as an important part of the healing process any therapy represents. Often I suggest that the client beginning therapy acquire a brand-new journal as part of the starting-up. This may be a new volume for a regular journal-keeper, or a first time acquisition for one new to journals. I suggest that the book be chosen carefully, with some appropriate symbolism: a purchased book may have a special illustration or design on the cover that's meaningful; a created notebook may have pictures of the client's choice glued on the front.

I suggest to the client that the journal be used as a central gathering place for everything to do with the therapy that's tangible. Various assignments I give can be done in the journal, or, if on separate sheets, kept in the journal. Other items may be included: letters, family photographs, anything that's part of what the client is working on.

Often, in the beginning, I suggest assignments, particularly to someone new to therapy, journal-keeping, or both. Two typical beginners are: to write the answer to "Who am I?" ten times, uncensored, without much premeditation; and to write a list of goals for therapy. Later, this last assignment can be amplified into short-term and long-term goals, action plans and timetable for both, as well as contracts for accomplishing them step by step: i.e., "By next Tuesday, I will have a new resumé ready."

This kind of practical use of the journal works best, I believe, when deeper, more emotional clearing out is also happening. I tell clients to use the journal to pour in all kinds of feelings: grief, rage, fear—uncensored. Then, after getting it all out, they can continue to write, perhaps the next day, about what to do next, what feelings are left over, what insights have been gained.

The journal is also an excellent tool for dealing with the past, the explorations and understanding of which also forms a large part of most therapies. The letter device is one I most often use, asking the client to write an unexpurgated letter (which she contracts not to mail!) to her mother, father, or to the one around whom the current work is being done. Clients may use this for any past hurt or trauma, including incest, parental alcoholism, or physical abuse. Sometimes many letters are needed, or many drafts of the same letter. Letters may be ripped up, burned, or scribbled over as a way to release feelings. Letters of accusation, anger, love and forgiveness may all follow in turn, depending on what is appropriate for each client.

Another use of the letter written into the journal is to create a rough draft for letters that actually will be sent, communications dealing with current situations. For example, a young lesbian client of mine wrote many versions of "coming out" letters to her parents and to a sister in her journal until the final drafts were approved and mailed. The eventual loving and accepting replies (she was fortunate) to her letters were then kept in her notebook along with her copies of her letters. Thus a complete chronicle of this crucial passage in her life was created and preserved.

Writing in the journal about childhood memories of certain events is also useful and may provide valuable insight. A client may write stream of consciousness, or focus in on a specific event and ask herself questions about it. In all of the situations described so far, the therapist needs to remain flexible about how much of what is actually written is shown to her or read, word for word, out loud. Some clients prefer to paraphrase or simply to report that the writing was done.

Of course, the dream journal, which has been well documented in various sources on dreams, is highly valuable. Another way to use a journal, especially one in a large blank-paged sketchbook, is to have the client draw (no previous talent necessary), using many colors of pencils or markers: draw herself in a certain situation, herself in a particular relationship, her feelings. I have had clients draw their "angry selves", "loving selves", "critical selves". It is then possible to try a drawing of a state to be achieved: compromise, hope, peacefulness, healing.

Clients who have been keeping journals already on their own may wish to bring them in to read or paraphrase sections about certain past events. One client of mine brought in her high school journal-cum-scrapbook, which was quite a facilitative tool for what we were working on at the time.

A journal may also be used for writing affirmations: positive statements which serve as a nudge to the subconscious which may be engaging in sabotage of the conscious mind by dishing out constant negative feelings. For example, someone who has broken up with a lover and feels lonely and undesirable could write fifty times, "I am totally loveable and desirable." She could then write an additional fifty times, "I am enough for myself."

As is obvious, the journal is a versatile and highly useful tool for the process of psychotherapy as well as for the process of living itself. Fruitful journal keeping!

Book Reviews

Alexander, Eveline S. *Cavalry Wife: The Diary of Eveline S. Alexander, 1866-1867.* Edited with an introduction by Sandra L. Myers. College Station, TX: Texas A & M University Press, 1977.

What distinguishes *Cavalry Wife* from many other journals that record a woman's life in the westward movement is its author's own joyous spirit, which breezes through the pages like a mild southwestern whirlwind. She can laugh about treefrogs she found in her bed, because they were not as bad as "a couple of little polecats snugly ensconced" in the pallet of one of the wagoners. She can spend a nostalgic Fourth of July by holding an imaginary political meeting in her tent, with her husband as the only orator. "I had to applaud from time to time with energy," she wrote, "and part of the speech, if it failed to bring the house, brought down the bed."

Twenty-three-year old Eveline had been married two years when she accompanied her husband, Andrew, an inspector general and chief of staff to General George Stoneman, to the New Mexico Territory with the Third Cavalry. She kept the journal with the idea of copying off pages to send to her mother whenever she reached posts where mail might be sent eastward. It is, as the editor subtitles the diary, "a Record of Her Journey from New York to Fort Smith to Join her Cavalry-Officer Husband, Andrew J. Alexander, and Her Experiences with Him on Active Duty Among the Indian Nations and in Texas, New Mexico, and Colorado."

For a girl who had grown up in a well furnished two-story home amid a close-knit family in New York, Evy was remarkably contented, even proud, to be the Lady of the Tent while the regiment was on the move. "My tent," she described, "is lined with blue army blankets, which not only protect it from dampness and make it much cooler on hot days, but subdue the light. . . . I have a buffalo skin for a carpet and my bed is covered with (a) red blanket."

In such a home she managed with grace the social amenities required of an officer's wife. When General Tecumseh Sherman came to dinner, she entertained him without apology by seating him on a trunk at her right at the table, assuring him that accidents like spilling coffee presented no problems on a dirt floor. She also entertained Kit Carson, or rather, was entertained by him as he told Indian legends concerning the second coming of Montezuma.

Without benefit of regiment chaplain, the Alexanders kept the Sabbath regularly according to the Dutch Church ritual. When a young soldier was killed accidently while cleaning his gun, Andrew read the funeral service from Evy's prayer book. "Never has the burial of a stranger affected me so deeply," she recorded.

Death also came to her dog Fan, who left a litter of five puppies. Eveline, in bittersweet tenderness, tied black mourning ribbons around the orphans' legs.

Her listing of the number of miles travelled daily runs like a *leit motif* though the diary. The regiment marched toward water sources, but climatic conditions also governed a day's journey. On July 31, 1866, Eveline wrote:

> Marched twenty-two miles. The greater part of our journey was over a tableland. . .entirely destitute of water and trees. . . . We think we have crossed into New Mexico. . .but how near we are to our journey's end is a conjecture. . . I am beginning to believe we are to wander in this wilderness forty years or more till we have expiated the sins of the regiment or until this generation shall have died off.

The regiment does eventually reach its destination, but the journal ends abruptly with the January 17, 1868 entry telling of a visit to a Navajo reservation. Eveline described the architecture of the Indian "snow houses," the charm of Indian children, and the beauty of the

219

rug being woven by "the mistress of the mansion." In earlier entries she had written of seeing tribes of Creek, Choctaw, Cherokee, and Utes. She saw, also, her first Negro troops who, under the command of Colonel Marshall S. Howe, made the trek with the regiment.

At the diary's end, the editor continues Eveline's biography by drawing on previously unpublished family letters. The Alexanders left New Mexico for "the States" four months after the last journal entry. A year later, however, they were in the Arizona Territory when their first child was born. The little girl lived only six years. A son, born in 1875 died in 1910. After more service in New Mexico, Texas, and Montana, Andrew retired from the Army in 1885, for health reasons, and died the following year. Eveline went home to Willowbrooke, New York, where she lived on her widow's pension until her death in 1922.

The original diary is in the Bancroft Library of the University of California, where it was discovered in a manuscript collection in 1970. The editor regularized some of the spellings; otherwise, the diary is just as Eveline wrote it. Myres, a professor of history at the University of Texas at Arlington, has thoroughly annotated, in highly readable end notes, references to historical persons and to the events occurring in Southwestern history at the time of Eveline's entries. The diary, therefore, is a personal portrait of a charming young woman, as well as an authentic handbook on a time and place in the history of the American frontier.

Olivia Murray Nichols

Antrim, Louisa, Lady. *Louisa, Lady in Waiting: The Personal Diaries and Albums of Louisa, Lady in Waiting to Queen Victoria and Queen Alexandra.* Edited by Elizabeth Longford. New York: Mayflower Books, 1979.

When is a diary also a commonplace book and a scrapbook? When it is the visual journal of Louisa, Countess of Antrim, which is a combination of the three.

Louisa was lady-in-waiting to Queens Victoria and Alexandra. The daughter of General Charles Gray, private secretary to Prince Albert, she knew her way around court when Victoria chose her in 1880. As qualifications for the position, a lady in waiting had to have a good handwriting and the ability to play the piano because she would be expected to assist the Queen with her correspondence and to entertain at informal parties. Other duties included attending the Queen at public and private functions and arranging accommodations for visiting dignitaries.

At the time of her appointment, Louisa had been married for five years to William, Earl of Antrim, whose family estate was Glenarm, some thirty miles from Belfast. In time, they had three children, but theirs was not an extremely happy marriage. Because of his personality, the Earl was called "Buzzard" by those who knew him best. Also, the responsibilities of a lady in waiting can put a strain on the most compatible of couples. "Buzzard" died in 1918; Louisa, in 1949, at the age of 93.

This visual diary is, in part, an album of pictures of the Antrims, the Royal Families, and other personages now famous for the parts they played in early twentieth century history. It is also a scrapbook of engraved and handwritten invitations and the sort of fill-in-the-blank card, printing the necessary information of time and place, with the recipient's name inked in.

Louisa kept and mounted menus and place cards from Royal dinners, dance cards, greeting cards, fashion sketches, newspaper clippings, and cartoons. She preserved personal letters, many of them black-bordered because of tragic news in the text or because the correspondent was in mourning. Louisa's collection of autographs is also reproduced throughout the journal.

The book is divided into twenty dated segments relating to significant periods in Louisa's life and service. The divisions are marked by prose passages supplied by the editor, who details events of history at the time, and quotes from the little brown books which were Louisa's conventional diaries. Journal keeping as such is a no-no for royal attendants, but Louisa recorded the number of days she spent in waiting, the books she read, and the times she went to church. She also complained of weariness at standing in the background through reception lines and at the Queen's evenings "At Home." She wrote of the friendships she formed with fellow ladies and with members of the Royal Family, especially Princess Beatrice of Battenburg.

Louisa's appointment ended in 1910, with the death of King Edward VII, but her albums continue to preserve memorabilia from his funeral and the coronation of Geroge V in 1911.

Lady Antrim's visual journal is a detailed and charming view of life at court and comments on related current events. As such, it is also a pictorial history.

Olivia Murray Nichols

Baldwin, Christina. *One to One, Self-Understanding Through Journal Writing.* New York: M. Evans and Company, 1977.

Rainer, Tristine. *The New Diary, How to Use a Journal for Self-Guidance and Expanded Creativity.* Los Angeles: J. P. Tarcher, Inc., 1978.

In 1977 and 1978, two books were published by women who wanted to give anybody interested the tools and skills with which to write a journal or diary. The first, *One to One, Self-Understanding Through Journal Writing* is by Christina Baldwin, a free-lance writer and counselor who conducts journal therapy seminars. The second, *The New Diary* is by Tristine Rainer, a writer and teacher of creative writing and journal keeping.

Each woman believes that through diary writing a person may gain a greater understanding of the self; this understanding is then taken back into the world to contribute to a happier, more productive life. Baldwin declares that "The journal provides a place for us to uncover our secrets, admit them to ourselves, deal with our reactions, and ground ourselves in a reality that includes them." Rainer claims that "Writing the diary makes you aware of how you see the world, and you begin to choose what sorts of perceptions you wish to have in your life as in your diary."

Both women presume a remarkable ability on the part of the writer to probe meaningfully and to make psychologically sound interpretations. To do this successfully, the writer must be totally dedicated to discovering his inner self. Both believe that keeping a journal in depth can give the writer a much greater control of his own world.

Both authors believe that there are basic attitudes and emotions which must be dealt with in the journey to self-knowledge: the influence of memory, the voice of the child within us, awareness of our own sexuality, the need for privacy, and the interpretation of dreams and fantasy. Each encourages the writer to be totally honest with himself, and each suggests ways to break down inhibitions and other blocking attitudes. Each wants the writer to be able to work through his problems by exploring them in the diary.

Baldwin's main technique is to have the writer ask herself a series of questions about her emotions and attitudes. These questions help the writer to cut through cultural restraints so she may listen to her inner self. She illustrates each of her subdivisions with excerpts from her own diary to show how the technique actually works. She assumes we can have a "relationship with our minds... [which] will be intelligent and basically benevolent." She gives attention to coping with attitudes toward mortality and immortality. Her style is straightforward and persuasive in its simplicity. She includes in the end a list of three or four books of extra reading on each of her subdivisions of emotions and attitudes.

Rainer synthesizes the contributions of four great diarists, Jung, Milner, Progoff and Nin, with her own research to offer a more detailed how-to book. She includes a large number of examples from a great variety of diaries to illustrate her points. While she too believes in questions and dialogues, she explains in detail eleven basic techniques and devices, such as free intuitive writing, lists, portraits, maps of consciousness, altered point of view, and unsent letters which may be used to unravel the writer's real feelings and help her to resolve her problems. Her best chapters are those on transforming personal problems and discovering joy because they are clearly explained, not overly cluttered with examples, and probably the most significant in terms of their contribution to a happier life. She includes in the end an excellent chapter on the values of rereading, showing how one can learn from discerning patterns in one's writing. There is also a long checklist of questions to help the writer make the most creative use of her diary, and comments on how to use a diary in conjunction with professional therapy. She has a bibliography of more than seventy titles of interest to diarists.

The psychological basis from which these authors make their claims seems sound to the uninitiated. But because they assume such wisdom and dedication on the part of the diarist, their claims for the therapeutic value of such writing seem often exaggerated. However, their techniques are clearly presented and would undoubtedly be helpful to either the novice or the experienced journal writer. Anyone willing to follow their guidelines in depth would have a reasonable expectation of substantially increased self-knowledge.

Jennifer Prescott McLean

Blankenship, Jane. *In the Center of the Night. Journey through a Bereavement.* New York: G. P. Putnam's Sons, 1984.

Jayne Blankenship is an American photographer, one of whose early shows was "Women Looking at Women." In this publication of her diary, however, her show and her photography are only mentioned in passing. The focus is on the three years after the death of her husband, Harvey Kantor, of leukemia, and it was written as a means to help her deal with her loss and grief. It is a vividly told and gripping account of the effects of this trauma on her life. She is able to engage the reader in her struggles to meet both her physical and emotional needs, which lead to involvements with her therapist and another man. The result is a perhaps unconsciously wished-for pregnancy, but the rational woman realizes that she can hardly care for herself and her young son. The knowledge that she would not be able to care for another life leads to the decision to have an abortion, which increases the emotional grief. Only the passage of time, and involvement with work and projects outside her old life, bring about the necessary healing.

In addition to her accounts of day-to-day happenings, the author, by means of flashbacks, explores various personal relationships: with her widowed, re-married and divorced mother, which seems blocked by a lack of communication that bordered on cruel indifference to the daughter's needs; with her dearly loved, and also recently deceased father; with her mother-in-law, who seems insensitive to the needs of the non-Jewish wife of her son; and to the son/husband himself, re-living the horrors of the disease as it progressively destroys the man she loves. There are touching scenes with the small boy who is too young (he is three years old) to understand either his father's death or his mother's grief. Nevertheless, the child's instinctive comforting also contributes to the healing process.

Blankenship finds guilt one of the most difficult things to deal with. She writes, "Those miraculous recoveries built false hopes, prevented me from recognizing the genuine onset of his dying. Oh, God, if only I could have seen it coming. If only I had spent that last night with him. I had stayed over before, in fear, but when it really counted, I was blind. I failed him."

She hangs onto every reminder of the man who was: "Ever since I came home from the hospital the morning Harvey died there has been an indescribable but quite palpable difference to these rooms, like when you get a new pair of glasses and can't tell if the floor is six inches closer or the walls off square or what. That morning there had been a red balloon tied to the back of one of the kitchen chairs. I sat down and stared dumbly at where it had hung. That was Harvey's breath caught inside."

In the early stages of her grief she writes, "My inner life is a shambles. Thinking muddled. Loss of structure, of will. Entire psyche rotates, still, around Harvey—only his human force is not here to balance mine. Incessant depletion—strength sucked into a black hole. Directionless floundering. My work is disrupted too—

a smaller, but genuine problem. The women's exhibit I put together, focus of eight months' concentration, ended for me with the opening the week before he died, momentum lost once it was framed and hung."

This diary is also a record of dreams: the nightmares, that recur after the death of her husband, dreams of longing, and finally dreams of finding and losing new loves. These are recounted and explored at some length and offer insight into the ways in which the subconscious deals with conscious problems.

Blankenship's grief is so intense, that it is with relief that one is told that healing is indeed possible. "So much seems possible to me now, . . . I am disappointed by my relapse into old habits of mind . . . The return of bad dreams and fatigue. . . . Dreams about lost purses and Harvey and Daddy.

"Yet despite this slipping back, I seem now to be able to pluck an hour out of a day's despair and declare it a sanctuary, an hour for yielding, opening, learning."

Jane DuPree Begos

Bonfield, Lynn A. *Jailed for Survival. The Diary of an Anti-Nuclear Activist.* San Francisco: Mother Courage Affinity Group, 1984.

This is a record of fifteen days in the Santa Rita Jail, kept from June 20 to July 4, 1983, by a woman arrested for participating in a blockade of the highway around the Lawrence Livermore Laboratory for nuclear weapons in California. Bonfield belongs to the Mother Courage Affinity Group, one of many small, organized anti-nuclear protest groups. Her purpose in writing this journal is not to persuade anybody to do as she did, or to enlist new people to her cause. She simply recorded the facts of what happened while she was in jail, and the result is a booklet that might be a sort of handbook for those contemplating a jail term for civil protest, so that they might know what to expect.

Bonfield describes the rules of the peace camp into which the women were first put (about five hundred of them, with the same number of men near by); she tells what they were given to eat, and about the simple logistics of trying to stay clean and warm. She records their efforts to remain and move as a unit, and to avoid arraignment until their demands of no fines, and no probation were met. But the most interesting part is her description of their frames of mind. The women organized constant workshops to keep their spirits up; they gave talent shows, sang songs, created a band out of make-shift instruments, and staged a lesbian parade. Most of all, they listened to each other talk, and supported each other. They expressed no bitterness when some chose to leave early because of other commitments. Day by day their ranks dwindled, but our author was among those who chose to stay in jail for as long as it took to be released with no fine and no probation. These women were moved for the last four days to a "real" jail, although for the most part they were kept separate from the regular prison population, most of whom the protesters felt were probably not a threat to society and should not be in jail.

The journal ends with the author stating her firm belief that what she did was effective, and will be repeated. She felt that she had enormous support not only from her own group, but from the outside as well. She was not angered by her experience, but rather determined to go fighting against nuclear weapons.

Jennifer Prescott McLean

Brooks, Anne M. *The Grieving Time: A Month by Month Account of Recovery from Loss.* Wilmington, DE: Delapeake Publishing, 1982.

Brooks is an author of children's books (*The Bird's Nest Ear*), and was the wife of H. W. Brooks, a plastic surgeon, with whom she traveled extensively. When her husband died of cancer, she found it therapeutic to put her feelings down on paper for the first six months after he died. This book is divided into six sections, and for each month, she has written roughly five to seven hundred words poignantly expressing, concisely and precisely, her grief.

Because this book is so short and because Brooks has been able to choose exactly the right words with no extras to explain her feelings, her words have tremendous impact. She involves the reader completely without quite wearing her out.

Brooks traces the stages of grief from the raw alternatives of numbness and physical hurt in the first month, to the guilt resulting from at last being able to bear the hurt in the sixth month. She touches on the difficulties of dealing with friends who do not know what to say to her, and explains how the idea of suicide becomes relegated to a future alternative instead of a consuming desire. She likens the whole recovery process to playing a part in a play one hates.

This is a sensitive but not sentimental book, emotional but not maudlin, and one I should think would be of great comfort to anyone going through similar circumstances. The black and white, slightly impressionistic drawings do not seem terribly relevant.

A subsequent version which presents a full-year's account of Brook's stages of grief was published in 1985 by The Dial Press, Doubleday & Company, Inc., Garden City, NY.

Jennifer Prescott McLean

Cooper, Mary. *The Diary of Mary Cooper, Life on a Long Island Farm 1768-1773.* Edited by Field Horne. Oyster Bay, NY: Oyster Bay Historical Society, 1981.

Mary Wright Cooper's diary starts when she was 54 years old, and ends when she was 59, five years before she died. Daily entries are short, rarely more than half a dozen sentences, the first of which is always a weather report. While she ignores the mounting turmoil in the colonies, and mentions her husband only a few times, her five years of entries do present an abbreviated account of what life was like on a busy farm just before the Revolution.

Mary Cooper records the chores which absorbed so much of her time and energy: boiling soap, combing flax, making candles, salting meat and drying all kinds of produce. She speaks of going to town to buy what she herself cannot produce, and of itinerant salesmen. More happily, she mentions quilting "frolics," and days at the races. But Mary Cooper's real joy in life is her church and her belief in a wise and personal God. She belonged to the New Light Baptist Church, and faithfully records the texts on which the sermons were based. She also mentions blacks and Indians as members of the congregation, and the fact that members would speak aloud when moved, in the manner of Quakers. The meetings she found exhilarating in spite of the fact that she had often to walk through terrible weather and wade through streams to get to them. She feels totally discouraged and disappointed when, towards the end of the diary, the congregation splits in two.

The clearest portrayal in Mary Cooper's diary is her own infinite weariness. The hard work was endless, and time and time again, she describes herself as "tired almost to death," or "Hurried, dirty and distressed." She records sorrowfully the anniversaries of the birth and death dates of her little sons who never grew to adulthood. Her grief seems fresh, although the anniversary she is marking may be the eleventh or even the seventeenth. She mentions, without any joy, that she has been married for forty years and has "seene littel els but hard labour and sorrow, crosses of every kind." Her daughter's depressions worry her, and she is frightened of smallpox. Her house is always full of visitors, to the point that she says she is tired of cooking for them and waiting on them. Some she admits to disliking; others she says nothing about. But the numbers of those who came and went made her farmhouse seem like an inn.

Mary Cooper's terminology is often interesting, as when she calls a woman in labor "unwell," or refers to her friends going to "Yorke." To cross Long Island Sound is to "go to New England." Although Mary Cooper's diary was private, from it emerges a limited picture of both the woman herself, and the time and place in which she lived.

Jennifer Prescott McLean

Crouter, Natalie. *Forbidden Diary: A Record of Wartime Internment 1941-1945.* Edited by Lynn A. Bloom. New York: Burt Franklin Press, 1980.

"I shall never be able to express how I have widened my mind and horizon in the confinement of this prison camp," wrote Boston-born housewife Natalie Crouter in 1942. With her husband, 12-year old daughter and 10-year old son, she had been captured during the Japanese invasion of the Philippines in 1941 and interned north of Manila with 500 other British and American prisoners.

Crouter wrote her secret diary on scraps of paper, wrapped them in square packets and concealed them in food tins. After the war she spent two years transcribing the scraps into a 5,000 page manuscript. Years later she heard a speech by Lynn A. Bloom, biographer of Dr. Spock, and decided she had found the perfect editor for her diary. She was right, and the result is well worth the wait. *Forbidden Diary* is a fascinating historical, literary and human document.

Just as we tried to guess how captivity affected the American hostages in Iran, *Forbidden Diary* provides some important clues. We have seen the phenomenon of hostages becoming attached to their captors. Crouter remembers that she felt "no joy or relief, only deep sadness" at the moment of release. Also, the act of writing a diary can be a technique for survival. Bruno Bettelheim used writing as a way "to protect against a disintegration" of his personality. Crouter called her diary a "safety valve."

As Bloom's excellent introduction explains, Crouter recognized that the imprisonment probably would be the most significant event in her life and in her family's life together; she wrote to preserve a record of that experience for her children and for future generations. She also felt a kinship with all the world's victims of oppression, injustice and war: "I often think of poverty and the thousands of women who endure it all their lives. . . bringing up their children in hardship, . . . I keep thinking of Vanzetti in that awful Charles Street jail for seven years before he was electrocuted."

The Crouters were relatively lucky as prisoners. Camp Holmes, near Baguio, was a mountain resort with a pleasant climate and soothing views of surrounding hills. Rokuro Tomibe, the camp's commander for most of the war, was a kind Japanese officer who made sure the Red Cross packages reached the prisoners, at times fed the prisoners out of his own funds, and ignored orders that they be shot when the American's recaptured the islands. As shortages made life desperate, the Crouters received food and clothing from their former Filipino maid—the individual most responsible for their survival.

Despite these ameliorating conditions, the long imprisonment brought suffering—psychologically from fear and lack of privacy and physically from chronic malnutrition. Each family member experienced at least one critical illness. Natalie Crouter's husband, Jerry, a successful businessman in the Philippines before the war, and a loving family man as portrayed in this diary, suffered permanent damage to his health and died in 1951.

The drama and politics of camp life provide some counterpoint to the warm and touching accounts of family life. Crouter's venom is reserved for those who abused their power or failed to do their share of work under camp rules that allowed some self-governance. At first the camp was run by an all-male committee, but after months of objections by Crouter and others, women were allowed to be heard. The other major controversy was over the question of whether families should be permitted to live together rather than be segregated by sex and age. Celibacy was considered necessary because camp members had agreed that only "previously conceived" babies should be born in captivity. Crouter fought a long battle to enable families to share quarters.

In spite of a few selfish people, most prisoners worked hard to remain civilized. Japanese soldiers played baseball with Americans and were introduced to pumpkin pie; voice and violin provided "I Know That My Redeemer Liveth" for Easter Services; the camp put on a production of "Our Town," and teachers set up schools for all levels, so that June Crouter obtained a degree from "concentration" junior high.

Natalie Crouter is an engaging narrator with an eye for significant moments—the thoughtfulness of a guard covering a sleeping child; the excitement as a husband brings back food; the stubborn resourcefulness of the women who sewed the rips in paper bags to make them last; the laughter of guards and prisoners over a musical satire called "Life Behind Barbed Wire."

The author's humor, wit and sense of incongruity make her a "lens" through which we may view painful events with perspective.

Lynn Bloom, a former St. Louisan who is an English scholar and a prolific writer, reduced the diary to less than one-tenth its manuscript length, eliminating much repetition—including the record of every scrap of food the constantly hungry diarist consumed during the internment. Besides her introduction, Bloom also added an illuminating epilogue. The diary, plagued for many years with difficulties between the editor and the original publisher, is now available by mail only. Ordering information may be obtained from Frederick Crouter, 66 Hollywood Avenue, Fairfield, New Jersey 07006.

Susan Waugh

Culley, Margo, editor. *A Day at a Time. The Diary Literature of American Women from 1764 to the Present.* With an introduction by Margo Culley. New York: The Feminist Press at the City University of New York, 1985.

Margo Culley, professor of English and Women's Studies at the University of Massachusetts in Amherst, has carefully selected excerpts from a wide chronological and functional range of diaries to present to her reader some idea of the variety that exists. She also thoroughly documents her conclusion that women's diaries have changed fundamentally from historical, semi-public chronicles to today's explorations in search of self. The excerpts are just long enough (from three to ten pages) to interest the reader, a fact which is often frustrating because they end just when the reader has become involved. They should be read one at a time, so as not to detract from the richness and originality of each.

One of the most interesting features of this collection is its variety. Among eighteenth century diaries, one records births and deaths, and another deals with incest. There are diaries written during the American Revolution, and during World War I. Another eighteenth century excerpt records how many yards its author wove in a given day, while a twentieth century one reports on what it is like to work in a canning factory. There are travel diaries including some written by women on the way West in the middle of the nineteenth century, another by a woman who did white water canoeing for long distances in the back woods of Maine in 1889, and one by Paul Robeson's wife telling about her travels in Africa. There are diaries of servants and socialites, jailed protesters, and homesteaders. They are written by wives, single women, lesbians, young girls and older women.

Culley includes a brief bibliographical sketch of the author of each diary, which is most helpful. Some excerpts are from published books, which the reader may be able to find in libraries. Others are quoted from periodicals, often old and difficult to locate. But even if the originals are hard to come by, this collection of excerpts is enough to stimulate and interest both the diary buff and the scholar. It is, in any case, an excellent introduction to the genre. The extensive bibliography lists other bibliographies, books about diaries, and diaries themselves. This book is a particularly good beginning for anyone interested in how women think and react to their surroundings.

Jennifer Prescott McLean

Cullwick, Hannah. *The Diaries of Hannah Cullwick, Victorian Maidservantt.* Edited by Liz Stanley. New Brunswick, NJ: Rutgers University Press, 1984.

This diary, together with that of the author's husband Arthur Munby (*Munby, Man of Two Worlds*, London, John Murray, 1972), present a detailed picture of Victorian England and an extraordinary romance. Arthur Joseph Munby, born in 1828, was a minor poet and a senior clerk in the office of Ecclesiastical Commissioners. A compulsive diarist and a dedicated observer of social customs, he frequented a world of literary figures and his diaries are full of descriptions of social gatherings with his friends Rossetti, Ruskin, and Swinburne. He discusses theatre, national celebrations and current books. But what gives his diaries an unusual sociological slant is his obsessive interest in working women whom he wrote about, interviewed, and photographed. While the Liberals were passing bills to protect women ironworkers by preventing them from working at night, Munby was out talking to them and discovering that they felt hurt by the bill, and resentful of the fact that they would no longer be allowed to earn extra money by night work. He gives detailed descriptions of the Yorkshire cliff climbers (hunting for mussels), acrobats and colliery-workers. But his favorites were always the milkwomen. He embarrassed his friends by stopping on the street to talk to the lowest classes of working women, and his approaches were frequently misconstrued by their subjects. Munby was fascinated by women's dress, their speech and above all by their skin texture, hands and muscles.

Munby fell in love with Hannah Cullwick when he was twenty-five, charmed by her strength, the redness of her hands, and often by the blackness of the dirt she was covered with. Hannah, born in 1833, worked full time as a kitchen maid from the time she was eight until she was an old woman. For nineteen years Munby and Hannah loved each other in secret, often pretending they did not know each other when their paths crossed in public. Munby's father reacted so violently to the idea of his son marrying a maid that Munby retreated and could never again speak to him of Hannah. However, he did finally marry Hannah in 1873, when he was forty-four and she was thirty-nine, although neither of them particularly wanted that change in their relationship. Only three of Munby's closest friends, and Hannah's family, ever knew of the marriage.

For almost five years Hannah lived in Munby's London house as a servant to most of the world, but as a wife to him—although he never could persuade her to share his meals. In the beginning, she traveled with him occasionally, dressed and behaving as a "lady."

But as time passed, it became increasingly evident to them both that Hannah did not like these abrupt changes in her image, and that she much preferred to live as his servant, loving him by caring for him. "I've long resolved in my own mind & felt that, for freedom & true lowliness, there's nothing like being a maid of all work." She loved the freedom of wearing comfortable clothes with her sleeves rolled up, of not worrying about how her hands looked, of being able to go out by herself in the streets anywhere at any time of day. She found playing the part of a lady enormously constraining. Munby was never able to resolve his dilemma of loving Hannah the most when she was doing the dirtiest hard labor, and his wanting her to go about with him and play the lady, too. More and more often he would go out to social functions while Hannah, by choice, remained at home cleaning. The strain on their relationship increased and in 1877, Hannah moved to the country. While they remained married for thirty-six years, and continued to love each other, they never lived together for more than a few weeks or months at a time after 1877.

Munby's diaries are the work of a man who loved, and was comfortable with, language. Hannah's diaries were written because Munby insisted that she write them not because she wanted to, and they stop shortly after they were married. Yet Hannah's show a greater growth than Munby's. Her diaries begin as almost a list of chores accomplished, and end with a great deal of description and introspection. The result is that she is the more appealing personality. Her diaries portray a woman who has great integrity and warmth. She takes joy in using her muscles and doing a good job, even if it is of the lowest kind of work. She is kind-hearted and often intellectually curious. She was content to serve Munby, and in quite a modern vein, never felt the need of formalizing the relationship. Hannah's diary is both a portrait of a sympathetic personality and a moving description of the hard work involved in being a maid in a particular time and place. Munby's diary presents a much less sympathetic personality and a much more detailed, broader picture of an era.

Jennifer Prescott McLean

Curd, Samuella. *Sam Curd's Diary. The Diary of a True Woman.* Edited by Susan Arpad. Athens, OH: Ohio University Press, 1984.

Samuella Curd began her diary in May of 1860, when she married and moved with her husband from her family home in Virginia to Fulton, Missouri. She wrote for two years, commenting on the buildup, in her town, of conflicting feelings on the Civil War, on the birth of her little girl, and on the lingering death of her husband from consumption. Sam has no heroic stature, but rather seems representative of many women of her time caught up in forces they could not control, and as such is a sympathetic figure.

Susan Arpad, Associate Professor of Popular Culture and Director of Women's Studies at Bowling Green State University, has written both an introduction and an epilogue which give background material and the editor's interpretation of many of Sam's entries. Arpad believes that Sam was searching for her own identity, a search helped by the writing of the diary. She maintains that Sam lost much of her identity when she left her family in Virginia, and lost even more when her husband died. But this reader does not feel that that interpretation should be given too great an emphasis.

It seems entirely natural that a young girl taken so far from her family should feel desperately homesick at times when communication, by our standards, was at best poor. Neither does it seem strange that she should feel so lost when her husband died; many a widow has initially felt that life was not worth living. Sam seems to have had a happy marriage, and the anguish she suffered watching her husband die and then feeling his absence seems entirely believable. Her comments on the war escalating around her are both interesting and sympathetic. She feels tossed around by life, and tries to find some stability in visiting with friends and in her religious faith. The diary ends five months before her little daughter dies.

The diary is replete with tedious entries of who visited whom, but over all it is more of a heartwarming picture of ordinary life at such a different time in our history. Sam is a brave girl, trying to hide her homesickness from her husband's family, trying to cope with difficult circumstances inflicted by the war, and struggling with the hopeless battle to save her husband. She is both believable and likable.

Jennifer Prescott McLean

Farnsworth, Martha. *Plains Woman, the Diary of Martha Farnsworth, 1882-1922.* Edited by Marlene Springer and Haskell Springer. Bloomington: Indiana University Press, 1986.

This diary is a delight to read. First, Martha Farnsworth is a thoroughly sympathetic character, both likable and interesting. Also, she was willing to record a great many of her feelings and opinions as well as the events of her life. Finally, she lived through dramatic personal traumas as well as through historical changes in the country, all of which are interesting in themselves.

Martha's mother died when she was three. She loved her father, but found her stepmother thoroughly unpleasant, critical and demanding. As a teenager, Martha was clearly a belle in her small Kansas town, attracting the attentions of many boys whom she often treated whimsically and callously. She seemed flighty because she was at once pleased and irritated by her frequent conquests. She became engaged a number of times, and finally married the wrong man. The account of this marriage is the most interesting part of the diary.

Martha turned from a light-hearted party girl into a woman of great strength of character—loving, compassionate, and dedicated to doing what she believed was right. What brought about this change was her misery in her marriage and the death of her beloved baby girl. Martha's husband, a "letter carrier," took some years to die of consumption, and while doing so, "cruelly abused" and "cursed" Martha day in and day out. She lived in constant fear of his fits of temper and rage against her which she had in no way earned. However, she complained only to her diary; she put on the most cheerful appearance she could muster, and stood by him until he died. The intensity of her unhappiness in this marriage was matched by the intensity of her joy in her little baby, and the reader becomes completely caught up in her agonies when the child dies. Martha marked every anniversary of that baby's death, and all her life spoke wistfully of her.

The second chapter of Martha's life describes her happy marriage to a good man and their life together in Topeka. Their great sorrow was in not having any children of their own but Martha made up for her childlessness by taking into her home collections of people from her niece to members of her Sunday school class of boys. She cared deeply about "her boys" who kept in touch with her after they grew up and went off to war. She often fed great numbers of people: family, friends, her Sunday school boys, whole troops of children from the Juvenile Court, and anyone else she deemed in need of loving care.

Martha worked hard all her life, cleaning, cooking, preserving, helping sick friends and family, and teaching. She worked for temperance and sometimes for politics, although she did declare "I am not going to mix in Politics this year; these men will work you to death in their own interest and yet refuse you the ballot." She was a member of a government club which supported women's suffrage, and discussed what it was like to get indoor plumbing and a telephone. Martha had amazing stamina which was little diminished by a badly broken arm, a severe cataract, and her increasing age.

The editors of this diary, both professors of English at the University of Kansas, maintain that although Martha showed her diary to nobody, she was writing as if she thought it might someday be read. She wrote in such quantity that it is clear she wrote for her own pleasure, and I am convinced the diary was good therapy during her most difficult years. Even though the editors have cut out some entire years and parts of others, they have presented a character in depth. All the Marthas are interesting: the romantic, the abused wife, the political activist, the temperance worker, the deeply religious woman, and the thoughtful, compassionate, hardworking frontier woman. Martha's diary is energetic and entertaining

Jennifer Prescott McLlean.

Fisk, Erma J. *Parrots' Wood*. New York: W.W. Norton & Company, 1985.

This is the journal of a field trip taken by Erma "Jonnie" Fisk, an "ornithological researcher" as she calls herself when pressed. The purpose of the trip, sponsored by the Cape Cod Manomet Bird Observatory,of which she is a trustee, was to study "one of the, more accessible barometers of change in the biological world, the song-birds Passeriformes." Roughly a dozen people comprised the group which went into the jungle of Belise (half of the former British Honduras) in Central America.

This journal should be read on many levels. At first, it seems to have been deliberately written to entertain a reader. It is informal, chatty, composed of run-on sentences with constant interjections of "Have I told you?" or "Did I mention?" Because Fisk has an engaging personality filled with wit and warmth and a deep appreciation of life, it is delightful to read as such.

On another level, the journal is a fascinating account of flora and fauna, with evocative descriptions of bees, birds, weather, plants, snakes and insects which draw the reader into a natural world she may never experience. Fisk writes with such tenderness and respect for the objects of her study that one cannot help but be caught up in her enthusiasm.

On the third level, this journal is a recreation of a long and active life, looking for some personal meaning in activities and, above all, in personal relationships. It is as if the field trip were a loose frame on which to hang memories, a catalyst for side trips of introspection and analysis. Fisk reluctantly accepts some of the limitations of her age (nearly 80) and leaves some of the more arduous field trips to the younger members of the group while she stays at camp to bake bread and do other useful chores. At times she rails against the frailties of her body, while at other times she declares that "There are a lot of things you don't have to do in this world, though it may take you years to arrive at this wisdom." Her musings search for a constantly changing self. She ponders on the nature of love, loneliness, aging, and people's protective covers. Some of her ramblings are full of cosmic questions, and some are a cry of anguish for the loss of her own stamina and people she has loved. But underneath the complaints and questions is a remarkable resilience which will never give up. "What matters deep down, what carries us through our days, however selfish, is what life gives us in the way richness and satisfaction." And for Fisk, that is a lot because she is never afraid to try something new; to her, life is a constant and desirable challenge by the new and unknown to be eagerly accepted at any age.

Jennifer Prescott McLean

Fisk, Erma J. *The Peacocks of Baboquivari.*   New York: W. W. Norton & Company, 1983.

"I didn't plan to write this journal," declares Mrs. Fisk. "It arrived uninvited, like a stray dog by my stove, demanding attention, nourishment; offering companionship. Phrases turning around and around, like a dog underfoot—under my tongue, under my hand, until finally they and I became comfortable together. . . When you are alone your interior landscape is as important as the exterior, so I also build stories in my head about what I think and feel—all discarded when finally I find a bird in a net and must concentrate on picking out claws and wings while its bill hammers on my thumb, its eyes watch me, bright with apprehension."

This delightful and sensitive book is a record kept by a seventy-three year old woman whom the Nature Conservancy persuaded to spend five winter months in the foothills of Baboquivari, a mountain southwest of Tucson, Arizona. Her job was to count, identify and band birds in that location. Her circumstances were quite extraordinary in themselves: at her age with a "gimpy" hip, she hiked miles each day setting nets to catch birds; she disentangled those caught, identified, banded, and then released them. She had no electricity, and no radio for communication. She lived in a simple cabin seventy-five miles from the city, and had to pack in all her supplied the last two miles to the abandoned ranch where she lived and worked. The weather was more often than not cold and rainy, with occasional bursts of snow or hail. Her company consisted of a band of peacocks, visits from the man in charge of the Arizona branch of the Nature Conservancy, occasional hikers, and a near-by rancher. Otherwise, she was alone.

The journal includes several letters written to members of her family and friends. It is a comfortable balance of chronological reporting of the facts of her work with the birds, and cosmic musings on everything from birds as environmental monitors to man's place in the universe and the meaning of the different stages in her own life. The journal is written with charm, a sense of humor, and a deep appreciation of nature. Mrs. Fisk is an engaging narrator, entertaining her reader while persuading her of the importance of every small creation of nature and the balance between them. The book is a joy to read.

Jennifer Prescott McLean

Hampsten, Elizabeth. *Read This Only To Yourself, the Private Writings of Midwestern Women, 1880-1910.* Bloomington: Indiana University Press, 1982.

Elizebeth Hampsten is Associate Professor of English at the University of North Dakota. Her purpose in writing this book is to "retrieve a genuine history of people who so far have largely been unaccounted for." Roughly one third is excerpts from letters and one diary of women who lived primarily in the Dakotas. Approximately two thirds of the books is the factual background of her correspondents, and her own interpretations of, and conclusions drawn from, her reading. The material is divided into subcategories by subjects such as housing and Indians, school and grammar books, sex, men, and death.

In the beginning of the book, Hampsten questions the methodology of some of her colleagues (Unruh, Faragher and Jeffrey) in their studies of chronicles and raises questions about how to read and interpret letters and diaries. She then offers her own theories, such as "that theories of literary criticism about regionalism are not pertinent to women's writing," and that working women "have had much to say about sexuality, disease, and dying."

Although Hampsten emphasizes the importance of a whole work to the understanding of any part of it, she rarely offers us more than a paragraph at a time to support her theories. Within her subdivisions, she is apt to draw generalizations such as, ". . .women's descriptions of men are apt to be blurred, just out of focus or to one side." Or, "Death is written about less as a substitute for sexuality, I think, than as a means to erotic experience in itself." Or, "She writes so sympathetically about plants, I think, because they were apart from the purely economic scramble that she saw the whole Dakota settlement becoming." This reader found these statements unsubstantiated by the texts offered for example. Hampsten's conclusions may read too much into the letters, as when she says of two correspondents, "They strain to keep cheerful." It is just possible these women had sanguine dispositions and were not straining at all, just as it is possible that the woman who wrote about plants did so because she genuinely loved them.

Although the conclusions drawn in this book often seem dubious, it is a worthwhile source of valuable questions to be asked by anyone studying historical correspondence.

Jennifer Prescott McLean

Hampsten, Elizebeth, editor. *To All Inquiring Friends.* Grand Forks, ND: University of North Dakota Press, 1979.

This collection of primary sources by Elizabeth Hampsten includes letters, diaries and essays in North Dakota, dating from 1854 to 1950. Although men are considered to be the makers of history, Hampsten points out in her preface that "women have done more of the writing about every day living," and that is the value of this collection. The topics are universal: life and death, sickness and health, friends and relatives, daily chores and special social gatherings, courting and getting married. The details are different because the environment is different. Homesteading is part of the record, and life takes place in a sod house. "In North Dakota, the weather is everything," states Hampsten, and the diaries and letters deal with the weather at great length.

Excerpts from five diaries are included; three by women, two by men. The first of the women's diaries is that kept by Julia Louise Gage Carpenter, who starts with her wedding trip from Syracuse, New York to a preemption claim in LaMoure County, Dakota Territory.

The second diary, inscribed "Miss May Bethia Roberts," begins with her family's arrival at the homestead claim north of Devil's Lake in the spring of 1884, and ends when she leaves the University of North Dakota in December 1889 after a single term.

The third diary is one of the most unusual because it is the diary of a hotel chambermaid. Louisa Wanner left her home in Renville, Minnesota for a job at a hotel in Tintah. The first few entries are full of references to homesickness, all the more poignant as it was the Christmas season. Her work seemed to consist largely of washing and ironing, but included doing the dishes and the chambers.

Jane DuPree Begos

Jackson, Nannie Stillwell. *Vinegar Pie and Chicken Bread.* Columbia, MD: University of Missouri Press, 1983.

The immediacy of the diary of Nannie Stillwell Jackson points up the dreariness of daily farm life in Desha Country, Arkansas in 1890. Edited by Margaret Jones Bolsterli, this slim volume is valuable precisely because it was kept by a nobody in a time and place where nothing was happening. Most of the facts mentioned in the diary are worth recording only in the context of a circumscribed world; however, it is important to remember that millions of people shared such a circumscribed world.

Dull at first glance, the text merits a careful reading for the light it sheds on many aspects of late nineteenth century rural life. For instance, a formal code of manners is indicated by the forms of address; even in her diary, Mrs. Jackson always refers to her husband as Mr. Jackson, though he is ten years younger than she is. Her social equals are "Mrs." or "Miss;" blacks are called by their first names, as are children and her closest friends.

According to the editor's well-presented background information, Nannie Jackson wrote with pencils in a small ledger. It was, in fact, worth noting in the diary that brother Jim "gave Fannie & the children some lead pencils & they gave us all 2 a piece which made 8, I am so glad to get them for I was needing a pencil so bad. . ."

Although Nannie is pregnant when she starts this diary, that fact is never mentioned. When she occasionally writes of feeling tired or unwell, the reason is unexplained until her son is born. Even when she feels very bad indeed, she only writes, "I have not felt well today am afraid I am going to be sick I went up to Fannies a little while late this evening & was talking to her, & I told her to see after Lizzie & Sue if I was to die & not to let me be buried here have me taken to Selma & put beside Mr. Stillwell & I want Lizze & Sue to have *everything that is mine,* for no one has as good a rite to what I have as they have I have been married to Mr. Jackson just 11 months to day & it seems like a heap longer time, maybe if we had got a long better the time would not seems so long."

Mr. Jackson was Nannie's second husband, whom she married as a widow with three children, apparently for purely practical reasons. He was an uneducated man and a little lower on the social scale than her first husband. We are somehow encouraged to learn that matters improved between the Jacksons after the birth of their son. He helped with the dishes and she began to educate him: "Mr. J. has begun to practice writing & I think he will succeed."

In addition to her description of farm and household chores, Nannie also gives us a fine account of what today is known as a women's support group. She and her friends helped each other in times of need, and they regularly cared for each other by cooking special dishes for themselves, by making small gifts, by visiting to break the monotony of the day and to comfort each other by sharing confidences. Her friendship with one Fannie Morgan was such a close one that her husband felt threatened by it. The relationship, however, was too valuable for her to give it up: "... Mr. Jackson got mad at me for going there 3 times this evening said I went to talk about him. . . I just talk to Fannie & tell her my troubles because it seems to help me to bear it better when she knows about it. I shall tell her whenever I feel like it."

This document is a testimony to the back-breaking work, the struggle to survive, and the limited prospects most people had. One must be reminded that the Jacksons owned a farm in a part of the country where the soil was fertile and rock-free, and that the living they got from it was the realization of the American rural dream. The tedium of the daily life it depicts is the fabric which supports the so-called big events of history.

Jane DuPree Begos

Kaufman, Polly Welts. *Women Teachers on the Frontier.* New Haven: Yale University Press, 1984.

Women Teachers on the Frontier consists of letters and one long diary written by women sent west to teach, with a commentary by Polly Welts Kaufman, who is Coordinator of the Library Program of the Boston Pubic Schools. For each of her teachers, she supplies biographical material not readily apparent in their letters and diary. She adds historical perspective and statistics about the movement west to teach. Catherine Beecher developed and publicized the National Board of Popular Education specifically to train girls for this purpose. The Board would accept, however, only those evangelical Protestant girls who had confessed to a sincere religious conversion experience. The diary and letters were written by students trained at the school in Hartford where they studied music, calisthenics, spelling, physiology, English composition, and algebra, and heard lectures (we can't help wondering why) on the deaf and insane. They were then placed in schools in Ohio, Missouri, Illinois, Indiana, Iowa, and a few in Oregon.

Of the many reasons girls had the courage to leave home and start new lives, the most important seems to have been a sincere religious zeal. They believed they could take the responsibility for their lives away from themselves and their families and hand it over to God's authority. At the same time, many had a real financial need to support themselves, and teaching jobs were often scarce in the east. Others had no close family ties to keep them home, and all were somewhat touched by the romantic publicity about the west circulating at the time.

The documents included in this volume are remarkable for their authors' willingness to be candid about their own feelings, and their ability to express their emotions as well as vivid descriptions of their experiences. They are an articulate group; they have fascinating stories to tell, and they tell them well. Half the book is comprised of the diary of Arozina Perkins, kept from November of 1848 to June of 1851. A native of Massachusetts, she completed her training in Hartford, and then went, against her family's wishes, to teach in Fort Des Moines, Iowa. She writes of her determination to go: "I *must* go out in the Spring class of the National Board, and my dear mother *must* give her consent and blessing, and I *must* improve my time till then in learning. . ." She is openly depressed and lonely at times: "Why is the faint sunlight of joy, which, so cautiously breaks upon us here, so quickly obscured by the cold, dull, leaden clouds of reality? Why are we just learning to prize sympathy and friendship when they are suddenly withdrawn from us forever!' Arozina has a sensitive appreciation for natural beauty: "The moon rose, while there; the motion of the boat causing it to appear as tho' dodging up from behind the trees then back again to see what the world was about before she would lend us her lamp." She also has a lovely sense of humor. She writes about how hard it is to teach when the children are cold, and are interested only in huddling near the stove: "I claim the merit of having discovered a new law of attraction not mentioned in any philosophy I ever studied—that of heat, which

246

proves here completely irresistible when exerted upon certain bodies coming within the sphere of its influence." Another time, reflecting upon her experiences, she declares, "Believe I have seen most of the curiosities that I wished to, now, except it be wolves. I have seen none of these unless they wore sheep's clothing." She is responsive and humble, admitting on her trip out that "I learned some lessons which I shall never forget, and not be be gained in any other way. I never before knew so much of the continual employment of boat hands, their recklessness of life, disregard of truth, profanity and gambling; and I have learned sympathy for them." This from the girl who was initially shocked by any lack of Sabbath observances! Arozina returned home to Massachusetts, for reasons unknown, and died at the age of 28.

Most of the teachers sent to the middle west by the National Board encountered a variety of problems, from finding that the school to which they had been assigned already had a teacher, to being fought over by rival Protestant sects, to being met with suspicion by the local people. They coped with the discomforts of being boarded around in different families, and the difficulty of teaching, with inadequate supplies, a group of up to forty "scholars" ranging in age from 3 to 23. Their hours were long, their pay poor, and yet they felt they were doing God's will and helping to bring civilization to those who needed it. One teacher, anticipating objections to her reading the Bible in her school, determined that, "I shall teach the scholars the golden rule & many other Bible percepts, whether I tell them where I found them or not."

This book testifies to the good will and fortitude of a dedicated group of women. It also includes, for those who would like to persue the subject further, four appendices, an annotated list of over two hundred teachers by name, and a bibliography.

Jennifer Prescott McLean

Lane, Rose Wilder and Helen Dore Boylston. *Travels with Zenobia: Paris to Albania by Model T Ford.* A Journal by Rose Wilder Lane and Helen Dore Boylston. Edited by William Holtz. Columbia MO: University of Missouri Press, 1983.

Rose Wilder Lane was the daughter of Laura Ingalls Wilder, popularly known for her *Little House on the Prairie* books. Lane was an author in her own right; she published biographies of Henry Ford and Herbert Hoover, two novels, a travel book, and numerous articles and stories in magazines. She met Helen Dore Boylston, who had been a field nurse in France during World War I, on a trip to Poland in 1920, when both had assignments there. By 1926, they had become friends, both disenchanted with America, both remembering fondly what they perceived as a romantic, almost medieval, world in Albania which they had earlier visited independently. To go and live there for a while seemed an answer, a resolution to their dissatisfactions with both America and Europe.

This book includes a foreword by William Holtz who fills in biographical information on the two women, and builds a political and cultural frame of reference into which to fit their journal, which consists of alternate entries by the two authors describing their trip from Paris to Albania. The book concludes with a few letters from Lane describing their house, and something of their way of life in Albania.

Both authors are accomplished writers (Boylston later wrote the Sue Barton nurse stories for girls). Lane has the more cosmic view of life and is more thoughtfully analytical. Boylston relished every crisis and writes with vivid, immediate enthusiasm. Both have unerring eyes for detail, local mannerisms, and the humor potential in a difficult situation. Their journal duet is a joy to read; it is clever, precise, often hilarious, sympathetic and totally entertaining.

The journey itself was fraught with difficulties of the kind all travelers experience: car breakdowns, poor maps, incompetent directions, poor food and nonexistent hotels, stolen luggage, and trunks not delivered. One acquires a profound admiration for these two brave women, accompanied by their French maid, coping by themselves in all kinds of predicaments. They demonstrate great courage, patience, humor, and resourcefulness. When the car broke down,

Lane thought nothing of attacking it with tools, determination and some knowledge. Both show endless perseverance, whether it is in finding a particular town, searching for typing paper in Albania, or breaking through assorted language barriers. Through all these vicissitudes they are able to laugh at both themselves and the world around them. While constantly disillusioned, they are never discouraged. The journal officially ends when they reach Albania, but one wishes it would go on for several more years at least.

Jennifer Prescott McLean

Lee, Agnes. *Growing Up in the 1850's, the Journal of Agnes Lee.* Edited, with a foreword by Mary Custis Lee deButts. Chapel Hill: The University of North Carolina Press, 1984.

Agnes Lee was the third daughter and fifth child of Robert E. Lee and Mary Anne Randolph Custis Lee. The entries in this journal start in December, 1852, and continue until January, 1858. Although she often skipped weeks and even months between entries, Agnes emerges clearly as an intelligent, warm-hearted and appealing young lady. Born into a world of privilege, she is nontheless grateful for all she has, and is forever striving to make herself a more "worthy" person. She derives her greatest joys from her love of her family. We see her in the beginning as child of twelve playing in the gardens of her family's house at Arlington, and in the end as a young lady who has decided, after some soul searching, to be confirmed. Underlying all her themes is a current of cheerful optimism, and of introspection.

Agnes spent two winters at West Point when Lee was superintendent there. At first she was shy and miserable; later she looked back on those winters with enthusiasm and longing. But the growth was not always smooth. "To be surrounded by several cadets at once is no very peasant feeling, but I am overcoming my bashfulness a little. I don't know it is any great advantage in one so young. I fear I am getting corrupted by the world." The new cadets had her total sympathy. "Poor fellows, they are teazed, tormented and tricked almost out of their lives. . . All, the other cadets say for their good they have had their turn & feel all the better for it. Perhaps a little would do no harm but I know it is carried too far & tell them it is only out of revenge for what they have suffered."

At Arlington, Agnes enjoyed visiting numerous members of her family and friends, and even dared to instruct some of the slave children, which was illegal at the time. She adored her Custis grandparents, and suffered miserably when they died. And always she worried about herself as a person. She prayed that "Our Father in Heaven would. . .satisfy that longing within me to do something to be something. . . . But now I am as bad nay worse than ever. Will I ever be a Christian? Ever be worthy of the love and esteem of anyone? O I hope so— but I am afraid not."

Agnes went to school at the Virginia Female Institute in Staunton. The letters she writes from there have a timeless quality and she sounds like any school girl. "I can't study tonight. Geometry is 'Greek' or worse but indeed I feel as if I can't write either." When she writes to her father that it is entirely too hot and the girls can think only of going home, he answers her that she cannot know what hot is until she joins him on the plains of Texas. He also adds that he wonders why he bothered to send her to school if all she can think about is going home! Agnes missed her father sorely during his long absences, but he made time to answer her letters.

One wishes Agnes had continued the journal through the Civil War because her descriptions are shrewd, full of humor and sensitivity. Her journal is a fascinating picture of aristocratic, pre-war life. Agnes never married, but died in 1873 at the young age of 32 (the book does not give the cause.)

The book includes not only Agnes's journal, but some letters to her parents and their replies, a few reminiscences from her younger sister about her, and an introduction by the great-great-grandson of Robert E. Lee as well. The editor is Agnes's niece.

Jennifer Prescott McLean

Lifshin, Lyn, editor. *Ariadne's Thread. A Collection of Contemporary Women's Journals.* New York: Harper & Row/Colophon, 1982.

In this unique collection of diaries and journals by contemporary women, the editor has divided fifty-three selections into seven subject headings: work, self, love and friendship, family, being somewhere else, society, and nature. The final division consists of selections from her own journal and deal with working on the anthology. Here she plots the work from conception to packing it off to the publisher, and touches on the agony of making the final selections from the near overwhelming amount of material— good material, all of it.

Lifshin states in the introduction that she wanted "a variety of experiences and concerns from women of all ages and differing backgrounds, women who were unknown and unpublished as well as those whose work in different fields [she'd] long admired." In this cross-section, she has achieved an interesting mix of entries that range from deeply personal, inward looking reflections and meditations to laconic accounts of everyday life. Among the known authors included are Gail Godwin, Maxine Kumin, Marge Piercy, Alix Kates Shulman, Rita Mae Brown and Denise Levertov.

Although the selections can, and should, speak for themselves, Lifshin, in her introduction, pinpoints the themes she encountered: writing, expected since many of the women are writers; an obsession with mother; problems with time; men as "the other;" a feeling of disappointment with the body, often linked with an obsession with food; concerns with money; aging; and dealing with a life-threatening illness. The introduction also includes the editor's synthesis of the replies to a questionnaire she sent to contributors. The answers are sometimes expected, sometimes revealing, and always interesting.

Jane DuPree Begos

The McKaig Journal, A Confederate Family of Cumberland. Edited and annotated by Helene L. Baldwin, Michael Allen Mudge, and Keith W. Schlegal. Baltimore: Gateway Press, 1984.

The McKaigs were a prosperous, socially prominent family who lived in Cumberland, Maryland. William Wallace McKaig a lawyer, state legislator, and president of the Frostburg Coal Company, began keeping this journal in 1851. His wife continued it right through the Civil War. The editors have included a Preface which explains many of the incidents and personalities in the war and their effect on Cumberland, and which gives genealogical information about the family. They also continue their annotations alongside the journal throughout, explaining people, battles and events. Their Conclusion tells what became of the members of the family after the journal ends.

As the journal begins, it is hard for the reader to know whose voice is recording, husband or wife. Throughout, dates are difficult to keep track of because entries are often dated "Monday the 2nd" without month or year, and weeks and months are frequently left unrecorded altogether. However, the journal is a particularly good record of domestic economics since the McKaigs kept detailed records of what monies were paid to whom, how much was sent to their sons for their educations, and exactly what was spent on food stuffs and grains, materials and clothes.

Mrs. McKraig's chief concern was for the welfare of her four sons, two of whom fought for the Confederacy (one was captured), and one of whom had epilepsy. She recorded at length the weather conditions and her own poor health. She told how she sent clothes, food and money to soldiers in prison camps, and how she visited her own sons behind enemy lines. She coped admirably when she had to travel around Virginia because she was banished form her house in Cumberland during the Union occupation of the town. She seemed a brave, compassionate woman who managed in whatever circumstances were dealt her, whether they were illnesses, lack of servants, exile, or worry over the sons' well being.

What is frustrating to the modern reader is her lack of emotion, or even willingness to discuss the great events taking place around her. She can record the death of a brother, the fall of Richmond, the surrender of Lee and Lincloln's assassination without so much as one comment of her own. She lives in a town torn apart by sympathizers of both North and South, and makes no mention of loss of friends or any difficulties which might have resulted from such tension. Instead, she talks about the weather and who called upon whom. So the journal as a whole becomes a timeless record of a mother's anguish for her sons at war rather than historical reaction to a time and place. The events to which she scarcely alludes are described in detail by the editors. And still many questions are left unanswered. Why wasn't her husband banished with her? How was she able always to have plenty of money while she was traveling? Why did there seem to be no shortages of the materials, food and goods they wanted during the war?

Mrs. McKaig's lack of involvement in ideas outside of her family, and the details left unexplained, tend to dull the reader's commitment to her account.

Jennifer Prescott McLean

Mallon, Thomas. *A Book of One's Own*. New York: Ticknor and Fields, 1984.

Thomas Mallon has written a brilliant introduction to a tremendous variety of significant diarists of the last three centuries, a book in which he 'suggst[s] the waterfront more than cover[s] it." The common thread among these diverse people is time: "Time is the strongest thing of all, and the diarist is always fleeing it. He knows he will eventually be run to earth, but his hope is that his book will let each day live beyond its midnight, let it continue somewhere outside its place in a finite row of falling dominos." Mallon discusses roughly one hundred twenty-two diarists, of whom approximately thirty-eight are women, and classifies their diaries loosely by function.

The Chroniclers are those who try to "hold on to it all, to cheat the clock and death of all the things that [they] had lived," and include such notables as Samuel Pepys, Elizabeth Wynne, the Goncourt brothers, G. T. .Strong, and Evelyn Waugh. The Travelers include explorers and the women moving West on the Oregon Trail (Amelia Stewart Knight, Lydia Allen Rudd, Jane Gould), Queen Victoria in Scotland, Simone de Beauvoir, and Clara Milburn of England with her war-time diaries. The Pilgrims are those in search of self or of spirituality, or those who try to lose the self, or simply to endure. Among these we find Thoreau, May Sarton and Anaïs Nin, C. S. Lewis, Annie Dillard and Pope John XXIII.

In his section on Creators, Mallon shows how closely the thoughts and images in a diary are allied to the final work of art, whether it is a poem, a painting, a building or a dance. The notebooks of an artist have often been used ". . .not just to prod himself toward his creations, or to map them out, but to commemorate them as well." The Apologists are those who ". . .wished to make the world sit up and take notice of their suffering or simply of their existence; unappreciated artists; nebbishes turned killers; those denied their dreams because they were the wrong age or the wrong sex, or just in the wrong place; those trying to lead upright lives when their nations were on sprees of violence." They want to make ". . .history prick up its ears and take notice, however briefly," and include Nixon, Nijinsky, Harold Nicolson, the Lindberghs, Trotsky and others. Next we meet the Confessors who include teenaged girls, homosexuals, tattle tales, criminals, and notables like Stendahl and Byron. The last of Mallons' groups is Prisoners: of spirt, of disease, of failure, or of circumstance. Some few are actually in jail (Dreyfus and Albert Speer) while others, like Anne Frank, are prisoners of circumstance. While the Chroniclers' " . . . lack of suspicion toward life made them happy to rake and bag all of its details, the prisoners of one sort or another . . .require room great enough in which to hide from the world. . ." so they both share a voluminousness.

What makes this book so successful, so entertaining, and so captivating are the author's skillful balancing of his own interpretations with quotes from the actual diaries, his sense of humor, and his ability to organize so many millions of words into satisfying, small bites. Transitions from one diarist to another, or one classification to another, are smooth and insightful: "The diarists we've just met were dispossessed by the traditional blind spots of their civilizations. Others, ordinarily content, have become internal exiles only during periods of national history so unusually dark that they were ashamed to be living in them." Or, "Until now we have been looking at people serving or opposing things larger than themselves—causes, tyrannies, revolutions, obsessions, anonymous prejudices, armies, and secret police. But most of the battles we fight aside from those within ourselves, are fought for and against the individual beings we know best."

Mallon's book is a marvelously comprehensive introduction to a world of diarists. Even though he can touch on only a few of the centuries' totals, he does give the reader a forceful sense of the different functions of diaries, and the wide variety of personalities and professions they have served.

Jennifer Prescott McLean

Manning, Nicola. *Historical Document.* Long Beach, CA: Applezaba Press, 1979. Introduction by Gerry Locklin, 1981.

This is a journal written for two months in 1959 by a young woman struggling against madness, a young woman who does not win the struggle. It is compelling, poignant, and heart breaking.

The introduction, which is short and confusing, tells us nothing we want to know about the author except that she had written some poetry. We do not know how old she is precisely, or what happens to her eventually. We can surmise from hints dropped in the journal that she lived in California, shared an apartment with another girl, and took some courses at a community college.

What we do read is the confusing attempt of a disturbed mind to sort out and make sense of the people around her. Manning believes that the world is peopled by Android Russians and Gestapo who are trying either to hypnotize or brain damage the rest of the world. Our troubled author is convinced she is being spied upon by everybody, and will be arrested because she resists hypnosis. When she is taken to the mental hospital, she believes she has been arrested; the hospital becomes the Gestapo Headquarters, and assorted doctors, social workers and technicians are the secret service. She calls her medications "industrial fluids." She is quite certain they will kill her in the end. She records her own diagnosis as Chronic Undifferentiated Schizophrenia.

There is no punctuation at all in this journal which often makes it a little difficult to decide where one sentence ends and the next begins, and to realize that "shed" is really "she'd." But more important is the fact that Manning writes with a dynamic insistence and a kind of clarity in the confusion which makes the journal impossible to put down. Her reasoning, while absurd, is understandable and sympathetic.

This is a chance to step inside the mind of a singularly articulate mental patient. Some people may find it too close an association. But for anybody interested in mental health or psychology, this account is riveting. The author's mind is disturbed, but it is such a good mind in many ways. One aches for the doctors unable to help her, and for the helplessness of society when confronted with this sort of illness. The reader is overwhelmed with compassion for the girl who struggles so hard against her perceived evils.

Jennifer Prescott McLean

Nin, Anaïs. *The Early Diary of Anaïs Nin*, vols. I-III. Harcourt, Brace, Jovanovich, 1978, 1982 and 1983.

ANAÏS, An International Journal, edited by Gunther Stuhlmann and published by The Anaïs Nin Foundation, 2335 Hidalgo Ave., Los Angeles, CA 90039.

Since Anaïs Nin's death in 1977, works by or about her have continued to be published. This review is an attempt to describe that continuous activity for the benefit of readers who might not be aware of it.

First some background to put the Early Diaries into perspective. The first diary that Anaïs Nin felt she dared to publish began in the year 1931 (she was 28), when, as she once thought, her life became exciting. She was then in the throes of her relationships with Henry and June Miller and receiving recognition for her study of D. H. Lawrence. Volumes I-VII cover Nin's life until shortly before her death. By then, public acclaim was such that Nin considered publishing the diaries written before 1931. These have been planned in four volumes and are distinguished from the later Diaries by being called *The Early Diary of Anaïs Nin*.

The first three volumes of The Early Diary are now available. Volume one is entitled *Linotte* and covers her life from age 11, when she started the diary to age 17. "Linotte" means "little bird", a term Nin dubbed her idealistic adolescent self, struggling to learn how to fly. This diary was translated from the French and Spanish Nin used as a child. It starts when Nin's mother left Barcelona for America after her father abandoned the family, and she began to write it as a means of searching for her lost father.

The second volume of the Early Diary documents Nin's life from 1920-3, when at age 20 she is on the threshold of marrying Hugh Guiler. These early diaries dispel any notion that Nin's life was eased by wealth. In America, Nin's mother ran a boarding house to support her three children, and Anaïs' top priority was helping her mother with chores and coping with the family problems to the extent that she even felt she could not marry because it would take her away from her mother's side.

Volume III of The Early Diary covers the first years of her marriage to Hugh Guiler and their move to Paris, when she is 20 to 24. These early diaries are of significance for the way they reveal the true origins of Nin's relationship with her parents, her brothers, her cousin Eduardo, her husband, as well as the development of her writing. In this third Early Diary she has written her first novel, *Aline's Choice*, when can be read in the Special Collections department of the Northwestern University Library. She wrestles with her tendency to write more fully and honestly in the journal than in her fiction and she attempts to get those around her to keep journals also. Volume IV of the Early Diary will close the gap between 1927 and 1930, when the first published Diary began.

One may wonder what more can be said about the life of Anaïs Nin to justify the beginning of a literary journal focused on her life and work. But we now have 2 issues (1983 & 1984) of , ANÄIS, An International Journal, edited by her agent Gunther Stuhlmann. Offered are unpublished excerpts from Nin's diaries, memoirs by friends and relatives, and substantial critical pieces. For those of us who want to know more about the people and facts of Nin's life, much of the material is illuminating.

In the first issue, Stuhlmann writes informatively about Nin's critics and translators. There are pieces by those close to her, including Ian Hugo (the adopted name of Hugh Guiler), Rupert Pole, James Leo Herlihy, and Otto Rank. In the second issue, a history of Nin's Gemor Press is provided by Philip Jason and others, as well as her relationships with Lawrence Durrell and Caresse Crosby. The formerly unpublished excerpt from Nin's diary concerns a time when she was 27 years old, devastated by her husband's criticism of a piece of work, feeing the intense pressure of unwanted and unfulfilled desires, and facing nervous collapse. The value of a publication, such as this, is in its extension of scholarship as well as its assembling of tidbits fascinating to Nin readers. For example, we are given an excerpt Nin wrote at the age of 25, comparing herself to Colette, which not only is evocative and incisive about Colette's style but also distinguishes Nin's.

The publishing of these Early Diaries and the Journal ANÄIS, enable the reader to come very close to the life of a particular woman with perhaps unprecedented psychological depth and historical range. It is not just to learn about *her* life that these works are meaningful, but because they allow us to identify with her struggles in creation and relationship and inspire us in our own lives.

Valerie Harms

Origo, Iris. *War in Val D'Orcia, An Italian War Diary 1943-1944*, with an introduction by Denis Mack Smith. Boston: David R. Godine, 1984.

From January, 1943, to July, 1944, the Marchesa Iris Origo (who has written books on Byron, Leopardi and St. Bernardino among others), an Englishwoman married to an Italian, kept a diary recording the effects of the Allied invasion and the German retreat on the valley in Tuscany where she and her husband lived. She wrote it in an attempt to find peace of mind amid the isolation and tension, and to try to make some sense out of what was happening all around her. She decided not to alter the diary in any way for publication forty years later.

The 7,000 acre estate on which the Origos lived was almost feudal in its self sufficiency and the interdependence of its fifty-seven farms with each other and the main house. This economic structure made them more able than many, certainly more than people in the cities, to cope and survive as the destruction of the war increased. They lived on much of their own produce, buried in the garden to keep the Germans from confiscating all of it. They wove fabric from the wool of their own sheep, made their own soap, and made shoes from their own animal skins. But they were providing not only for themselves, their two tiny daughters (one of whom was born during an air raid in 1943), and their farmers, but also for twenty-two children sent to them from Turin and Genoa for protection, for great numbers of partisans hiding in their woods, and for streams of refugee soldiers and civilians who had no other place to turn for food and clothing.

"Our problems," wrote the Marchesa, ". . . arose from a continual necessity to weigh, not between courage and cowardice or between right and wrong, but between conflicting duties and responsibilities, equally urgent. Every day the need for deciding between them would arise: the request for the lodging of a p.o.w. would have to be weighted against the danger to the farm which sheltered him, the dressing of a partisan's wound against the risk to the nurse and to the other patients in her charge, the pleas of the starving townsfolk who, in the last weeks before the liberation of Rome, came all the way from the city to beg for food, against the needs of the children and partisans whom we must go on feeding here." Always she was compassionate, giving whatever they had, spending their money on supplies, when they could find them, to help others.

Eventually, the Germans forced them out of their house; then their only possessions were what they wore on their backs. In a ragged band of sixty, four of whom were babies in arms and twenty-eight others children, they walked eight miles through the battle lines between the mines to another village where they were housed until the Allies finally reached them. When they returned home ten days later, they found the walls of their house standing, but total devastation inside. Now, with the same quiet determination with which she had faced the Germans, the Marchesa set about reconstruction.

Iris Origo writes cooly and objectively with quiet anguish rather than dramatic emotionalism. He diary relates facts and incidents of their day-to-day existence, interlaced with judgments concerned more with understanding than blaming. "But in the great mass of the nation, the keynote still appears to be a dumb, fatalistic apathy—an acceptance of the doom falling upon them from the skies, as men living in the shadow of Vesuvius and Fujiyama accept the torrents of boiling lava." Or, "As the circle in which our life moves grows smaller and smaller, and the immediate menace more threatening, our mental horizon shrinks to that of the peasants; and with this narrowness creeps in something of their skepticism towards all vague schemes for the future, all remote Utopias."

In the worst hours of the war on their own land, she states quite simply: "This glimpse of a tiny segment of the front increases my conviction of the wastefulness of this kind of warfare, the disproportion between the human suffering involved and the military results achieved. In the last five days I have seen Radicofani and Contignana destroyed, the countryside and farms studded with shell holes, girls raped, and human beings and cattle killed. Otherwise the events of the last week have had little enough effect upon either side: it is the civilians who have suffered."

Later she concludes that, "When I look back upon these years of tension and expectation, of destruction and sorrow, it is individual acts of kindness, courage or faith that illuminate them; it is in them that I trust. . .the shared, simple acts of everyday life are the realities on which international understanding can be built. In these. . . we may, perhaps, place our hopes."

The Marchesa tells her story simply, with poignant clarity. As incident after incident of human cruelty is documented in these pages, the reader's admiration for the author's self discipline and compassion, energy and determination, mounts. This diary is one more valuable testimonial to the best kind of resourcefulness, as well as to the evil, in human nature.

Jennifer Prescott McLean

Parkerson, Julia Etta. *Etta's Journal, January 2, 1874 -July 25, 1875.* Edited by Ellen Payne Paullin. Canton, CT: Lithographics, Inc., 1981.

Julia Etta Parkerson's diary is a poignant account written by a most sympathetic girl in her early twenties. Etta was born deformed; her spine was misshapen by scoliois and she never grew to be more than four feet tall. When she was four, her mother died. Her younger sister was quickly adopted by her mother's brother, but Etta, who was not expected to live long, stayed with her father who married again. She helped to bring up her half brothers and sisters, spent a semester at Kansas State Agricultural College, and then kept house for an uncle in Neosho Falls, Kansas.

Etta's journal starts while she is in college, and continues while she works (for $1.00 a week) for her uncle. It is candid and soul searching, and reveals a girl who is intelligent, hard working, compassionate and enormously likeable. It also reveals the anguish she suffered over her deformity, and her irresolution as to whether or not she should marry the man (30 years older than she) who so patiently courted her day after day. She was afraid of marriage because she believed the resulting childbirth combined with her deformity would kill her. But her journal warmly describes her deepening commitment to her suitor: "I believe I am learning to love Alvin more and more every day; he is so kind. It doesn't seem as if God would ever have let us love each other so, if it wasn't right." She was also determined to cure him of his love for tobacco! She was deeply religious, believing that God would guide her in all ways, and make firm her resolution to be a better person. But she had a sense of humor as well: "Last Monday evening I took a meddlesome streak and attempted to fix uncle's old clock, and spoilt it so that it will never go any more." She had days when nothing went right, and we can easily identify with her. When she was irritated with a nosey neighbor, the reader shares her exasperation. Above all, she worked hard, and was angry with herself for complaining.

Fortunately, the editor tells us that after the diary ends, Etta does marry Alvin, and does give birth to two sons. She dies suddenly, aged 36 of "lung congestion." The editor also gives good supplementary notes identifying people and places.

But it is Etta's own words which give warmth and magic to this diary. She was so concerned when somebody died young and left small children, or when a farmer was wiped out by grasshoppers; she was so endearing when she fought against her own exhaustion from hard work, and struggled so hard to do the "right thing." This journal is a touching love story, and a tribute to the strength of a woman who worked so hard to bring warmth and goodness to the people around her.

Jennifer Prescott McLean

Pender, Rose. *A Lady's Experiences in the Wild West in 1883,* with a forward by A. B. Guthrie, Jr. Lincoln: University of Nebraska Press, 1978.

In the spring of 1883, Lady Rose Pender spent four months with her husband and a few friends traveling in the United States. She wrote a detailed account of her travels as soon as she returned to

England. We do not know how old she was at the time of this trip, but we do know she died an old woman in 1932. Her husband, James, was one of many British who invested in ranching in the United States, although his venture was not a success.

Lady Rose's trip began in New York City, continued to Washington, D. C., and ultimately included visits to Texas, California, Salt Lake City, Cheyenne, and the Dakota Territory, with countless trips in between. Her account is interesting and appealing because the author wrote with both great detail and fervor. She brought with her the English prejudices against central heating and any people who were not white. She also brought courage and resilience. She was never afraid or too tired to go somewhere. She hiked through waist-deep snow, and loved to get out of any stage or wagon she was in to walk on ahead on her own two feet. She was enthusiastic about the things she loved: American bread, clear air, lovely views and windflowers. She was equally vehement about the things she hated: dirt, bugs, rudeness, and cruelty to animals.

Lady Rose's adventures included climbing Pike's Peak in deep snow against the advice of her guides, and with her feet tied up in burlap sacks. She visited Yosemite, was caught in a sand storm in the Mohave Desert, stayed in the most primitive of accommodations, and very nearly lost her life when she was swept away by the current while crossing a river. When she was in the northeast corner of Wyoming, she declared that ". . .the Americans pride themselves rather on not making things comfortable, so as to enhance the 'roughing.'" But the American's were unable to daunt her. "Sun Dance was a filthy den, and I declined to sleep in the place we 'ladies' were given, a sort of outhouse where fleeces and general rubbish were stored away, and I dragged my buffalo robe and blankets outside, where it was fresh, and a dear old colley came and snuggled down by me all night and kept me warm."

Lady Rose seemed to recognize a balance between the difficulties of traveling and the rewards to be earned by putting up with them. "Never in my life had I enjoyed anything half so much as our wild rough life of the past few weeks. The delicious pure air, the scenery, the strange sights and experiences, the sense of utter freedom and independence, and above all, the immunity from any ailment what-ever—a feeling of such well-being that to rise in the morning was a delight and to live and breathe a positive luxury—made our few weeks' drive over the prairies a happy time for me to look back upon for all my life."

Jennifer Prescott McLean

Pepin, Yvonne. *Cabin Journal*. Berkeley: Shameless Hussy Press, 1984.

"*Cabin Journal* is a real account of my life at age eighteen as I bra-zenly and oftentimes awkwardly set out to define my relationship to myself and others. Now, eleven years later, I have transcribed twenty-four spiral notebooks, the actual journals, and compiled art work from this past to complete *Cabin Journal* . . . . What started out to be a school project has evolved into a mode of self-exploration, discovery, and has become my companion when there has been no one to be my friend," writes Pepin about her book. This diary tells two stories: one is the story of a girl determined to prove herself in a man's world of heavy and dangerous machinery, cutting down trees, and building a log cabin. The other story concerns Pepin's coming to terms with her own sexuality, with her lesbianism.

At age eighteen when she was no longer a ward of the state, Pepin bought, with money from her deceased parents, land on an Oregon mountain to which she moved from Minnesota. There she lived in a tent while, with the help of a friend and a wandering carpenter, she learned how to build, and did much of the actual work involved in building, her own log cabin. She takes tremendous joy in her accom-plishments which are considerable for her ninety-nine pound frame (and size three work boot). She drives herself to learn the techniques necessary, and to do the work required, much of which is monoto-nous, more of which is both dangerous and difficult for her. Her pleasure in her acquired skills, and appreciation of the nature around her, are intense and compellingly expressed. We can share

264

her muscle fatigue and her excitement in the sound and smells and feel of the wildlife around her.

Complicating this enjoyment is her unresolved relationship with a woman with whom she had lived for two years prior to her move to Oregon. This woman moved with her as her lover, but then left her to live with a man. This journal is an exploration of what it means to be lesbian, and what it is like to be rejected. It is filled with probing self analysis. Pepin asks for nobody's approval of her life style but her own. She enjoys alcohol in excess, marijuana, sex, working naked, and apologizes for nothing.

Only after two months of winter is she able to understand her own need for other human beings, and to appreciate at the same time her own self-sufficiency. Once she has built the cabin and lived in it, she is ready to go back to civilization to take courses at a community college. She wants to be involved with other women, and particularly with lesbian groups.

The book, written in a tone of self inquiry, is filled with honest reporting of day to day incidents, and a sprinkling of poems. Pepin also includes her own pen and ink drawings, many of which are of a surrealistic nature. The combination allows one to know her personality to an extraordinary degree.

Jennifer Prescott McLean

Schlissel, Lillian. *WOMEN'S DIARIES OF THE WESTWARD JOURNEY*. New York: Schocken Books, 1982.

Lillian Schlissel, author and Director of American Studies at Brooklyn College, has drawn on the diaries and letters of 103 women who traveled west from 1840 to the 1960s to present a fascinating narrative interpretation of their experiences.

Schlissel organizes the first part of the book by connecting lengthy excerpts by theme and time period, and concludes with four short diaries in their entirety. We learn how the early travelers were more concerned with finding the right trail than the later ones who had far worse problems with the Indians. We are immersed in the heartache of women who went against their own will because their husbands decided they should go. We see frightened women counting graves of those killed by the cholera epidemic they thought they had left behind. We share the anguish of those split from other members of their families because of illness or a poorly built wagon. We share their apprehension for their children who died of illness and accidents along the way. We begin to understand the difficulties of being exhausted, too cold or too hot, constantly soaked, poorly fed, and above all, lonely for the life they knew.

But few of these women complained. They did the best they could with the resources available to them. Schlissel's interpretation helps us to understand all that the diaries leave out, such as any mention of pregnancies, or the connection of a mother's death with the birth of her child a day before. Her grouping the excerpts by theme contributes to a poignant understanding of the bravery and determination of these women. It is wholly absorbing reading and sheds a dramatic new light on such significant part of our country's history.

Jennifer Prescott McLean

Sprigg, June. *Domestick Beings.* New York: Knopf, 1984.

June Sprigg here uses excerpts from the diaries of seven New England women to give an impression of the every day lives of women in the eighteenth century. As she notes in her introduction, the selections are personal, not representative, and she also points out that these particular women did not speak for all women in America. For one thing, they were definitely in the minority in that they were educated enough to keep a written record, and in that minority, they were among the few who had the gift of self-expression. But the themes are universal: marriage, motherhood, home management, wearing apparel, entertainment, and the state of health.

The diarists whom Sprigg quotes are an interesting cross-section of eighteenth century women. Martha Ballard, a midwife who delivered over 900 babies in her career, was distressed at "the first woman that died in childbed which I delivered." Jemima Condict was a farmer's daughter and her diary is a record of chores and Sunday sermons, as well as a place to explore thoughts about marriage. Molly Wright Cooper was the typical farmwife, whose life contained more drudgery than seemed bearable without the release and comfort of her fundamentalist religion. Nanny Green was a 10-year old school girl who kept her journal as a letter to tell her parents of her life away from home. Abigail May was a young woman in ill-health, who kept a journal of her summer at Ballston Spa, New York, where she went in an attempt to regain her health. Rebecca Dickinson, a spinster, laments in her journal that "God only knows there is no person in the world who loves Company more than me. . . how it come about that others and all the world was in Possession of children and friends and a hous and homes while I was so od as to sit here alone?" And finally, Abigail Adams, wife of the second president, whose level of education and experience far exceeded that of most women of her time.

Sprigg gives a brief biography of her "scribblers," as she calls them, and sets each section solidly in an eighteenth century context. She has also illustrated the book with beautiful pencil drawings of authentic eighteenth century artifacts that formed a part of the woman's world. But this reviewer found the excerpts tantalizing in their brevity. What happened between May 7, 1769, when Molly Cooper wrote: "I am much distrest. No clothes irond, freted and tired almost to death and forst to stay at home;" and December 15, 1769, when she seems in better shape: ". . .I have got some clean cloths on thro mercy. Very littel done to clean the house." More of the same, or did she have one good day somewhere between having no clothes ironed and having some clean clothes on? Also, on another page, there are three selections from the diary of Martha Ballard, the first at age 70, when she is thankful that she can still do the washing; the second, on the anniversary of her 73rd birthday; and the third, at age 63, when she is worried about the state of health of her husband. Was she a widow on her 73rd birthday, or did Mr. Ballard survive even though her "hopes almost vanished that he will recover"?

But these are questions that intrigue the scholar. The general reader will be enchanted with Sprigg's selections and especially with her illustrations.

Jane DuPree Begos

Vaughan, Elizabeth. *The Ordeal of Elizabeth Vaughan: A Wartime Diary of the Philippines*. Edited by Carol M. Petillo. Athens, GA: University of Georgia Press, 1985.

Women's diaries, even May Sarton's landmark *Journal of Solitude*, exhibit a pervasive concern with communities. Elizabeth Head Vaughan, a sociology graduate student who interrupted her doctoral study in 1938 to marry civil engineer Jim Vaughan, had a professional interest in the Philippine Island communities into which she moved as a newcomer from Georgia.

However, as *A Wartime Diary of the Philippines* reveals, the community of Vaughan's first allegiance was her family. Unfortunately, Jim was in Manila on a business trip when World War II began, and was permanently cut off from his wife and their infant children (Beth, 2 and Clay, 1). He joined the United States Army and survived the Bataan death march only to die of dysentery in a military prisoner of war camp in July 1942. His wife did not learn of his death until a year later. She began the diary as an extended letter to her husband, and continued it after his death as a record for their children. This primary community becomes a lonely frame of reference for the diarist, because Vaughan's very young children, only 5 and 4 at the war's end, could never provide the intellectual reciprocity and emotional nurturing she enjoyed with her husband.

The diary itself focuses on four communities. At *Bacolod*, the capital and trade center (1939 population, ca. 58,000) a sugar producing Negro Occidental province, Vaughan was "the only American-born woman" in a foreign population. Here in a disorienting prelude to the gradually escalating way, Vaughan spent an "interminable"

December, 1941, plagued with concerns that were to consume her strength and resourcefulness throughout the next three years. Where was her husband? Would they ever meet? Would she and the children escape? How could she feed them and keep them safe? Where would she get money to live on?

At *Silay*, and *a Camp in the Hills*, December 25, 1941, to June 6, 1942, Vaughan and her children joined a community of one British and five American managerial families employed by the Hawaiian-Philippine Sugar Central (a plantation and mill), nine miles from Bacolod. As outsiders, for their first three months they nonetheless enjoyed the in-group hospitality, which consisted of a well-stocked house, servants, bridge, and dinner parties. The fall of Bataan, on April 9, 1942, made the Vaughans exiles and outsiders again, as the sugar mills closed and the families went into hiding in the nearby hills. Danger eroded the fragile communal bonds. Although the women were united in their fear of torture and rape ("The U.S. Army advises white women not be be captured alive."), some became preoccupied with making sure "that no one else gets more than they"—another infernal, eternally divisive theme through the rest of the war.

Bacolod Camp, June 7, 1942 to March 9, 1943, was an enforced community of some 125 civilians (including doctors, nurses, and seven priests), gradually rounded up by the conquering Japanese and confined to an abandoned elementary school. All the internees had to cope continually with unremitting tropical heat, flies, contaminated water, dysentery, shrinking food rations, overcrowding, lack of privacy, and the indignity of being bossed around by their former employees: "We think [Yasamori] the former carpenter. . . was placed here to humiliate us." The internees also had to contend with each other's jealousies, backbiting, tattling, goldbricking, selfishness, and unequal resources—having irritations soothed by spouses (whom Vaughan understandably envies), or by venting them in diaries such as Vaughan's.

Santo Tomas Internment Camp, March 10, 1943 to March 9, 1945, was an enormous camp of "3,500 internees of mixed races,colors, and creeds," housed on the campus of the University of Manila, where Vaughan had once taught English. She was assigned to share a small room with eight other mothers and their dozen children. Their relationships ranged from resigned tolerance to open hostility, especially when Vaughan's children kept the others awake with their explosive whooping cough or frantic crying from earaches. Vaughan herself longed to write "a sonnet of hate" to express her loathing for one roommate, a bowlegged "creature so revolting that I cannot sleep even when darkness shuts her from my sight."

Typical of the impersonal community in Santo Tomas where internees spent innumerable hours waiting in line—to eat, to buy extras at the camp store, even to use the bathroom during water shortages—was Vaughan's experience on the day in July, 1943, when she learned via a smuggled note of her husband's death: "A mother bumped into me with a baby tub of warm water as she passed down the corridor, always crowded with children and mothers. Instead of apologizing she swore at me for standing so stupidly in the middle of the corridor. . . . 'No one knows, no one cares.' I realized the awful loneliness as I went from duty to duty, like the other people, always in motion, around me."

The war, which lasted far longer than either side ever imagined, wore everyone out. The internees, starving on a rice diet (flavored with rock salt) during the war's last four months, entertained themselves by watching "daily raids, dogfights, parachutes, planes careening wildly, throwing off smoke as they crash." In February, 1945, they were liberated, though their four top Executive Committee members were shot by vindictive Japanese in retreat. They went home, Vaughan to compete her Ph.D. at the University of North Carolina, and then to teach at southern colleges until she died of cancer in 1957.

We could wish for more analytic commentary on the sociological and political aspect of these confined communities. But given the somber nature of Vaughan's experience, we can appreciate her survival, and the survival of this memorial of her "persistent, tenacious, relentless" character.

Lynn Z. Bloom

Wainwright, Sonny. *Stage V: A Journal Through Illness*. Berkeley, Acacia Books.

Sonny Wainwright is a writer, poet, and Assistant Principal of an East Harlem junior high school in New York City. Her journal, written in 1983, when she was fifty-three, describes one of her battles against cancer, and is an affirmation of her lesbianism.

The first part begins six and a half years after her second mastectomy while she is awaiting the diagnosis of her bone marrow cancer. The second largest section of the journal records her experiences during several months of hospitalization. The third part is written after she is released, close to remission.

Because the first and third parts of the journal allude to many other aspects of Wainwright's life than her illness, they are harder to follow and lack the intensity and continuity of the middle section. They include frequent intrusions of poems, quotes and allusions so the reader must search for understanding of relationships and details loosely mentioned.

The middle section detailing Wainwright's treatments and hospital stay is powerful. Through it emerges a portrait of a strong, intelligent and kind woman who is deeply committed to writing (stories, journals, poems), to her family and friends (and the Lesbian Illness Support Group), and to her own independence. Writing her journals gives her great satisfaction in otherwise unsatisfying circumstances. Her friends supported her and comforted her through each treatment with an experimental drug. They made telephone calls, paid her bills, organized her life, and most of all, gave her their time and their blood. Always she appreciated them and was grateful.

While she fought the illness, she fought for some control over her treatment and her medications. She had to endure some few doctors and nurses who were insensitive, rude and abusive, and hospital bureaucratic delays and inefficiencies. She encountered one psychiatrist who refused to understand or acknowledge the existence of Lesbian concepts of family and marriage. Yet she never wallowed in self pity and rarely complained. Wainwright ends on a note of triumph as she seems well on her way to control of the disease.

271

This journal makes no pretense of being a total portrait of a person and the incomplete picture is often confusing and tends to diminish the reader's involvement. But one can certainly admire Wainwright's bravery and strength in fighting the cancer.

Jennifer Prescott McLean

Wetherby, Cornelia, Harriet Wetherby and Berentha Chandler Hagadorn. *If Our Earthly House Dissolve, a Story of the Wetherby-Hagadorn Family of Almond, New York, Told from their Diaries and Papers.* Edited by Helene C. Phelan. Alfred, NY: The Sun Publishing Company, 1973.

Helene Phelan has cut, spliced and interpreted diaries and letters from three generations of a family who lived in western New York State. They start with a woman born in 1815, and end with her grandson who writes as late as 1917. Phelan has wisely chosen to leave out many repetitive details which do not, she thinks, shed a great deal of light on the personalities or times involved. Instead she presents entries expressing opinions, records of prices and activities, and the business of a country doctor. This editing allows the reader to have a more cosmic view of the family, and the change in personalities and life styles. The diaries are arranged chronologically and are run together when they overlap on dates in common.

The first diary is written by Berentha Chandler Hagadorn (starting in earnest about 1837) who expresses her irritation and discontent with an irresponsible husband who drinks too much and delays providing her with the promised and much-desired house. It is full of the weariness of constant moving and the problems of a hard life.

The second is the diary of a nineteen-year old girl, Cornelia Wetherby. Instead of the rather factual, forthright reporting of Chandler's diary, Cornelia's is primarily a collection of extremely self-conscious, contrived, over-dramatic essays. She groans and moans and exclaims over problems which do not seem very significant to the reader.

Cornelia marries Berentha's son Will, whose diary presents a picture of the life of a country doctor. Dr. Will rarely expressed an opinion, so it is usually hard to tell what he is thinking. Running concurrent with Dr. Will's diary is that of his mother-in-law, Harriet Wetherby. Hers is the most interesting of the diaries because over the course of years its entries change from short, factual records of activities to rather longer, more thoughtful expressions of opinion. Mrs. Wetherby does, however, refuse to mention or comment upon many of the most significant events in her life (filled in by the editor), and her diary is often more frustrating for its omissions than satisfying.

There is also a short, joint diary written by two of the sons of Cornelia and Dr. Will, written when the boys were young teenagers. The book concludes with letters written by one of these boys when he is a young man.

This collection is interesting because of the interrelationship of the diarists. It is cleverly edited and spliced. Still, one wishes the writers had expressed more opinions. The result is a record of hard working people, more interesting for their dedication than for their own characters.

Jennifer Prescott McLean

Whitely, Opal. *Opal, The Journal of an Understanding Heart.* Adapted by Jane Boulton. Tioga Publishing Company, 1984.

This enchanting book is adapted from a diary kept at the turn of the century by a mysteriously precocious six-year-old. Between punishments and chores imposed on her by "The Mama," Opal Whitely, as she was called by the Oregon lumber camp family to whom she was given after her parents died, nourished a radiant inner life by printing out her thoughts with hoarded crayons on stray wrapping papers and sacks.

A bit too Dickensian? No. By the act of naming, Opal transforms bleak and loveless circumstances into a life-affirming fable, both magical and real. As I read, I thought of Thoreau, E. B. White, Kenneth Grahame, Annie Dillard. But there is no one like Opal.

Opal's companions in her loneliness are everything the natural world offers, from spiders and lichen ("lichen folk talk in grey tones") to the pictures steam makes on the window panes of the cabin. She entertains philosophical discussions with potatoes who are "very interesting folks. / I think they must see a lot of what is going on in the earth./ They have so many eyes." Among her many animal friends are "a lovely woodrat" Thomas Chatterton Jupiter Zeus, Lars Porsena, her pet crow, and Peter Paul Rubens, the pig who follows Opal to school to her teacher's displeasure. "I did ask her what she was looking long looks at me for./ She said, 'I'm screw tin eysing you.'/ I never did hear that word before. . . I think I will have uses for it."

Such charm easily might veer toward the cute or sentimental; but Opal's shimmering celebration of the oneness of nature also copes with loss and mourning, the real text of this document. A hired boy shoots Lars Porsena. The grand tree, Michael Raphael, in whose branches Opal confided her troubles, is chopped down. Peter Paul Rubens is slaughtered. "The girl who has no seeing" dies in a fire.

With small ceremonies, Opal says good-bye to her friends, incorporating their memories into her being, just as she carries with her always "Angel Mother and Angel Father," the lost parents.

To some readers, Opal's diary may seem too artful in its insights, plot unfoldings and unconscious wit to be the spontaneous writing of child. First printed in 1920, by Atlantic Monthly Press, reprinted in 1976, by Macmillan, the authenticity of the diary has always aroused controversy. It seems that when Opal was twelve, a spiteful foster-sister tore the diary to bits. Later, when the *Atlantic* editor asked if she's ever kept a diary, Opal burst into tears and spent nine months painstakingly reconstructing the pitiful scraps. Did the twenty-year-old Opal improve on the six-year-old?

Some of the artfulness comes from the shaping hand of Palo Altan Jane Boulton, Opal's present editor, herself a gifted poet and diarist. All the words are Opal's but Boulton has broken the sentences into poetic lines. For dramatic flow, she has rearranged some events and the introduction of certain characters. There are wonderful sub-plots as we meet "the man that wears grey neckties and is kind to mice" and Elsie, the neighbor who gets the wrong baby.

Whatever the circumstances of its creation, this book works. There could be no counterfeiting the emotional truth at its heart. Small Tioga Publishing Company is to be commended for this handsomely produced edition which includes photographs, a postscript by Opal, splendid line drawings of the creatures in Opal's world, and a new afterword by the editor that tells of Opal's lifelong search for her parents.

Mary Jane Moffat

Selected Bibliography

*T*he bibliography to this volume is selective and does not pretend to be complete in any way. Diaries and works dealing with diaries that are mentioned in the text are included, as well as those published since 1977, when I privately published the first *Annotated Bibliography of Published Women's Diaries*. Since that time, many other excellent and more extensive bibliographies have been published and there is no reason to duplicate their efforts.

BIBLIOGRAPHIES

Addis, Patricia K. *Through a Woman's I. An Annotated Bibliography of American Women's Autobiographical Writings, 1946-1976.* Metuchen, NJ & London: The Scarecrow Press, 1983. 2217 listings of personal narratives including autobiographies, letters, diaries & journals, memoirs, reminiscences and travel accounts.

Aitken, James, ed. *English Diaries of the XVI, XVII and XVIII Centuries.* Harmondsworth, Eng. & New York: Allen Lane, Penguin Books, 1941

_____. *English Diaries of the XIX Century, 1800-1850.* Harmondsworth, Eng.: Penguin Books, 1944.

Arksey, Laura, Nancy Pries, and Marcia Reed, eds. *American Diaries: An Annotated Bibliography of Published American Diaries and Journals.* Detroit, Mich.: Gale Research Co., 1983. 2 vols.

Batts, John Stuart. *British Manuscript Diaries of the Nineteenth Century: An Annotated Listing.* Totowa, NJ: Rowman & Littlefield, 1976.

Begos, Jane DuPree. *An Annotated Bibliography of Published Women's Diaries.* Pound Ridge, NY: Privately Printed, 1977.

_____. *An Annotated Bibliography of Published Women's Diaries.* Supplement I - "European Sources." Pound Ridge, NY: Privately printed, 1984

_____. *Subject Bibliography No. 1 - Artists, Photographers, Visual Diaries.* Pound Ridge, NY: Privately Printed, 1986.

Bitton, Davis. *Guide to Mormon Diaries and Autobiographies.* Provo, Utah: Brigham Young University Press, 1977.

Brinton, Howard Haines. *Quaker Journals; Varieties of Religious Experience Among Friends.* Wallingford, PA: Pendle Hill Publications, 1972.

Briscoe, Mary Louise, Barbara Tobias, and Lynn Z. Bloom, ed. *American Autobiography 1945-1980.* Madison, WI: University of Wisconsin Press, 1982. Contains 5000 annotated entries, including many women's diaries, journals and travel accounts, a large number of which cover periods before 1945, as reprints and new issues of old manuscripts were included.

Fairbanks, Carol and Sara Brooks Sundberg. *Farm Women on the Prairie Frontier: A Sourcebook for Canada and the United States.* Metuchen, NY & London: The Scarecrow Press, 1983. Includes references to many diaries and journals.

Forbes, Mrs. Harriette, comp. *New England Diaries, 1602-1800. A Descriptive Catalogue of Diaries, Orderly Books and Sea Journals.* Topsfield, MA: Privately printed, 1923. Reprinted in 1976 by Russell & Russell, New York.

Goodfriend, Joyce D., comp. *The Published Diaries and Letters of American Women. An Annotated Bibliography.* Boston: G. K. Hall & Co., 1987.

Hinding, Andrea, ed. *Women's History Sources: A Guide to Archives and Manuscript Collections in the United States.* Greenwich, CT: R. R. Bower, 1980. 3 vols.

Huff, Cynthia. *British Women's Diaries. A Descriptive Bibliography of Selected Nineteenth-Century Women's Manuscript Diaries.* New York: AMS Press, 1985.

Matthews, William, comp. *American Diaries: An Annotated Bibliography of American Diaries Written Prior to the Year 1861.* Berkeley, CA: University of California Press, 1945.

_____. *American Diaries in Manuscript, 1580-1954. A Descriptive Bibliography.* Athens, GA: The University of Georgia Press, 1974.

_____. *British Diaries: An Annotated Bibliography of British Diaries Written Between 1442 and 1942.* Berkeley, CA: University of California Press, 1950.

_____. *Canadian Diaries and Autobiographies.* Berkeley, CA: University of California Press, 1950.

ANTHOLOGIES

Culley, Margo, ed. *A Day at a Time. Being The Diary Literature of American Women from 1766 to the Present.* New York: The Feminist Press at the City University of New York, 1985. (Reviewed)

Dunaway, Philip and Mel Evans, eds. *A Treasury of the World's Great Diaries.* Garden City, NY: Doubleday & Co., Inc. 1957.

Franklin, Penelope, ed. *Private Pages: Diaries of American Women 1830s-1970s.* New York: Ballantine, 1986.

Goodfriend, Joyce D. and Claudia M. Christie. *Lives of American Women. A History with Documents.* Boston: Little, Brown and Company, 1981.

Hampsten, Elizabeth, comp. *To All Inquiring Friends.: Letters, Diaries and Essays in North Dakota.* Grand Forks, ND: University of North Dakota Press, 1979. (Reviewed)

Holliday, Laurel, ed. *Heart Songs: The Intimate Diaries of Young Girls.* New York: Methuen, 1980.

Lifshin, Lyn, ed. *Ariadne's Thread. A Collection of Contemporary Women's Journals.* NY: Harper & Row, 1982. In hardcover and paperback. (Reviewed)

Moffat, Mary Jane and Charlotte Painter, eds. *Revelations: Diaries of Women.* New York: Random House, 1974. Issued in paperback in 1975 by Random House/Vintage, New York.

GENERAL WORKS

ANAIS, An International Journal. Los Angeles, CA: The Anaïs Nin Foundation. Pubished annually. (Reviewed)

ANTAEUS. Journals, Notebooks & Diaries. No. 61 (Autumn, 1988). New York: The Ecco Press, 1988.

Baldwin, Christina. *One to One, Self-Understanding Through Journal Writing*. New York: M. Evans and Company, 1977. (Reviewed)

Benstock, Shari, ed. *The Private Self. Theory and Practice of Women's Autobiographical Writings*. Chapel Hill, NC: University of North Carolina Press, 1988.

Blanch, Lesley. *The Wilder Shores of Love*. Harmondswroth, Eng.: Penguin Books, 1959 (c1954). (Life in a Foreign Culture - North Africa, Middle East)

Bolitho, Hector. *A Biographer's Notebook*. New York: The Macmillan Company, 1950. (Quaker women)

BOOK FORUM. Essays Diaries Letters. Vol. IV, no. 3 (1979). Rhinecliff, NY: Hudson River Press, 1979.

Capacchione, Lucia. *The Creative Journal. The Art of Finding Yourself*. Chicago: The Swallow Press. 1979.

Cargas, Harry J. and Radley, Roger J. *Keeping a Spiritual Journal*. Garden City: Doubleday/Nazareth Books, 1981.

Clinton, Catherine. *The Plantation Mistress. Woman's World in the Old South*. New York: Pantheon Books, 1982.

Faragher, John Mack. *Women and Men on the Overland Trail*. New Haven: Yale University Press, 1979.

Fischer, Christiane, ed. *Let Them Speak for Themselves: Women in the American West, 1849-1900*. Hamden, CT: Shoe String Press, 1977.

Fothergill, Robert A. *Private Chronicles: A Study of English Diaries*. New York: Oxford University Press, 1974.

Fraser, Antonia. *The Weaker Vessel: Women's Lot in Seventeenth Century England*. New York: Alfred A. Knopf, 1984.

Friedman, Jean E. *The Enclosed Garden. Women and Community in the Evangelical South, 1830-1900*. Chapel Hill, NC: University of North Carolina Press, 1985.

Green, Harvey. *The Light of the Home. An Intimate View of the Women in Victorian America*. New York: Pantheon Books, 1983.

Holmes, Kenneth L., ed. *Covered Wagon Women: Diaries and Letters from the Western Trails, 1840-1890*. Glendale, CA: A. N. Clark Co., 1983 -. 7 vols. to date.

Jelinek, Estelle C., ed. *Women's Autobiography: Essays in Criticism*. Bloomington, IN: Indiana University Press, 1980.

_____. *The Tradition of Women's Autobiography: From Antiquity to the Present*. Boston: Twayne Publishers, 1986.

Jensen, Joan, M. *Loosening the Bonds: Mid-Atlantic Farm Women, 1750-1850*. New Haven: Yale University Press, 1986.

_____. *With These Hands. Women Working on the Land*. Old Westbury, NY: The Feminist Press, 1981.

Jones, Katharine M., ed. *Heroines of Dixie: Confederate Women Tell Their Story of the War*. Westport, CT: Greenwood Press, 1984.

Kagle, Steven E. *American Diary Literature, 1620-1799*. Boston: Twayne Publishers, 1979.

_____. *Early Nineteenth-Century American Diary Literature*. Boston: Twayne Publishers, 1986.

_____. *Late Nineteenth-Century American Diary Literature*. Boston: Twayne Publishers, 1988.

Kaufman, Polly Welts. *Women Teachers on the Frontier*. New Haven: Yale University Press, 1984. (Reviewed)

Kelsey, Morton T. *Adventure Inward. Christian Growth Through Personal Journal Writing*. Minneapolis: Augsburg Publishing House, 1980.

Kolodny, Annette. *The Land Before Her. Fantasy and Experience of the American Frontiers, 1630-1860*. Chapel Hill, NC: University of North Carolina Press, 1984.

Leavitt, Judith Walzer. *Brought to Bed. Childbearing in America, 1750 to 1950*. New York: Oxford University Press, 1986.

Lebsock, Suzanne. *The Free Women of Petersburg: Status and Culture in a Southern Town, 1784-1860*. New York: W. W. Norton & Co., 1984.

Luchetti, Cathy and Olwell, Carol. *Women of the West*. St. George, UT: Antelope Island Press, 1982.

Lyons, Robert. *Autobiography. A Reader for Writers*. New York: Oxford University Press, 1977.

Mallon, Thomas, *A Book of One's Own*. New York: Ticknor and Fields, 1984. (Reviewed)

Morris, Jill. *The Dream Notebook*. Boston: Little, Brown and Company, 1985. (Applications)

Myres, Sandra L. *Ho for California: Women's Overland Diaries from* the *Huntington Library*. San Marino, CA: Huntington Library, 1980.

Nirenststein, Virginia King. *With Kindly Voices: A Nineteenth-Century Georgia Family*. Macon, GA: Tullous Books, 1984.

Pocock, Guy Noël, ed. *Some English Diarists*. New York: E. P. Dutton, 1924.

Ponsonby, Arthur. *English Diaries; A Review of English Diaries from the Sixteenth to the Twentieth Century with an Introduction on Diary Writing*. London: Methuen & Co., Ltd. 1923.

_____. *More English Diaries: Further Reviews of Diaries from the Sixteenth to the Nineteenth Century with an Introduction on Diary Reading*. London: Methuen & Co., Ltd., 1927.

Rainer, Tristine. *The New Diary, How to Use a Journal for Self-Guidance and Expanded Creativity*. Los Angeles: J. P Tarcher, Inc. 1978. (Reviewed)

Rothman, Ellen K. *Hands and Hearts. A History of Courtship in America*. New York: Basic Books, Inc. 1984.

Schlissel, Lillian. *WOMEN'S DIARIES OF THE WESTWARD JOURNEY*. New York: Schocken Books, 1982. (Reviewed)

Scott, Anne Firor. *The Southern Lady: From Pedestal to Politics*, 1830-1930. Chicago: The University of Chicago Press, 1970.

Sears, Clara Endicott. *Gleanings from Old Shaker Journals*. Boston: Houghton Mifflin Company, 1916.

Shea, Daniel B., Jr. *Spiritual Autobiography in Early America*. Princeton, NJ: Princeton University Press, 1968. (Quaker Diaries)

Simons, George F. *Keeping Your Personal Journal*. New York: Paulist Press, 1978.

Spalding, Philip Anthony. *Self-Harvest. A Study of Diaries and the Diarist*. London: Independent Press, 1949.

Sprigg, June, *Domestic Beings*. New York: Alfred A. Knopf, 1984. (Reviewed)

Spruill, Julia Cherry. *Life and Work of Women in the Southern Colonies*. Chapel Hill, NC: University of North Carolina Press, 1938.

Stanton, Donna C. ed. *The Female Autograph. Theory and Practice of Autobiography from the Tenth to the Twentieth Century*. Chicago: The University of Chicago Press, 1987 (c1984).

Stein, Leon, ed. *Fragments of Autobiography. Women in America from Colonial Times to the Twentieth Century.* New York: Arno Press, 1974.

Sterling, Dorothy. *We Are Your Sisters: Black Women in the Nineteenth Century.* New York: W.W. Norton & Co., 1984.

Sternburg, Janet, ed. *The Writer on Her Work.* New York: W. W. Norton & Co., 1980.

Stowell, H. E. *Quill Pens and Petticoats. A Portrait of Women of Letters.* London: Wayland Publishers, 1970.

Ulrich, Laurel. *Good Wives: Image and Reality in the Lives of Women in Northern New England, 1650-1750.* New York: Oxford University Press, 1983 (c1982).

Van Kirk, Sylvia. *Many Tender Ties. Women in Fur-Trade Society, 1670-1870.* Norman, OK: University of Oklahoma Press, 1983 (c1980).

Watkins, Owen C. *The Puritan Experience.* London: Routledge and Kegan Paul, 1972. (Quaker Diaries)

Welter, Barbara. *Dimity Convictions: The American Woman in the Nineteenth Century.* Athens, OH: Ohio University Press, 1976.

Wharton, Anne Hollingsworth. *Colonial Days and Dames.* New York: Arno Press, 1977.

Whitman, Ruth. *Becoming a Poet. Source - Process - Practice.* Boston: The Writer, Inc. 1982.

Wright, Luella M. *The Literary Life of the Early Friends: 1650-1725.* New York: Columbia University Press, 1932 (Quaker Diaries)

INDIVIDUALS

Alexander, Eveline M. *Cavalry Wife: The Diary of Eveline M. Alexander, 1866-1867.* College Station, TX: Texas A & M University Press, 1977. (Reviewed)

Antrim, Louisa, Lady. *Louisa, Lady in Waiting.* New York: Mayflower Books, 1979. (Reviewed)

Arden, Cathy. *My Sister's Picture.* New York: Simon & Schuster, 1986. (Journals of Cathy and Doren Arden. Death of a Sibling - Cancer)

Ashbridge, Elizabeth. *Some Accounts of the Life of Elizabeth Ashbridge.* Philadelphia: Friends Book Store, n.d. (Quaker)

[Balano, Dorothea] Balano, James W., ed. *The Log of the Skipper's Wife.* Camden, ME: Down East Books, 1979. (Travel - Sailing Ship.)

Barnard, Anne, Lady. *The Letters of Lady Anne Barnard to Henry Dundas, from the Cape and Elsewhere, 11793-1803, together with her Journal of a Tour into the Interior, and certain other letters.* Cape Town: A. A. Balkema, 1973. (Travel - Cape of Good Hope.)

Bauman, Janina. *Winter in the Morning: A Young Girl's Life in the Warsaw Ghetto and Beyond 1939-1945.* New York: The Free Press, 1986. (Based on Diaries - Holocaust.)

Bayard, Martha Pintard. *The Journal of Martha Pintard Bayard, London 1794-1797.* New York: Dodd, Mead & Co., 1894. (Life in a Foreign Culture)

Berenson, Mary. *Mary Berenson. A Self-Portrait from her Diaries and Letters.* New York: W. W. Norton & Co., 1983. (Ex-patriate - Italy)

Berkeley, Maud. *Maud. The Diaries of Maud Berkeley.* London: Secker & Warburg, 1985. (Visual Diary)

Bevington, Helen. *The Journey is Everything: A Journal of the Seventies.* Durham, NC: Duke University Press, 1983.

Bishop, Isabella Bird. *This Grand Beyond. The Travels of Isabella Bird Bishop.* Selected by Cicely Palser Havely. London: Century Publishing, 1984. (Travel - Selections from Each of Her Books)

Bisland, Elizabeth. *A Flying Trip Around the World, in Seven Stages.* New York: Harper, 1891. (Travel)

Blake, Mary E. *On the Wing. Rambling Notes of a Trip to the Pacific.* Boston: Lee & Shepard, 1883. (Travel)

Blankenship, Jayne. *In the Center of the Night. Journey through a Bereavement.* New York: G.P. Putnam's Sons, 1984. (Reviewed)

Bogan, Louise. *Journey Around My Room: The Autobiography of Louise Bogan.* New York: Viking, 1980. (With Journal Excerpts)

Bonfield, Lynn A. *Jailed for Survival. The Diary of an Anti-Nuclear Activist.* San Francisco: Mother Courage Affinity Group, 1984. (Reviewed)

Bradford, Ruth. *"Maskee!" The Journal and Letters of Ruth Bradford, 1861-1872.* Hartford, CT: The Prospect Press, 1938. (Travel - China by Clipper Ship)

Branson, Ann. *The Journal of a Minister of the Gospel in the Society of*

Friends. Philadelphia: Wm. H. Piles Sons, 1892. (Quaker)

Brooks, Anne M., *The Grieving Time: A Month by Month Account of Recovery from Loss.* Garden City, NY: The Dial Press/Doubleday & Company, Inc. 1985. (Reviewed)

Chesler, Phyllis. *With Child. A Diary of Motherhood.* New York: Thos. Y. Crowell, 1979. (Pregnancy and Childbirth)

[Chestnut, Mary] Woodward, C. Vann, ed. *Mary Chestnut's Civil War.* New Haven: Yale University Press, 1981. (The Original Diary)

Clark, Eleanor. *Tamrart. 13 Days in the Sahara.* New York: Stuart Wright, Publisher, 1984. (Travel - North Africa)

Clarke, Caroline Cowles. *The Diary of Caroline Cowles Richards, 1852-1872, Canandigua, New York..* Rochester, NY: Privately Printed, 1908.

Clarke, Elizabeth Dodge Huntington. *Joy of Service. Memoirs of Elizabeth Dodge Huntington Clarke.* New York: National Board of the YWCA, 1979. (Based on Diaries. Life in a Foreign Culture - Turkey)

Clawson, Augusta. *Shipyard Diary of a Woman Welder.* New York: Penguin Books, 1944. (World War II)

Cooper, Mary, *The Diary of Mary Cooper, Life on a Long Island Farm 1768-1773.* Oyster Bay, NY: Oyster Bay Historical Society, 1981. (Reviewed)

Cooper, Susan Fenimore. *Rural Hours. Journal of a Naturalist in the United States.* Syracuse, NY: Syracuse University Press, 1968. (Facsimile of the 1887 edition - Nature Diary)

Coppola, Eleanor. *Notes.* New York: Pocket Books, 1980 (c1979). (Travel - Philippines)

Courtney, Kate. *Extracts from a War Diary.* Chelsea, London: Printed for private circulation by Victor Press, 1927. (World War I)

Crouter, Natalie. *Forbidden Diary: A Record of Wartime Internment 1941-1945..* New York: Burt Franklin & Co.,1980. (Reviewed)

Cullwick, Hannah. *The Diaries of Hannah Cullwick, Victorian Maidservant.* New Brunswick, NJ: Rutgers University Press, 1985. (Reviewed)

Curd, Sam[uella]. *Sam Curd's Diary. The Diary of a True Woman.* Athens, OH: Ohio University Press, 1984. (Reviewed)

Davidson, Robyn. *Tracks.* New York: Pantheon, 1981. (Travel - Australia)

Day, Dorothy. *By Little and by Little. The Selected Writings of Dorothy Day.* New York: Alfred A. Knopf, 1983. (With Diary Excerpts - Spiritual)

_____. *On Pilgrimage.* New York: Catholic Worker Books, 1948. (Journal for a Year - Spiritual)

[de Cleyre, Voltairine] Avrich, Paul. *An American Anarchist. The Life of Voltairine de Cleyre.* Princeton, NJ: Princeton University Press, 1979. (Based on Journals)

Dodwell, Christiana. *In Papua New Guinea.* London: The Oxford Illustrated Press, 1983. (Travel)

_____. *A Traveler in China.* New York: Beaufort Books, 1986. (Travel)

[Donovan, Jean] Carrigan, Ana. *Salvador Witness: The Life and Calling of Jean Donovan.* New York: Simon & Schuster, 1984. (Based on Her Diary - Life in a Foreign Culture - Salvador)

Dow, Peggy. *Vicissitudes in the Wilderness; Exemplified in the Journal of Peggy Dow.* Norwich, CT: Printed by W. Faulkner, 1833. (Pious Memoir)

Dufferin, Hariot, Lady. *My Canadian Journal 1872-1878.* Don Mills, Ont.: Longmans Canada Ltd., 1969. (Travel)

[Duniway, Abigail Scott] Moynihan, Ruth Barnes. *Rebel for Rights, Abigail Scott Duniway.* New Haven: Yale University Press, 1983. (Includes 1852 Journal of her Overland Trip.)

Edmonds, Amanda Virginia. *Journals of Amanda Virginia Edmonds, Lass of the Mosby Confederacy, 1859-1867.* Stephens City, VA: Commercial Press, 1984. (Civil War)

Edwards, Amelia B. *A Thousand Miles Up the Nile.* Los Angeles: J. P. Tarcher, 1983. (Travel - Egypt, 1873)

Eggleston, Hazel. *St. Lucia Diary. A Caribbean Memoir.* Old Greenwich, CT: Devin-Adair Co., 1977. (Life in a Foreign Culture - Caribbean Islands)

Ellice, Jane. *The Diary of Jane Ellice.* Toronto: Oberon Press, c1975.

Farnsworth, Martha. *Plains Woman, the Diary of Martha Farnsworth, 1882-1922.* Bloomington, IN: Indiana University Press, 1986. (Reviewed)

Fell, Sarah. *The Household Account Book of Sarah Fell of Swarthmoor*

Hall. Cambridge, Eng.:Cambridge University Press, 1920. (Quaker)

Ferland, Carol. *The Long Journey Home.* New York: Alfred A. Knopf, 1980. (Personal Illness - Nervous Breakdown)

Fernea, Elizabeth Warnock. *A Street in Marrakech. A Personal Encounter with the Lives of Moroccan Women.* Garden City, NY: Anchor Press/Doubleday, 1980. (c1975. (Life in a Foreign Culture - Morocco)

Field, Joanna. *A Life of One's Own.* Los Angeles: J. P. Tarcher, 1981 (c1976). (Applications)

[Fields, Annie] Howe, M. A. DeWolfe. *Memories of a Hostess. A Chronicle of Eminent Friendships Drawn Chiefly from the Dairies of Mrs. James T. Fields.* Boston: Atlantic Monthly Press, 1922.

[Fiennes, Celia] Morris, Christopher, ed. *The Illustrated Journeys of Celia Fiennes.* London: MacDonald & Co., 1982. (Early English Diary)

[Fish, Mary] Buel, Joy Day and Richard Buel, Jr. *The Way of Duty: A Woman and Her Family in Revolutionary America.* New York: W. W. Norton & Co. 1984. (Pious Memoir)

Fisher, Lois. *A Peking Diary. A Personal Account of Modern China.* New York: St. Martin;'s Press, 1979. (Travel)

Fisk, Erma J. *Parrots' Wood.* New York: W.W. Norton & Co., 1985. (Reviewed)

_____. *The Peacocks of Baboquivari.* New York: W. W. Norton & Co., 1983. (Reviewed)

French, Emily. *Emily: The Diary of a Hard-Worked Woman.* Lincoln, NB: University of Nebraska Press, 1987. (19th Century Working Woman)

Frobel, Anne S. *The Civil War Diary of Anne S. Frobel of Wilton Hill in Virginia.* Florence, AL: Privately Printed, 1986.

Gellhorn, Martha. *Travels with Myself and Another.* New York: Dodd, Mead, 1979. (Travel - China, Russia, Israel, the Caribbean)

Gilcrist, Ellen. *Falling Through Space: The Journals of Ellen Gilcrist.* Boston: Little, Brown, 1988. (A collection of Radio Monologues)

Giles, Nell. *Punch in, Susie! A Woman's War Factory Diary.* New York: Harper and Bros., 1943. (World War II)

Gladstone, Mary. *Mary Gladstone, Her Diaries and Letters.* New York: E.P. Dutton and Company, Inc., 1930.

Greene, Ruth Altman. *Hsiang-Ya Journal.* Hamden, CT: Shoe String Press/Archon Books, 1977. (Life in a Foreign Culture - China)

Gregory, Lucy. *My Beloved is Mine and I am His: Extracts from the Diary of Lucy Gregory, 1829-1876.* Leominster, Eng.: Orphans Printing Press, 1877. (Quaker)

Grove, Harriet. *The Journal of Harriet Grove for the Years 1790-1810.* London: Privately printed, 1932.

Gurney, Elizabeth. *Elizabeth Fry's Journeys on the Continent 1840-1841 from a Diary Kept by Her Niece Elizabeth Gurney.* London: John Lane the Bodley Head Ltd., 1931. (Quaker)

[Hagadorn, Berentha Chandler and Cornelia Wetherby] Phelan, Helene C., ed. *If Our Earthly House Dissolve: A Story of the Wetherby-Hagadorn Family of Almond, N.Y., from their diaries and papers.* Alfred, NY: The Sun Publishing Co., 1973.

Hampsten, Elizabeth, *Read This Only To Yourself, the Private Writings of Midwestern Women, 1880-1910.* Bloomington: Indiana University Press, 1982. (Reviewed)

Hardy, Emma. *Emma Hardy's Diaries.* New York: Mid Northumberland Arts Group and Carcanet New Press, 1985. (Travel - Europe, 1874-1897)

Harrell-Bond, Barbara E. *Diary of a Revolution Which Might Have Been.* Hanover, NH: American Universities Field Staff, 1980. (Travel - Africa)

Harrison, Michelle, M.D. *A Woman in Residence.* New York: Random House, 1982. (Single Parent)

Harvey, Margaret B. *A Journal of a Voyage from Philadelphia to Cork: in the Year of Our Lord 1809 together with a Description of a Sojourn in Ireland.* Philadelphia: West Park Publishing Company, 1915. (Quaker)

Havens, Catherine Elizabeth. *Diary of a Little Girl in Old New York.* New York: H. C. Browne, 1919. (Childhood)

Helm, Edith. *The Captains and the Kings.* New York: G. P. Putnam's Sons, 1954. (White House Social Secretary under the Roosevelts)

Hoby, Lady Margaret. *Diary of Lady Margaret Hoby, 1599-1605.* London: Routledge & Sons, 1930.

Hundon, Sarah Raymond. *Overland Days to Montana in 1865; the Diary of Sarah Raymond and Journal of Dr. Waid Howard.* Glendale, CA: A. H. Clark Co., 1971.

Hersey, Jean. *A Widow's Pilgrimage.* New York: A Continuum Book/ The Seabury Press, 1979. (Death of Spouse)

Hillesum, Etty. *An Interrupted Life: The Diaries of Etty Hillesum, 1941-1943.* New York: Pantheon Books, 1983. (Holocaust)

Holdren, Shirley and Susan. *Why God Gave Mr Pain.* Chicago: Loyola University Press, 1984. (Death of a Child - Leukemia)

Hubbell, Sue. *A Country Year. Living the Questions.* New York: Harper & Row/Perennial Library, 1987. (Nature Diary)

Hunt, Sarah. *Journal of the Life and Religious Labors of Sarah Hunt.* Philadelphia: Friends Book Association, 1892. (Quaker)

Hyde, Nancy Maria. *The Writings of Nancy Maria Hyde of Norwich, Conn., connected with a sketch of her life.* Norwich, CT: Russell Hubbard, 1816. (Nineteenth Century Education)

[Jackson, Nannie Stillwell] *Vinegar Pie and Chicken Bread. A Woman's Diary of Life in the Rural South, 1890-1891.* Fayetteville, AR: University of Arkansas Press, 1982. (Reviewed)

[Jackson, Mother Rebecca] Williams, Richard. *Called and Chosen. The Story of Mother Rebecca Jackson and the Philadelphia Shakers.* Metuchen, NJ: The Scarecrow Press, Inc. & American Theological Library Assn. 1981. (Spiritual)

Jenks, Kathleen. *Journey of a Dream Animal: A Human Search for Personal Identity.* New York: Julian Press, 1975. (Dream Diary)

[Jesse, F. Tennyson] Colenbrander, Joanna: *A Portrait of Fryn: A Biography of F. Tennyson Jesse.* New York: Andre Deutsch, 1984. (Based on Diaries)

Journal of Anna May. Edited by George W. Robinson. Cambridge, MA: Privately Printed, 1941. (Nineteenth-Century Women's Education)

Keith, Agnes. *Three Came Home.* Boston: Little, Brown, 1947. (Internment Diary)

[Kinsley, Jessie Catherine] Rich, Jane Kinsley, ed. *A Lasting Spring. Jessie Catherine Kinsley, Daughter of the Oneida Community.* Syracuse, NY: Syracuse University Press, 1980. (Based on Diaries)

Lady, A. (M. E. P. B.) *Bubbles and Ballast. Being a Description of Life in Paris During the Brilliant Days of Empire; A Tour through Belgum and Holland, and a Sojourn in London.* Baltimore: Kelly, Piet & Co., 1871. (Travel)

Lady, A, of New York. *Over the Ocean, or Glimpses of Travel in Many Lands.* New York: Paine & Burgess, 1846. (Travel)

Lane, Rose Wilder and Helen Dore Boylston. *Travels with Zenobia: Paris to Albania by Model T Ford. A Journal*. Columbia, MO: University of Missouri Press, 1983. (Reviewed)

[Lange, Dorothea] Meltzer, Milton. *Dorothea Lange: A Photographer's Life.* New York: Farrar Stauss & Grioux, 1978. (Quotes Journals)

Langeloth, Valeria. *The Journal of My Trip Around the World.* Riverside, CT: Privately Printed, 1926. (Travel)

[Larcom, Lucy] Addison, Daniel Dulany, ed. *Lucy Larcom, Life, Letters, and Diary.* Boston: Houghton Mifflin & Co., 1895.

Lee, Agnes. *Growing Up in the 1850's, The Journal of Agnes Lee.* Chapel Hill: The University of North Carolina Press, 1984. (Reviewed)

Lee, Andrea. *Russian Journal.* New York: Random House/Vintage Books, 1981. (Life in a Foreign Culture)

Lee, Laurel. *Mourning into Dancing.* New York: E. P. Dutton, 1984. (Inspirational Journal)

Leitch, Mary and Margaret W. *Seven Years in Ceylon. Stories of Missionary Life.* New York: American Tract Society, 1890. (Life in a Foreign Culture)

L'Engle, Madeleine. *The Crosswicks Journal.* New York: Seabury Press/A Crossroad Book, 1980. 3 vols.

Leigh, Frances Butler. *My Ten Years on a Georgia Plantation.* London: R. Bentley, 1883. Also by Macmillan, New York, 1913. (Daughter of Fanny Kemble)

LePere, Gene. *Never Pass This Way Again.* New York: Adler & Adler, 1987. (Imprisonment in a Foreign Culture - Turkey)

Lerner, Gerda. *A Death of One's Own.* New York: Simon & Schuster, 1978. (Death of Spouse)

Lewis, Abigail. *An Interesting Condition. The Diary of a Pregnant Woman.* Garden City, NY: Doubleday & Co., 1950. (Pregnancy and Childbirth)

[Loomis, Vivienne] Mack, John E. and Holly Hickler. *Vivienne. The Life and Suicide of an Adolescent Girl.* New York: New American Library, 1982 (c1981) (Includes her Diary)

Lorde, Audre. *The Cancer Journals.* Argyle, NY: Spinsters Ink, 1981. (Life-Threatening Illness - Cancer)

Love, Helen Stewart. *Diary of Helen Stewart, 1853.* Eugene, OR: Lane County Pioneer-Historical Society, 1961. (Overland Journey)

Lynch, Dorothea. *Exploding Into Life.* New York: Aperture, 1985. (Life-Threatening Illness - Cancer)

McCormick, Anne O'Hare. *Vatican Journal 1921-1954.* New York: Farrar, Straus and Cudahy, 1957. (A Foreign Correspondent)

[McKaig, Pricilla] *The McKaig Journal: A Confederate Family of Cumberland.* Cumberland, MD: Allegany County Historical Society, 1984. (Reviewed)

Mackay, Helen. *Journal of Small Things.* New York: Duffiend, 1917. (World War I)

Malkiel, Theresa Serber. *The Diary of a Shirtwaist Striker, a Story of the Shirtwaist Maker's Strike in New York.* New York: The Co-Operative Press, c1910.

Malloy, Ione. *Southie Won't Go: A Teacher's Diary of the Desegregation of South Boston High School.* Bloomington, IL: University of Illinois Press, 1986.

Manning, Nichola. *Historical Document.* Long Beach, CA: Applezaba Press, 1979. (Reviewed)

Matschat, Ceclie Hulse. *Seven Grass Huts. An Engineer's Wife in Central-and-South America.* New York: Literary Guild of America, 1939. (Life in a Foreign Culture)

[Maynard, Constance Louise] Firth, C. B. *Constance Louise Maynard. Mistress of Westfield College.* London: George Allen and Unwin Ltd., 1949. (Based on Diaries)

Milburn, Clara. *Mrs. Milburn's Diaries. An Englishwoman's Day-to-Day Reflections 1939-45.* New York: Schocken Books, 1980. (World War II)

Mitchell, Maria. *Maria Mitchell: Life, Letters, and Journals.* Freeport, NY: Books for Libraries Press, 1971.

Mooney, Elizebeth. *In the Shadow of the White Plague.* New York:

Thomas Y. Crowell, 1979. (Death of Mother -TB)

Mott, Lucretia. *Slavery and "The Woman Question:" Lucretia Mott's Diary of Her Visit to Great Britain to Attend the World's Anti-Slavery Convention of 1840.* Haverford, PA: Friends' Historical Association, 1952. (Quaker)

[Newman, A. E.] *Evangeline. European Leaflets, for Young Ladies.* New York: John F. Baldwin, 1861. (Travel)

Newport, Elizabeth. *A Memoir of Elizabeth Newport.* Philadelphia: John Comly, 1874. (Quaker)

Nin, Anaïs, *Linotte. The Early Diary of Anaïs Nin, 1914-1920.* New York: Harcourt Brace Jovanovich,1978 .

_____. *The Early Diary of Anaïs Nin, Volume Two,1920-1923 .* New York: Harcourt Brace Jovanovich,1982

_____. *The Early Diary of Anaïs Nin, Volume Three, 1923-1927.* New York: Harcourt Brace Jovanovich,1983.

_____. *The Early Diary of Anaïs Nin, Volume Four, 1927-1931.* New York: Harcourt Brace Jovanovich,1985.

_____. *Henry and June: From the Unexpurgated Diary of Anaïs Nin.* New York: Harcourt Brace Jovanovich, 1986.

Oakes, Maud. *Beyond the Windy Place. Life in the Guatemalan Highlands.* New York: Farrar, Straus and Young, 1951. (Life in a Foreign Culture)

Oakley, Deborah. *Journal of a Trip to China, August 17 - September 6, 1977.* Ann Arbor, MI: University of Michigan Press, 1977. (Travel)

Origo, Iris. *War in Val d'Orcia - 1943-44: A Diary.* Boston: David Godine, 1984. (Reviewed)

Orr, Lucinda. *Journal of a Young Lady of Virginia, 1782.* Baltimore: J. Murphy, 1871.

Owen, Marget. *The Book of Maggie Owen.* New York: Grosset & Dunlap, 1941. (Childhood)

Parkerson, Julia Etta. *Etta's Journal, January 2, 1874-July 25, 1875.* Newington, CT: Privately Printed, 1981. (Reviewed)

Partridge, Frances. *Everything to Lose: Diaries 1945-1960.* Boston: Little, Brown and Company, 1985. (Bloomsbury Group)

_____. *Love in Bloomsbury. Memories.* Boston: Little, Brown and Company, 1981. (With Diary Excerpts)

Paz, Juana Maria. *The La Luz Journal. Autobiographical Account of Lesbian of Colour Land.* Fayetteville, AR: Paz Press, 1982.

Peabody, Barbara. *The Screaming Room. A Mother's Journal of Her Son's Struggle with AIDS.* San Diego, CA: Oak Tree Publications, Inc., 1986. (Death of a Child)

Peabody, Elizabeth Palmer. *Record of a School.* New York: Arno Press, 1977. (Reprint of 1836 edition) ((Nineteenth-Century Education)

Pember, Phoebe Yates. *A Southern Woman's Story.* New York: G. W. Carleton, 1879. (Civil War)

Pembroke, Anne, Countess of. *The Diary of Lady Anne Clifford.* London: William Heinemann, 1923.

Pepin, Yvonne. *Cabin Journal.* Berkeley, CA: Shameless Hussy Press, 1984. (Reviewed)

_____. *Three Summers. A Journal.* Berkeley, CA: Shameless Hussy Press, 1986.

Pepys, Emily. *The Journal of Emily Pepys.* Charlottesville, VA: The University of Virginia Press, 1984. (Childhood)

Pender, Rose. *A Lady's Experiences in the Wild West in 1883.* Lincoln, NB: University of Nebraska Press, 1978. (Reviewed)

Plath, Sylvia. *Johnny Panic and the Bible of Dreams.* New York: Harper & Row, 1979. (With Diary Excerpts)

[Plath, Sylvia] Alexander, Paul, ed. *Ariel Ascending: Writings About Sylvia.* New York: Harper & Row, 1984. (Includes Ted Hughes' Discussion of Her Journal)

Piozzi, Hester Thrale. *Thraliana, the Diary of Mrs. Hester Lynch Thrale (late Mrs. Piozzi) 1776-1809.* Oxford: Clarendon Press, 1942. 2 vols

Prentiss, Elizabeth. *The Life and Letters of Elizabeth Prentiss.* New York: Anson D. F. Randolph, 1882. (Pious Memoir)

Preston, Madge. *A Private War: Letters and Diaries of Madge Preston, 1862-1867.* New Brunswick, NJ: Rutgers University Press, 1987. (Civil War; Physical Abuse by Husband)

Pringle, Elizabeth Allston. *Chronicles of Chicora Wood.* New York: Charles Scribner's Sons, 1922. (Civil War)

Ramsay, Martha. *Memoirs of the Life of Martha Laurens Ramsay.* Boston: Samuel T. Armstrong, 1814. (Pious Memoir)

Read, Jenny. *Jenny Read In Pursuit of Art and Life. The Journals and Letters of a Young Sculptor, San Francisco, 1970-1976.* Burnsville, NC: Celo Press, 1982.

[Robinson, Mrs. Dorothy] Blake, Dorothy (pseud.) *The Diary of a Suburban Housewife.* New York: Wm. Morrow and Co., 1936.

Roe, Marion. *Home-Scenes and Heart-Tints: A Memorial of Mrs. Marion H. Roe.* New York: John F. Grow, 1865. (Pious Memoir)

Rogers, Mrs. Clara. *Journal-Letters from the Orient.* Norwood, MA: Privately Printed, 1934. (Travel)

St. Denis, Ruth. *Ruth St. Denis, An Unfinished Life. An Autobiography.* New York: Harper & Bros., 1939. (With Journal Excerpts)

[St. Denis, Ruth] Shelton, Suzanne. *Divine Dancer: A Biography of Ruth St. Denis.* Garden City, NY: Doubleday, 1981. (Based on Diaries)

Salisbury, Charlotte Y. *China Diary: After Mao.* New York: Walker and Co., 1979. (Travel)

_____. *Long March Diary: China Epic.* New York: Walker and Co., 1986. (Travel)

Sarton, May. *At Seventy: A Journal.* New York: W.W. Norton & Co., 1984. (Old Age)

_____. *The House by the Sea.* New York: W. W. Norton & Co., 1977.

_____. *Journal of a Solitude.* New York: W. W. Norton & Co., 1973.

_____. *Plant Dreaming Deep.* New York: W. W. Norton & Co., 1968.

_____. *Recovering. A Journal.* New York: W. W. Norton & Co., 1980.

Shalom, Sabina. *A Marriage Sabbatical.* New York: Dodd, Mead, 1984. (Based on Diaries)

Shannon, Elizabeth. *Up in the Park. The Diary of the Wife of the American Ambassador to Ireland, 1977-1981.* New York: Atheneum, 1983. (Life in a Foreign Culture)

Shin, Nan. *Diary of a Zen Nun.* New York: E. P. Dutton, 1986. (Life-Threatening Illness; Life in a Foreign Culture - France)

Shepherd, Laurie. *A Dreamer's Log Cabin. A Woman's Walden.* New York: Dembner Books, 1981. (A Year's Journal)

Simeti, Mary Taylor. *On Persephone's Island: A Sicilian Journal.* New York: Alfred A. Knopf, 1986. (Life in a Foreign Culture)

Sloane, Florence Adele. *Maverick in Mauve: The Diary of a Turn-of-the-Century Aristocrat.* Garden City, NY: Doubleday and Co., 1983.

Smith, Elizabeth. *A Woman with a Purpose. The Diaries of Elizabeth Smith, 1872-1884.* Toronto: University of Toronto Press, 1984. (Nineteenth Century Education)

Sparrow, Jane, *Diary of a Delinquent Episode.* London: Routledge & Kegan Paul, 1976.

_____. *Diary of a Student Social Worker.* London: Routledge & Kegan Paul, 1978.

Stein, Judith. *The Journal of Judith Stein.* Washington: Columbia Journal, Inc. 1973.

Stevenson, Fanny and Robert Louis. *Our Samoan Adventure, with a three-year diary by Mrs. Stevenson.* New York: Harper & Bros., 1955. (Travel)

Strachey, Julia. *Julia. A Portrait of Julia Strachey by Herself and Frances Partridge.* Boston: Little, Brown and Co., 1983. (Bloomsbury)

Stuart-Wortley, Victoria. *A Young Traveler's Journal of a Tour in North and South America during the year 1850.* London: T. Bosworth, 1852. (Travel)

Taylor, Janet. *Brigie: A Life, 1965-1981.* New York: St. Martin's Press, 1984. (Death of a Child)

[Thursby, Emma] Gipson, Richard McCandless. *The Life of Emma Thursby, 1845-1931.* Charlottesville, VA: The University of Virginia Press, 1981. (With Diary Excerpts)

Truitt, Anne. *Daybook. The Journal of an Artist.* New York: Penguin Books, 1986.

_____. *Turn. The Journal of an Artist.* New York: Penguin Books, 1986.

Tyndall, Mary. *The Diary of May Tyndall, One of the Early Quakers.* London: Hall and Company, 1876. (Quaker)

Vaughan, Elizabeth. *The Ordeal of Elizabeth Vaughan: A Wartime Diary of the Philippines.* Athens, GA: University of Georgia Press, 1985. (Reviewed)

Wainwright, Sonny. *Stage V: A Journal Through Illness.* Berkeley, CA: Acacia Books. 1984. (Reviewed)

Warwick, Mary, Countess of. *Memoir of Lady Warwick: Also her Diary from A.D. 1666 to 1672, now first published.* London: The Religious Tract Society, 1847.

Weingarten, Violet. *Intimations of Mortality.* New York: Alfred A. Knopf, 1977. (Terminal Illness - Cancer)

Wentworth, Barbara Copeland. *No Boughs On My Bonnet, The Journal of the Times of Barbara Copeland Wentworth of Cushing, Maine, 1811-1890.* Augusta, ME: J. S. McCarthy, 1984. (Farmwife)

White, Viola Chittenden. *The Journals of Viola Chittenden White, 1918-1941.* Taftsville, VT: The Countryman Press, 1979.

[Whiteley, Opal] *Opal, The Journal of an Understanding Heart.* Adapted by Jane Boulton. Los Altos, CA: Tioga Publishing Company, 1984. (Reviewed)

[_____.] Hoffman, Benjamin. *The Singing Creek Where the Willows Grow: The Rediscovered Diary of Opal Whiteley.* New York: Ticknor & Fields, 1986. (Childhood)

Whitford, Maria. *. . . And a White Vest for Sam'l.* Almond, NY: Privately printed, 1976. (Farmwife)

Willard, Emma. *Journal and Letters from France and Great Britain.* Troy, NY: N. Tuttle, 1833. (Travel)

Willison, Marilyn Murray. *Diary of a Divorced Mother.* New York: Wyden Books, 1980.

Wordsworth, Dorothy. *The Journals of Dorothy Wordsworth. The Alfoxden Journal 1798; The Grasmere Journals 1800-1803.* New York: Oxford University Press, 1987.

About the Authors

JANE DUPREE BEGOS has been working with both published and manuscript diaries and journals for the past fifteen years. She has created bibliographies, written articles in national and international journals, and conducted tours and workshops based on diaries and journals. She is currently editing and preparing a guide for a microfilm project for READEX on Southern Women's Diaries.

HARRIET BLODGETT, a native New Yorker, has taught at various campuses of the University of California and in the California State University System. She is currently an Affiliated Scholar at the Institute for Research on Women and Gender at Stanford University. She is author of *Patterns of Reality: Elizabeth Bowen's Novels* (1975), based on her doctoral dissertation, and *Centuries of Female Days: Englishwomen's Private Diaries* (1988).

LYNN Z. BLOOM, Professor of English at Virginia Commonwealth University, is currently writing *Autobiography, The Versatile Genre* and *Telling Secrets: Modes of Childhood in American Autobiography*, aided by a NEH Fellowship. She has written *Doctor Spock: Biography of a Conservative Radical* (1972), is associate author (with M. Briscoe, B. Tobias) of *American Autobiography, 1945-1980: A Bibliography* (1982), and editor of *Forbidden Diary: A Record of Wartime Internment, 1941-45* (1980).

SUZANNE L. BUNKERS is a native Midwesterner who has kept diaries and journals for over twenty years. She is currently completing a book based on her study of unpublished diaries by nineteenth century Midwestern American women; the book will be published as part of the University of Wisconsin Press's new series on American Autobiography. She teaches English and Women's Studies at Mankato State University in Mankato, Minnesota, and is the proud mother of Rachel Susanna.

CATHERINE DENNING is curator of the Annmary Brown Memorial, Brown University. She also received her M. A. from Brown University. Though the nature of her work usually keeps her attention confined to the fifteenth century, she enjoys the occasional foray into more modern times.

JILL ERICKSON is the Head of Reference at the Boston Athenaeum. She received her Master of Library Science degree from Simmons College in 1984. She has been keeping her own diary since 1973.

JOANNA BOWEN GILLESPIE is a Visiting Scholar at the Pembroke Center for Research on Women at Brown, has taught at Drew University and been a Visiting Assistant Professor at the College of William and Mary. She continues to publish essays on the eighteenth century women's diaries, and is working on a biography of Martha Laurens Ramsay, as well as a book of her articles on nineteenth century popular religious literature. She is also a member of the research team on twentieth century Episcopal women and the church, Lilly Endowment.

DURE JO GILLIKIN is an Assistant Professor in the Department of English, Speech, and World Literature at the College of Staten Island. She is the author of articles on the diary of Anne Rogers Minor,and is founding and current editor of the *CUNY Women's Coalition Journal.* She served as editor of the 1988-89 *Women's Studies Quarterly.*

EMILIE W. GOULD a native of New York State with close family ties to Nova Scotia, has had a varied career ranging from folklore to museum work to the computer industry. Along the way, she has been a curator of textiles and has worked with domestic craft in historic restorations.

VALERIE HARMS is an *Intensive Journal* consultant as well as the author of five books and many articles. Under her imprint Magic Circle Press, she published a book of stories by the noted diarist, Anaïs Nin. She has conducted tours and workshops based on diaries and journals, and in 1987, she was honored by the U. N. for her work with journals and writing.

CAROL ROLLOFF LANGWORTHY is a Research Associate at Carleton College and Director of Corporate/Foundation Relations at the College of St. Catherine, St. Paul, Minnesota. She is the editor of a volume of Neith Boyce's autobiographical writings, *The Modern World of Neith Boyce*, which is to be published by The University of New Mexico Press.

LYN LIFSHIN is an internationally known, award-winning poet and editor. More than seventy of her books and chapbooks have been published, and she has edited a series of books on women's writings. They include *Tangled Vines* (Beacon Press, 1978), *Ariadne's Thread* (Harper and Row, 1982), and *Unsealed Lips: Women's Memoirs and Autobiography*, to be published by Capra Press. She is also the subject of a documentary film "Not Made of Glass."

ANN L. MCLAUGHLIN teaches courses in writing and literature at American University, Washington, D. C. She has just completed a novel and is working on a series of stories. She continues to lead a reading group which discusses works of fiction by women.

JENNIFER PRESCOTT MCLEAN teaches writing courses at Manhattanville College. She is the author of numerous essays for the Westchester section of the Sunday *New York Times*, and a booklet entitled *The Jays of Bedford*. She was a regular contributor to *WOMEN'S DIARIES, A Quarterly Newsletter.*

MARY ANN MCNEIL is an artist who has lived and painted in New Zealand, Venezuela and Kenya. Her work has been exhibited in galleries and museums in the United States and Europe. She is also a teacher with experience in Michigan and New York in elementary schools, NEA Outreach Programs, Community Centers, universities, and a county jail.

MARCIA D. MILLER teaches English as a Second Language to elderly immigrants, edits a storytelling newsletter and studies the Chinese language and calligraphy. She has traveled to thirty countries, usually alone and always local class, crossing the Atlantic Ocean twelve times and the Pacific Ocean seven times. She spent one year teaching in a remote area in northeast China and has written and lectured widely about that experience.

MARY JANE MOFFAT, a poet and fiction writer, has taught creative writing at colleges and universities in the San Francisco Bay area. She was co-editor of *Revelations: Diaries of Women*, and editor of *In the Midst of Winter: Selections from the Literature of Mourning*. She is author of *The Times of Our Lives, A Guide to Writing Autobiography,* and *City of Roses,* a memoir.

AUGUSTA MOLNAR is a development anthropologist working for the World Bank and the Food and Agriculture Organization of the United Nations, consulting on social issues related to the implementation of forestry and watershed development projects in Nepal, India, and the Asia region. A key issue on which she has focused is the involvement of women in the management of their natural resources.

OLIVIA MURRAY NICHOLS is editor of *Literary Sketches,* a monthly newsletter about books and authors. A long-time resident of Dallas, TX, she keeps a journal herself and collects published journals and collections of letters.

VANESSA OCHS has taught writing at Colgate University, Yale University and at Hebrew University in Jerusalem. Her articles have appeared in national magazines and newspapers. She is currently working on a book for Harcourt Brace Javanovich entitled *Women of the Book,* which deals with women who are learned in sacred Jewish texts.

PATRICIA PENDERGRAFT began scribbling stories on school paper, always dreaming that one day she would be a "real" author. Now divorced and the mother of four grown children, she has just had her fourth children's book accepted for publication. She has been keeping a journal since 1979.

DOROTHY PERKINS, of Philadelphia, PA is a writer and independent scholar with a Ph.D. in Religion and a special interest in Japanese culture.

PATRICIA ROTH SCHWARTZ is a psychotherapist in private practice working from a holistic and feminist perspective. As a writer, she has published works of fiction, poetry and reviews. A volume of her short fiction is to be published by New Victoria of Norwich, Vermont.

SUSAN WAUGH is a Professor of English and Coordinator of the Liberal Arts Program at the St. Louis Community College at Meramec. She has received numerous awards and recognitions, published reviews and articles and is active in professional organizations. She is co-author with Diana Wyllie of *The Shape of This Century: Readings in the Disciplines,* to be published by Harcourt Brace Jovanovich in 1989.

SHARON WHITEHILL, a professor of English at Grand Valley State University in Michigan since 1970, teaches journal writing, personal narrative, and other forms of autobiography in several of her courses. She also gives journal-writing workshops off-campus and is a frequent lecturer on dreams, which she believes have a great deal to teach us about who we are. She is currently working on a biography of Mary O'Hara, author of *My Friend Flicka,* who based much of her fiction on experiences from her own life.

METTA WINTER is a freelance writer whose more than 150 articles have appeared in such national publications as *Ms., Working Mother, Delta Sky, The Los Angeles Times,* and *The Boston Globe.* She writes regularly for *The Christian Science Monitor.* The National Public Radio series, "A Private Space: the Personal Diaries of Women," which she co-authored with Saundra Hybels, won the first-place award in the entertainment category of the American Women in Radio and Television's 11th National Commendation Awards.

Afterword: a note from the designer-typesetter

*I*n April of 1972, Valerie Harms and I conducted a seminar at Wainwright House in Rye, New York called "Celebration With Anaïs Nin" in honor of the famed diarist who was our loved heroine. In August of that year we began Magic Circle Press and in 1973 published the book *Celebration With Anaïs Nin*, edited by Valerie and designed by myself.

Valerie and I also went to our first "Intensive Journal" workshop together in the Fall of 1971. Years later, living here in California, I used parts of my journals in a Ph.D. thesis on "Art & The Personal Symbolic Process." This work, called *Rainbow*, included dreams, poems, active imaginations, drawings and the obsessive out-pourings of my life as I observed it on a daily basis.

When I told Valerie I would like to typeset and design the cover for the book she was publishing for Magic Circle Press on women's diaries, I was struck by the continuous weaving of our lives that began so many years ago. And while I find typesetting a tedious job I thoroughly enjoyed reading the content of the book, word for word, comma by comma, as I painstakingly strung together the words of all these women, past and present into my Macintosh Computer. The magic continues to circle.

The illustration for the cover of this book is derived from a quilt pattern symbolizing the content of the book. As women have pieced quilts from bits and pieces of fabric so women's lives are pieced together, day by day, in their diaries. This pattern has been superimposed with designs I created from the last names of all the contributing authors of the book. The pattern is appropriately called "Album" and is comprised of twenty-five squares. There are twenty-two authors in the book plus the orchestrator for the entire project, Jane Begos. Two of the authors have written two articles each. This number worked perfectly in the twenty-five squares by assigning two squares each for the authors who wrote two articles, and fitting Jane Begos's name in the center.

Adele Aldridge

Mill Valley, California
May 12, 1989